The Indictment

By John A. Murphy

Brockston Publishing Company

Published by Brockston Publishing Company

ISBN 0-918052-03-3

Library of Congress Catalog Card Number: 99-091830

Dedication

To my grandchildren, Emily, Thomas, Warren and Caitlin

The grandchildren and great grandchildren of
William Estabrook Chancellor

Table of Contents

Foreword

Freedom of speech, the right to speak one's mind, and to publish without censorship is the true issue of this book. William Estabrook Chancellor forced to seek sanctuary in Canada, because of his point of view, was not the first person censored and will not be the last by the United States Government. The fact that a President made this issue is the surprise. Why this was not a concern in 1922, will remain a mystery cloaked by the shadows of time.

Every biographer of President Warren G. Harding mentions Chancellor but always in a racist tone. They place him as a bigot, a man who hates the black race, because of a book, erroneously credited to his name. This book, which you will become familiar with, dwells heavily upon Hardings ancestors that Chancellor says have a Negro parent in the family tree. Warren G. Harding never denied nor affirmed this allegation for reasons only known to him. One can speculate that Harding knew, but he was ashamed of his historical ties. This race issue overshadows the keen insight of Professor Chancellor's research into the background of the 29th president of the United States and the knowledge he had at his fingertips.

Biographers accepted what others said about Warren G. Harding and William Estabrook Chancellor as the truth. None researched the province of history for the truth. Just a rough review of the professor's background, reveals he was a literate man with many published books to his honor. They published him in the distinctive, *Who's Who* as early as 1904, many years before his altercation with Harding.

Yet, shamefully the historians accepted the obvious without investigation. The investigation into Chancellor's history was not easy, but it offered many astonishing discoveries as the mystery unfolded, a rare and enjoyable experience for a writer.

This research of the Chancellor brought me into direct contact with some really fine people and I know it is my duty to mention them, because to do otherwise would be wrong.

First is Donna Duggan-Young, who painstakingly went over the manuscript as a line editor, with intensity and dedication. A line editor checks for grammar errors, not content. Grammar errors within quotes remains. Typos we blame on the typesetter.

i

Anthony and Maryann Biggio of Wooster, Ohio who invited me to the privacy of their home and offered me boxes containing memorabilia of the professor. Harry S. McClarran is probably the most knowledgeable man about the history of Wooster, Ohio, was a tremendous help. Despite failing eye sight Harry sent to me reams of papers expounding some minute detail. His background information was very valuable.

Jeff Flonnery, archivist at the Library of Congress, who with patience helped to find the Winnipeg Manuscripts that were mis filed, deserves a nod and thanks. Denise D. Monbarren and her able assistant Ms. Synder started me in the right direction by making available all the material the archives the College of Wooster had on Chancellor. We must thank Kathy Bardor for finding microfilms of old newspapers at the Bucyrus Library, just when I was about to give up. Wayne T. De Cesar, of the National Archives, with his magic and knowledge found the exact reports I needed that solved a vexing problem about the Secret Service. James Hoff, S.J., James E Bundschuh, Father Felton and the entire staff of Xavier University whose kindness gave me a copy of a self portrait written by Professor Chancellor. Christian Yackley who refused to relinquish a xerox copier as she produced for me one copy after another which proved to be very valuable in my research.

Michael S. Hart, Executive Director of the on line Project Gutenberg whose goal is to have 10,000 e-text books available to the public on the net. It was his inquiry about the book allegedly written by Chancellor that started the whirlwind.

I cannot leave without mentioning the entire staff of the Ohio Historical Society's archivists who displayed immense patience with my questions.

CHAPTER ONE
THE MAKING OF A PRESIDENT

Qualifications of being the President of the United States are not demanding, as set forth by the Constitution. A candidate must be at least thirty-five years of age, a natural born citizen of the United States and must have been a resident of the United States for at least fourteen years. That is all.

Warren G. Harding setting type for the Marion Star, of which he was a part owner. At the age of twelve he learned typesetting working for the Caledonia Argus.
Credit Ohio Historical Society

Nothing in the constitution addresses the popular vote, although custom prevails that the popular vote has persuaded Electors. A candidate can get the popular vote but lose the election. The people do not elect their President. This system belies Abraham Lincoln's declaration that our government is "of the people, for the people and by the people."

Selection of candidates for the office of President, is removed even more from the average citizen. Political parties have a carnival like assembly called a convention and delegates vote to select their candidate for the coveted office. One person, who can gain the control of delegate votes can get his candidate nominated. If the times are right, one man can single handily produce a president. This happened twice.

Markus Hanna virtually pushed McKinley onto the people as President. Hanna, controlled McKinley and in fact, many thought he ran the country. This Hanna, a powerful Ohio political boss, had in his political machine a Harry M. Daugherty.

Daugherty, an attorney from Columbus, Ohio followed the same path as his mentor, Hanna, in the election of Warren G. Harding, the twenty-ninth president of the United States. One man influenced the system and gave us our worst President.

December 1919 at the palatial home of Harry M. Daugherty and Senator Warren G. Harding, of Marion, Ohio, talked about the up coming November 1920 election. We still find this house at four-eighty-three, East Town Street in Columbus, Ohio. This was not the first time that Daugherty asked Harding to toss his hat into the ring. The Columbus attorney had made several trips to Washington, D.C. to convince Senator Harding he would be a winner in the up coming presidential elections.

Daugherty said to Harding, "Warren, whoever gets elected at this summer's Republican convention will be the next president of the United States. None of the leading Republican candidates can triumph. General Wood will not get elected though a powerful and rich group of men have backed him. He reeks of the military and such a man will never see the White House. Business men are nervous about the growing demands of Labor and they do not wish to entrench themselves behind the invincible force of the bayonet and the machine gun. The scheme will not work as people are sick of war. Soldiers who saw action in France hate war will not vote for a general."

"Women will vote for the first time in this election. It would be suicide on that account to name a general for that reason alone. The Republican Convention will not do it. The smart people know all the money in the world would not buy a nomination for a man who wears a uniform in 1920."

Daugherty continued, "The other candidate is Governor Lowden who represents big money from the Pullmans of the *Pullman Coach Company*. He is the best man on the list, a power with whom we must reckon with, and I like him. He would make a fine president, but he will never have the reward of nomination. Lowden married into the Pullman family, which means railroad money. No party will name a railroad magnate for the office of president. Lowden is ready to spend more than a million dollars to get his nomination at the convention. The knowledge that he may buy his nomination will sink him."

"Then Hiram Johnson will slip in," offered Senator Harding.

"Never! We needed California to put Hughes in during the last presidential election, and Hiram Johnson won that state. He killed the Republican presidential hopes. The Republicans begged him not to run and back the ticket for Hughes. He refused and the party will never forgive him. Johnson has no chance at all."

Warren Harding nodded in agreement. Senator Harding listened carefully to Daugherty who was the mastermind behind his election to the Ohio State Senate, Lt. Governor of Ohio and as a Senator to Congress. "Warren," continued Daugherty, "we need a man who will listen and follow along. Warren, we need you to run for president."

That December night, Harding responded, "Come down to business, Harry, am I enough of a man for the race? You know it takes a great man to become president of the United States."

Harry Daugherty had one brown eye and one blue eye. The blue eye twitched and rolled aimlessly in its socket when he got excited. His obtrusive eye began to roll as the stocky Daugherty stood up, walked to a window and looked out. He said, "Warren, the party selects the president, not the people. Greatness in the presidential chair is largely an illusion."

Harding struggled from within. That struggle registered on his face and he said to Daugherty with dimmed eyes, "You know me better than any man in the world. Your opinion inspires me."

Daugherty turned and looked at Harding. "Remember," said Daugherty, "I am not presuming to decide this question. It is up to you. It is between you and your God. If you decide to run, I believe, you can get the nomination at the Chicago convention. You get the nomination and you will be our next president!" Warren shook his head slowly, "I wish I could see it as clearly as you do."

Daugherty sat in a chair opposite to Harding. "In my mind you are the man of the hour. We must name a candidate who can carry Ohio. This year, of all years, our state will be the battleground. Only one man had been elected president in half a century without the Ohio vote. The nation, I tell you, is sick of war and President Wilson's continued play for the League of Nations. Woodrow Wilson ignores the real needs of the people who are desperately trying to make a living."

"The Democrats will follow Wilson's line of thinking. Right now more than one half million workers are on strike for better wages. Growing dissatisfaction with the Democrats is evident everywhere I look. That fact is a big thing in your favor. You are a man of peace, human, friendly, genial, and popular."

"We will triumph at the convention in June! When General Wood and Lowden have worn each other to a frazzle at the convention, I will swing the delegates to you at the right moment! I know I can get you nominated!"

Warren Gamaliel Harding listened to Attorney Harry Daugherty for the rest of the evening. It was very late when he left. The next morning Warren Harding walked up High Street to the Huntington Building to Harry Daugherty's Columbus law office.

That morning Warren G. Harding committed to running for the presidency of the United States. Harding insisted that Daugherty had to be his campaign manager. Smiling, Daugherty said to Harding, "We need money. How much do you think you can raise in Marion?"

A professor of political science would see through the absurdity created by Daugherty. This scholarly man, an author of forty published books, contributed many articles to leading newspapers. His opinion on politics was well respected and he was not afraid to voice them either in speech or in his writings. This man was William Estabrook Chancellor.

Business had taken Professor William Estabrook Chancellor to Lima, Ohio, in June 1920. There in a hotel dining room, he sat at a table next to where they seated a party of men that Chancellor knew.

> Chancellor wrote, one of these men happened to be president of a small Ohio college and he belonged to a religious association that dealt with world questions. His name was Reverend John Wesley Hill. Reverend Hill went about the country making speeches for religious ends that always contained attacks upon the Democratic party.

The Presbyterian minister saw Professor Chancellor and he rose from his chair. In a very loud voice Mr. Hill told the roomful of dinners, "Well, I wish everyone to know that we are going to have a safe and sane president. He is an

Ohio man, and his name is Warren Harding. I have just seen him, and I am on my way to the Chicago Convention, which will nominate him!"

Hill and his party left the hotel dining room and Bill Chancellor and his lunch colleague watched them leave. Chancellor's colleague said, "I heard that Harding had Negro blood in his ancestry. This came out in the spring primaries."

Chancellor put on his rimmed glasses and peered at his lunch companion. "Yes, I have heard stories to that effect but I know very little about this man. During the spring primaries General Wood and his people tried to make race an issue, but it did not work."

"Professor, could a Negro be elected a president of the United States?"

Bill Chancellor smiled, "Yes, as God has made all the nations of men. The mixing and compounding of the bloodlines are forever going on. Sometimes there comes a man from a particular stock whom the world is in need. He may have the one trait, which made him great, that came from his race. We can never tell where the needed man will come from."

Chancellor's lunch mate sat back in his chair and smiled. "I should have known better than to ask a Hoge Professor of the College of Wooster such a leading question."

Chancellor gave his views of the upcoming Republican convention to his lunch mate. "Only three contenders of the Republican ticket matter. General Wood, who, if he is selected, will cause me to sign on as a Republican to help get him elected president. General Wood was the commander of the Rough Riders to whom Teddy Roosevelt belonged. He is an excellent candidate for president. Next in the running would be Governor Lowden of Illinois, followed closely by Hiram Johnson. Senator Harding has little chance of winning. He is weak compared with General Wood, Lowden or Johnson."

"Wood's strength lies in the fact that most of his delegates believe in him and come from states that had instructed them to vote for him as nominee. It will surprise me if any of Wood's delegates change their votes. Johnson's delegates are generally ready to abandon him. Governor Lowden is strong because he has bought and paid for his votes with his own money. Harding, like so many others on the Republican slate is considered a dark horse and not qualified. It will surprise me if Warren Harding gets the nomination."

The professor's lunch mate said, "Harry Daugherty is the campaign manager for Warren Harding and everyone knows he can pull an upset. Just two weeks ago Daugherty predicted that at 2:11 a.m. in some smoke filled hotel room a dozen men sitting together would pick the man and the convention would nominate him."

"You know," stated Chancellor, "that happened during the 1916 Republican presidential convention. They said that Hughes was selected in a smoke-filled room to break a dead lock."

The professor bid his friend good-bye and caught a train home to Wooster, Ohio. This chance meeting of Hill intrigued the professor of politics. The Republicans scheduled their convention to take place mid June 1920 in Chicago. Chancellor arranged to attend the convention in Chicago but only succeeded in getting there on the last day.

Professor Chancellor of the Political Science department at the College of Wooster was once a registered Republican but he had followed Teddy Roosevelt out of that party. Roosevelt's failure too win and the resulting split of the Republican party caused Chancellor to become a Democratic. He made copious notes about the candidates and included them in a book.

Chancellor wrote, Governor Lowden, a multimillionaire, sank large sums of money into his bid to become the leading Republican candidate. Later, they would discover that he had purchased delegates to vote for him, paying at least $2,500, and in few cases as high as $5,000. General Wood, the leading candidate, had the backing of Colonel Proctor of *Proctor and Gamble* fame. With Colonel Proctor's backing, Wood's war chest expanded to millions of dollars. Harding claimed he had only a small chest containing no more than a couple hundred thousand dollars. Still, by coincidence, Harding would get a large fund of money to spend for his presidential primary bid. It would come from Jake L. Hamon, an Oklahoma oil man.

Jake L. Hamon was a big bodied man some five feet nine inches tall. He claimed German and Indian blood, and had an indescribable complexion, like the Mississippi river at sunset. He may have had Spanish or Portuguese blood. According to the business standards and practices of Oklahoma and the oil country, he was an exceedingly able business man. At any rate, being on the ground floor from the start, he made and lost millions. They report Hamon's estate at five million dollars in assets, to a low of two million. Public opinion credits him with having conveyed, in trust, at least ten million in assets to others. This was done to insure an anchor to the windward in case of a smash up of his various speculative enterprises. At the worst, he is worth three million and more.

Ten years ago, he had a wife and children in Kansas. The wife was Georgia Harding, a cousin of Warren G. Harding. She was a Black person like Warren and made no claims to being anything else. The Hamons lived in a world of all races and of all mixtures of all races, Chinese and Mexican included. Color of the skin was nothing to those living out west, as race was considered a joke.

Nevertheless, Jake had the traits of his primitive people, one trait being that he was a born polygamist and woman chaser. Among other women he had taken was Clara Smith. This was as deliberate on her part as his. Jake met her in a store tending a customer. He followed her, took her to his office, and made a deal with her. Jake would educate her as his private secretary for the usual consideration exacted by loose young women. She was eighteen and understood what the affair was. Jake Hamon sent her to a private school in Lawrence, Kansas. While she attended school learning English and shorthand, Hamon would send for her often to see him in Topeka, for purposes easily imagined.

Clara, a brown-haired women and slight in person, had Negro blood. She used rouge and cosmetics and kept herself up despite expense. Hamon was making a million a year and often that much a month. Among all the women Jake fancied, Clara developed the most ability.

When sober, Jake was not only considerate, but even agreeable and polite, he was seldom more than a quarter drunk. The way the men on the street put it, he could hold booze with any man in Oklahoma. Still, occasionally he did get very drunk. Than he was a demon, an all furious Indian. Clara was the only one who could even partially tame him. Such sprees usually lasted several days.

Jake and Clara drove over the prairies and plains together, looking up petroleum, refineries, pipelines, railroads, and markets. They occupied adjoining rooms in hotels, or the same room. Eventually some rich eastern operators who were using Hamon to stalk yet bigger prey objected to his loose ways. For appearances sake, Jake married Clara off to a worthless nephew of his. Jake prevented the nephew from ever seeing Clara alone. After that, Jake and Clara traveled as uncle and niece, a very raw proposition, but in a very raw land.

Occasionally Jake visited his legal wife and she bore another child to him. Mrs. Georgia Harding Hamon agreed to accept a fine apartment, plenty of money, and to live in Chicago. Eventually she would marry a successful contractor.

Jake L. Hamon built the city of Rankin, Oklahoma, and he helped make the city of Ardmore. He was a power, a spender, a mixer, and sponsored Boy Scouts and YMCA's. When people complained about his morals, for he had women friends besides Clara stationed at various points. Men said, "Oh, its Jake's way, we cannot change him." Clara was the head of the harem. They ate together in hotels. They even went together to the homes of friends. Everyone knew the situation. Jake gave Clara the finest motor cars and clothes. She worked hard for him when she accompanied him, she wrote his telegrams and letters and mended his clothes. She developed an expert knowledge of oil and oil men.

Georgia Harding Hamon was delighted to hear the news that her cousin Warren was going to try to become president, Jake also heard about it. They met and talked over what they could do. Then they went to Ohio to see Warren. Warren sent them to Harry M. Daugherty, who said that what he needed most was money. We have been unable to get all the details of what Jake gave to Warren Harding's nomination campaign. Jake did not much care about the amount. He had enough to finish what he started.

Yet, the common report was that Harry M. Daugherty got only $200,000 and won most of the delegates with this money. He later claimed of spending only $100,000 at the Republican convention.

In Oklahoma, the delegation fight was a hot one. Jake won the state committee directorship at a cost of forty-six thousand dollars. Nevertheless, the Oklahoma delegates received instructions from the bosses, to support Lowden for the nomination at the Convention.

W. B. Nickels, many years later, testified at the hearings before the Committee on Public Lands and Surveys confirming some observations made by Chancellor. Nickels testified he had helped Hamon win the directorship of Oklahoma.

Warren G. Harding at age 21. His dark olive skin and kinky hair earned him the nickname of "Nig."

"We unseated James J. McGraw as National Committee Man of Oklahoma, " testified Nickels. "I also had asked Jake what he was going to get out of this." Jake said, "I could get a place if I wanted, like the Secretary of the Interior. With that position Jake Hamon knew he could control the leasing of government oil land and add millions to his estate."

Daugherty wrote about the convention, "We did not try, as a rule, to win leaders but individual delegates. An exception to this rule was my approach to Jake Hamon. I got Hamon to come to Washington because he controlled a block of fifty delegates. He was backing Lowden, but agreed he would switch his votes to Harding if his man could not make it."

During the train ride to Chicago Harding said repeatedly while playing cards that he did not expect too win the nomination. In Chicago he arranged to have his name filed in Columbus so that he could run for renomination for the Senate. When he heard this, Daugherty lost his temper. The two men argued and in panic Harding screamed at Daugherty, "You don't want me to give up the senatorship, do you? I haven't got a ghost of a chance for the Presidency!" Daugherty managed to calm Harding, but not until after the Senator made the call to Columbus to his friend George B. Harris. Harding told Harris, "Keep in touch with headquarters. If I get the nomination, do nothing. If I fail, use your own judgement. I don't care. I'm tired and sick of politics."

Before the primary campaign in Ohio and his meeting with Daugherty, Warren G. Harding always played the reluctant candidate. Harding wrote to the Republican State Advisory Committee, "I have had it in my mind to ask to run again for the Senate, provided my record will justify such approval by the Republicans of Ohio. As far as I was personally concerned, I had no particular objection to closing the door on the Presidency, for I never intended to seek a nomination for that place."

The Indictment

His ancestry, love affairs and Warren's natural concern about being qualified for the job of president made him a reluctant candidate. Born in Blooming Grove, Ohio, Warren Harding lived all his life being called "Nig." The local people believed Warren and his family to be black people. This fact did not prevent Warren to be elected twice to the Ohio State Senator, Lt. Governor of Ohio once and one term to the U.S. Senate. A business associate said of Harding's ancestry, "He may be Negro but he managed to live around it." Another deep concern of Harding was his love affairs with two women, Nan Britton and a Carrie Phillips, both from Marion, Ohio. He would meet his young lover Nan Britton in Chicago during the convention.

Ignoring Harding's lack of confidence, Daugherty spent every minute of his time lining up delegates and taking notes about how they planned to vote. As Daugherty worked, Harding had a friend drop him off at 6103 Woodlawn Ave in Chicago. Warren met Nan Britton, the young lady he had been secretly seeing for the last few years. Nan just twenty-five years old, a native from Marion Ohio had always admired Warren Harding. The two met and made love in a hotel room in New York City when Nan was just twenty years old. They had sex often in his Senate chambers and that was when she conceived their child according to Nan. She named the baby Elizabeth Ann.

Harding told Nan how proud he was that they had managed to keep their affair so secret. Nan wrote about Chicago, "The time we spent together was so brief. Warren gave me some money and made arrangements to get me tickets to the convention. I walked over to the EL with him and watched the tall, handsome figure of my sweetheart until he disappeared inside the station. This would be the last unguarded tryst we ever had, until he became president."

During the spring primaries, Daugherty carefully kept Harding out of public view as much as possible. Harding made very few speeches in Ohio, but did campaign in the adjoining state of Indiana. Harding spoke on the 27th of March in Indianapolis. He called himself an unwilling candidate and told the audience the country needed more honesty in life and not a League of Nations. From Indianapolis he went to Anderson, Muncie, Kokomo, and Huntington. Harding also entered the Iowa primaries, but never went there to campaign.

In the April primary election, Harding carried Ohio by a small margin. Daugherty knew the negative campaign of racial slurs by General Wood was a major cause for the close vote. With a slim majority of only fifteen thousand votes, Harding captured thirty-nine delegates of the forty-eight at large for the Republican convention. General Wood carried nine Ohio delegates, adding to the totals he won in other state primaries, which included Indiana, where Harding came in dead last. Warren Harding also came in dead last in the Iowa primary. The *Ohio State Journal*, a Columbus newspaper, eliminated Harding as a presidential candidate and discredited Daugherty as a politician. Daugherty undaunted, considered the results in Ohio as a great victory.

With Harding's disastrous showing in Indiana and Iowa, Boise Penrose, a Pennsylvania Republican boss, wrote Harding off as a serious contender. He looked around for someone else to beat General Wood and Governor Lowden at the Convention. The bosses wanted someone who would be willing to deal with them.

Daugherty ran in the Cincinnati area as a delegate-at-large to the convention and lost. Black voters stood solidly behind General Wood and called Daugherty "D.D." or dictator Daugherty. The lack of the black vote was fundamental to his failure, and the manager knew he must find a way to solidify the color vote in Ohio. He would do this during the run for presidency by Harding.

During the primaries, Harding went to Boston to speak at the annual dinner of the Home Market Club. As Harding read his speech, he mispronounced normality as "normalty." Reporters changed the error to read *normalcy* in their copy. Ironically, this error grew into a campaign slogan for getting America back to normalcy. Harding's propensity for mis pronouncing words would plague him for the rest of his life.

Harry Daugherty worked tirelessly after the primaries to get commitments across the country from Republican delegates. The Columbus attorney made deals for the second, third, and even fourth ballot and thought he could muster one-hundred-fifteen voters for Harding on the first ballot at the Convention. Daugherty thought he knew how each delegate would vote on the first four ballots. In Chicago, Daugherty continued to gather information. If a delegate mentioned he was obligated to vote for another candidate, they advised him to put Harding down as second, third or fourth choice. Daugherty grew optimistic while others thought Harding had no chance at all.

Chancellor wrote in his book. Daugherty had opened offices for Harding in Chicago, with more of Jake's money. We believe that the direct office expenses were seventy-eight thousand dollars.

Jake Hamon went to General Wood and declared his willingness to help the candidate. Hamon would help provided he got the inside track on the government oil reserves in the west. General Wood refused Jake's offer. The western oil man, Hamon, later told Bill Nickels he thought it was a raw deal and made up his mind to help get Harding elected.

Black delegates wanted civil rights added to the Republican platform. They wanted a Federal anti lynching law, more blacks in government, a force bill to allow blacks to vote in all the states and freedom to enter all businesses. In response the Republicans added the plank for anti lynching. The one hundred seventy black delegates were not happy but accepted this as a step in the right direction.

Those black delegates committed to General Wood would never waver and voted for him in every ballot. Most thought General Wood would be the winner of the nomination in six or fewer ballots. They thought of General Wood as a man with unimpeachable integrity and a true patriot, the ideal candidate for president. He was Teddy Roosevelt's commanding officer in the Rough Riders during the Spanish American War. Many thought he would carry through with Roosevelt's policies of the progressive party. However, as Daugherty said not enough money in the world existed to buy the votes Wood needed because he was a military man. The delegates proved Daugherty's insight correct on this count.

Frank O. Lowden was everyone's second choice. He enjoyed an excellent record as Governor of Illinois and he did well in the House of Representatives. He had plenty of money because of his marriage into the *Pullman Car Company* family. This gave him the independence of making his own political decisions. Penrose and other political bosses knew this and made plans to prevent him from getting the Presidential bid. The bosses wanted someone they could control. Daugherty would make a deal with Lowden and give him enough votes to tie or go ahead of Wood. Daugherty warned the Lowden people that once this happened it would be every man on his own. They agreed.

Hiram Johnson, without party backing, won seven out of the twelve state primaries he had entered. His success at securing more than one million popular votes surprised the political machine. The machine ignored the mandate of the popular vote, but they were worried about Johnson forming a partnership with Wood and dominating the convention. However, Johnson attacked Wood and Colonel Proctor for the misuse of big money. This attack on Wood prevented the Wood-Johnson ticket from materializing. Johnson also alienated all of Lowden's delegates. Daugherty watched as everything moved his way. The bosses now looked at Johnson and his delegates as a tool to block Wood and Lowden.

Oil companies had a room in an office building in Chicago. They would summon potential presidential candidates to the room and sound out their feelings about Mexico where they had discovered a vast amount of oil. If the candidate refused to come to the room, they eliminated him from consideration. They told delegates and candidates that oil was ready to back the Republican candidate in the fall election. This backing would be cash, needed to get votes. Jake Hamon visited the oil people constantly.

Boise Penrose of Pennsylvania could not make it to the convention because of ill health. They reported that he would at times fall into a coma, but once conscious, he called the convention hall to keep in touch with the latest events. Boise was a great believer in political favors for cash. Although he had a modest salary of just seven thousand dollars per year, almost a million dollars of cash would be found in his safety deposit box when he died. One bill was in the denomination of ten thousand dollars.

Penrose with the help of his Pennsylvania delegates wooed the oil interests. From his sick bed he offered to back Wood if the General would allow Penrose to hand select three cabinet members. Wood refused. Many thought General Wood sealed his fate in his run to be President by turning down the acknowledged leader of the Senate Cabal and the strongest political boss then. This cabal consisted of a strong coalition of senators.

Daugherty again tried to keep Harding out of view. He would not allow his nominee either heard or seen. At his Congress Hotel headquarters an Ohio reporter noticed Harding was unshaven, disheveled in dress and that he wandered unhappily about the streets. Harding looked more rancid every passing day. Harding keep telling reporters he was planning to quit politics, but Daugherty refused to listen to Harding in his moments of self pity and doubt.

Mrs. Florence Harding, became concerned about the outlandish amount of money being paid by Daugherty for the Congress Hotel rooms. She bitterly complained about the seven hundred fifty dollars a day rent for the assembly room. This did not bother Daugherty and he did not tell Mrs. Harding that Jake Hamon contributed twenty-five thousand dollars to pay that expense.

Insiders and outsiders paid little attention as Daugherty kept a spot map of every delegate's room. His men, numbering more than two thousand, dropped in to have a friendly word with each delegate. Daugherty refused to allow anyone in his team give out a press release. Like a dictator Daugherty ruled and orchestrated every move of the Harding team.

Professor Chancellor tried his best to keep in touch with the happenings in Chicago as he lectured at the summer class he gave at the College of Wooster in Wooster, Ohio. It had been twelve years since he had last been to Chicago. Then he was the Superintendent of Washington DC's schools and became involved in a bitter fight with the school board. He had eliminated outdated books and replaced them with books of his choice. Those in control disliked him for this action and they made a move to dismiss him from his job by suing him. While preparing for the lawsuit, the professor came down with a gallstone attack that hospitalized him for eleven weeks. On the witness stand, he fainted. This was in the spring of 1908.

Chancellor's wife Louise, then thirty-seven years' old, gave birth to his only son, David Beecher Chancellor, that year. David, a sick child, required special attention. Louise did not fully recover from the strain of giving birth and employed a house worker to care for the new born son. The house worker nursed the sick David back to good health. The Professor had to leave the family and accept temporary employment at the University of Chicago as a summer lecturer. While in Chicago, circumstances would give Chancellor bitter memories that he dealt with for the rest of his life.

Louise became very sick. The family tried in vain to notify Chancellor by mail, that his wife was becoming weaker every day with an acute case of Typhoid fever. One day while in class he received a telegram, informing him that his wife had died. After reading the telegram he grasped his desk and fell forward in a faint. It took him four days to get back to Washington. Eugene Francis Beecher and Chancellor accompanied the remains of his wife to Rhode Island and they buried her in the Beecher's family burial plot. Chancellor told his children to remember their mother as she was, happy, laughing, singing and playing the piano. The family believes to this day because of this incident the famous Beecher family stopped all communications with Chancellor family.

Despite his bitter memories the professor returned to Chicago the summer of 1920 to attend the Republican convention. He was there but one day.

About one thousand delegates and thirty thousand guests packed McCormick Hall to witness the election of the Republican candidate for president. A record-breaking heat wave drove outside air temperatures into the high nineties, and the temperature inside the hall was more than 110 degrees. Delegates opened collars and fanned themselves with folded paper to try to stay cool. The glass dome roof allowed light into the massive auditorium and the solar heat drove temperatures inside to an unbearable level.

The convention started that June week and Nan Britton met Harding in the lobby of the Auditorium Hotel and the senator gave her tickets to the Convention. Nan wrote, "I heard the nominating speech by Frank B. Willis. I remembered my high school days writing in the margin of my books, Warren G. Harding, President of the United States!" Harding's young lover was in total awe of the proceedings.

On June 11 the mass of humanity suffering in the heat of the coliseum heard nomination speeches. The gallery joined in the protracted demonstrations as each candidate became nominated. Managers closely orchestrated most demonstrations and many showed real enthusiasm. Ex Ohio Governor Frank B. Willis nominated Harding.

Chancellor wrote about the ex Ohio governor. Willis served one term as Governor of Ohio, during which his motto was "Let the people attend to their own business and the Governor will keep out of the fray." Many thought this resulted in the attitude, "What is everyone's business, is no one's, business." He was commonly considered the poorest Governor Ohio ever had. Yet, he was elected to the United States Senate. After serving a term or two in Congress, they defeated him. Willis wept tears in public. He vowed that he would never return to Washington, because he was the sentimentalist supreme.

Willis had a wonderful voice, the best voice of any speaker in American public life except William Jennings Bryan. His voice was loud and deep, marvelously loud, a foghorn voice, but pleasant. A thorough gentleman, an ardent prohibitionist and he remembered the faces of his friends and acquaintances. Frank Willis was a devout Methodist, scrupulously free of bribe taking and did not associate with corruptionists.

Willis did not secure the Presidency for Harding with his speech at the convention, though he seems to think that he did so. I have reports of many eyewitnesses that it was the saddest, most anxious, hottest mass of men ever gathered for any such purpose. Sadness overcame some because they realized what they were asking them to do. They experienced anxiety because they were afraid of being discovered doing the bidding of crooks. Willis' speech cheered them a bit just as any other vaudeville performer might have done. His speech required less ability than most of the stunts of acknowledged comedians.

Willis was not a close friend of Harding because their tastes are too different. Nevertheless, he lent his megaphone bass voice to the event. Like Julius Burrows, of Michigan, he rose to the Senate on his own wind. He nominated Harding in a speech ending with the exhortation, "Come on, boys and girls, let's make him President!" They said that Harding received the most spontaneous applause, partly because of Willis's gifts of oratory, grand opera and hog calling. The speech lasted but eight minutes.

Professor Chancellor discovered that after the nomination speeches, the first ballot found General Wood in the lead as expected. Daugherty expressed surprise at the number of votes he received. The Columbus attorney thought Wood could poll about 250 votes but he started with a resounding 287. Harding received just 61.5 votes about half what the president-maker Daugherty expected. Vote trading by delegates began in earnest to neutralize the lead of General Wood. After the fourth vote Daugherty saw just what he expected. Johnson and Lowden effectively blocked Wood from moving ahead. Henry Cabot Lodge the convention's chair called for a motion to adjourn. "Ayes" were few and scattered. So Lodge called for another motion to adjourn. A full voice arose from the floor, giving a resonant, "No!" Chair Lodge pounded his gavel and announced the motion to adjourn carried. The delegates did not protest, because a boss had spoken.

Boise Penrose, the Pennsylvania boss controlled votes from his sick bed.

Chancellor wrote in his book. The last night was sweltering hot, after a very hot day. All night, in rooms taken by Colonel George R. McClellan Harvey, the insiders had been working out the plan to land Harding that day. It cost them fifty thousand dollars to turn the Oklahoma delegation from Lowden to Harding. Runners came in from time to time to tell Harding, Harvey, Daugherty, and the others present how the business of getting the delegates was going forward. One delegate vote cost twenty-five hundred-dollars. One Republican leader came into Harding's suite, at midnight and said that he had three questions to ask before he would let his state swing to Harding.

First, the man asked, "Have you ever been bankrupt?"

Second, he asked, "Have you ever had any trouble, public trouble, over women?"

Third, he asked, "We heard a rumor among the Johnson men that you have Negro blood. We want to know if this is true."

To the first question, Harding answered a point blank, "No."

He had a long answer to the second, which went well enough.

Daugherty answered the third by saying, "Ohio elected Harding United

States Senator. Is not that enough?"

George Harvey, the editor, of the North American Review and intimate of J.P. Morgan took himself very seriously that hot night. At the Blackstone hotel, politicians drifted through his room and that of Will Hay's room. Medill McCormick, the Senator from Illinois, Watson of Indiana, and Weeks of Massachusetts were among those of the Senate cabal coming and going. As one reporter said, "They ran around like chickens with their heads off. They suggested candidates one at time. They mentioned Harding's name every time as second choice. One by one the Senate cabal, in the smoke, eliminated the suggested candidate. It was past two o'clock in the morning when the men in Harvey's room decided that Harding was the man to select. If the Senator could not make it in four or five ballots, they decided they would give another candidate their consideration. Medill McCormick was among the senators that selected Harding."

After 2:00 A.M. they decided that Harding would be the tie breaker and nominated as the Republican candidate for President. Daugherty's prediction that at eleven minutes past two, in a smoke-filled room a candidate would be selected and nominated the next day, came true. The politic smoke-filled room legend was born. The state leader went out and aligned men for Harding.

Senator Smoot gave an interview to a *New York Telegram* reporter. He said, "Harding was the man and the bosses would put him over the next afternoon after giving Lowden a brief run."

That night, Harry Daugherty must have sensed the cabal was eliminating candidates rather than selecting one. He insisted that Harding clean himself up by shaving and dressing in a business suit. The attorney, and gambler sensed that his dark horse was about ready to make a run for it.

Samuel Adams reported that Harding was seen leaving his hotel room with Myron T. Herrick an owner of Dayton, Ohio, *Journal*. Both were in good spirits. Herrick waved to the reporters and said, "they will nominate Senator Harding tomorrow!" This was before midnight.

Harry Daugherty had used his skills in Chicago like a master. Harry had spent weeks lining up votes without revealing his plan to anyone. This included a complete survey of the 984 delegates. He knew about their choices for a candidate through their fourth vote. The survey showed Harding on every ballot as second, third or fourth choice. This encouraged and excited the gambler. As Harding would later say, "We went in with a pair of deuces and drew into a full-house."

Daugherty later wrote that his first goal was not to alienate anyone. In fact he offered and gave locked in delegates to other candidates during the first ballots. Eighteen candidates were running to be the president elect for the Republican nomination.

Daugherty kept in the background, talking, dealing and consulting seemingly unimportant delegates. With promises and, of course, Hamon's money, each day Daugherty gained more of the delegates. The third ballots and others showed Lowden gaining strength and Wood losing as Daugherty lent his in pocket delegate votes to Lowden. Just what Daugherty wanted. Harding lost ground from the first vote.

At the hearings on Public Land and Surveys it was found that Jake Hamon promised $250,000 to Boise Penrose at the convention that night in the smoke-filled room. At these same hearings Nickels revealed Jake Hamon spent one million dollars to buy Harding the nomination. Daugherty, Will Hays, and Senator Hill received twenty-five thousand dollars each of the Hamon's money. After deducting the money he gave to Penrose, Daugherty, Hays, and Hill, the average price for a delegate vote was about one thousand dollars. This was a tidy sum in the year 1920.

Although Daugherty disagreed, it was determined in the smoke-filled room that Jake Hamon would be the Secretary of Interior. Daugherty knew the bosses had cut a deal before the convention that Senator Albert Fall would get that job. Jake Hamon's money would not change his mind on that point. The Harding people were taking advantage of the oil man and his money.

Black delegates asked Harding if he would support and address their concerns. Harding responded that all delegates were equal in his mind. Cottrell, a leading black delegate, said he would swing all his votes to Harding.

Saturday morning professor Chancellor, an active member of the New York Press club, found it easy to enter the McCormick convention hall for the first time. He was pleased to hear that General Wood still had a marginal lead after the fourth ballot just before the delegates adjourned the day before. However it was not until March 1921 that Chancellor got all the inside information. He spoke with Oklahoma oil men, members of the Oklahoma delegation, and witnessed things for himself at the convention. He would not learn about Harding's Negro ancestry until that fall. Many accused the professor of passing racist pamphlets at the convention, but this was the work of Johnson and Wood.

Chancellor wrote in his book, at 8:00 a.m., they had already told the delegates that they could go home, for Harding was the man. At noon they were a wretched, gloomy lot, anxious, fearing exposure, and many of them fearing defeat in the autumn. By the end of the day, they had experienced something worse than defeat. They had experienced the shame of discovering that under Harding they had but a shadow for president.

The first vote Saturday morning, the fifth ballot, Lowden pulled ahead of Wood and virtually stopped any chances of the favorite general to become a serious contender during the rest of the Convention. The game was going just as Daugherty had foreseen it.

On the sixth ballot, Harding gained eleven votes, which showed a small but, dramatic change to those at the convention. By the eighth vote, Daugherty started his move, by not voting his locked in delegates to Lowden. Harding now had 133.5 votes. Daugherty knew instinctively he had won. He sent his orders about the floor and "locked in"and paid for delegates were instructed how to vote on the next ballot. On the ninth ballot, Harding went into the lead with a small margin. The delegation chair, Henry Cabot Lodge, called for a recess. Daugherty complained unsuccessfully about this recess at four o'clock.

Daugherty learned ailing Penrose had ordered the recess from his sick bed in Pennsylvania. He received a call from Boise Penrose during the recess. The political boss said he was going to declare for Harding on the next ballot provided he got three choices for Harding's cabinet. Harry Daugherty agreed and told the Senator not to declare yet because it would look like a Boss controlled election. Penrose compromised and allowed the president maker Daugherty to continue his orchestration. At 4:46 the Convention reconvened for the taking of the tenth ballot.

Chancellor wrote later, the colored delegates, 176 in all, not counting the alternates, out of a total of not quite 1, 000 delegates, withdrew as usual to the sidewalk. They left their proxies in the hands of the chair of their state delegations. They voted in blocks according to the number of their state delegates. This solved a problem for the bosses. The Negro voting block represented one sixth of all the votes, or one third of the number necessary to nominate. No one knows how much they paid these colored brothers for their votes, except the bribers and the bribed. Nevertheless, a group told me that they were anxious to get home and spend their money. I asked them how much they got, and they said their traveling expenses, their board bills, their incidentals, and their wages. None left the convention empty-handed. They were serving the interests of their common country and ours by making a living in politics.

Frank Hitchcock dealt with the Negro delegates. The former United States Postmaster General, made a point every four years of fixing the Southern delegates in the Republican Convention. Hitchcock went to Washington to be a government clerk at sixteen hundred dollars a year in 1900. When finished with the election work in the 1912 Republican Convention, they estimated that he was worth about six hundred thousand dollars. Hitchcock, a bachelor, found his proper work in the field of national politics. Southerners and New Englanders traded in Negroes for plantation slaves for breeding stock, but Hitchcock had a new wrinkle. He traded in Negroes for political slaves to use in Republican conventions.

The Negroes voted for Harding as instructed with very great pleasure. They told them about Harding's Negro bloodline. They were also assured that Harding would appoint Negroes to many more offices than any other president had. Nevertheless, they were wise enough not to vote for their colored brother until they received the cash for doing so. The Negro was not in politics for his health.

Ballot after ballot, the strength slowly faded away from Wood, Johnson, and Lowden to Harding, who came through with a small majority by the ninth ballot. A swing to Harding continued as delegates delivered votes bought and paid for. To appease their angry consciences, they stampeded to Calvin Coolidge for vice president. The Oklahoma delegation, after a few ballots, abandoned Lowden for Harding for a price. They say this cost another fifty thousand dollars and they also bought other delegations. It was unknown how many votes that Harding won that Jake Hamon's money bought. The total amounts spent were about three hundred thousand dollars. It was not a convention of cheap men. Some delegates went home with net profits of twenty-five thousand dollars.

Jake Hamon, a wealthy oil man who was used by Harding.

Jake thought he had the definite promise of the inside track on the huge Naval oil reserves in Wyoming and California. In total Hamon spent from $900,000 to $1,500,000. Three persons knew how much Hamon spent, Harry M. Daugherty, Clara Smith, (now in the vaudeville field), and Ketchum, the manager of the Hamon estate. This raises the question of the debts of $1,800,000 Hamon borrowed from Standard Oil Banks and companies at the convention. Hamon, had the understanding that when he became Secretary of the Interior and opened Mexico and western oil reserves to the Standard Oil Interests, Standard Oil would forget the notes.

Daugherty knew his victory was in hand after talking with Penrose. The Columbus attorney looked to the galleries that were shouting themselves hoarse. He caught sight of Florence Harding. After sending a messenger to the Pennsylvania delegation to give sixty votes for Harding on the next ballot, he hurried above to sit next to Florence. He pulled a chair close and surprised her as he touched her arm. She complained to Daugherty about the yelling, bawling and cat calling. She said, "I cannot follow it."

Daugherty told Harding's wife that within a few minutes something was going to happen that may shock her. "I am here to keep you calm, " said Daugherty, "we have the votes. Warren will be elected on the next ballot!" In her hand she gripped two enormous hat pins. When Daugherty told, her Warren would be the winner on the next ballot and she jumped out of her chair. Florence may have intended to hug him but instead she drove both hat pins deep into his side. "I sprang back, " related Daugherty, "feeling the blood running down my legs into my shoes." Later the future attorney general found out it was sweat that filled his shoes.

Daugherty left Mrs. Harding in her gallery box and went back on the floor to hear Pennsylvania's vote, "we cast 60 votes for Warren G. Harding!" The cheers arose. He had won. Harding had 440 votes and would end with 692 votes as the other states jumped on the bandwagon. This was Saturday, June 12, 1920. Medill McCormick of Chicago, nominated Senator Lenroot for Vice President and Wallace McCamant of Oregon nominated Calvin Coolidge as Vice President. The vote for Coolidge was 674 to 146.

Nan Britton said, "I witnessed excitedly the balloting at the convention. I could not share with anyone, by the most extravagant verbal picture, the emotions I experienced. My eyes swam (with tears)."

Senator Brandagee sadly summed up the nomination of Harding for president: "This was not any 1880 or any 1904. We had no Shermans or Theodore Roosevelts. We had many second raters and Warren Harding was the best of the second raters."

CHAPTER TWO
HE LOOKS LIKE A PRESIDENT!

Harding possessed a prime qualification for any politician and that was the ability to remember names and faces. Besides having good table manners he was very careful about his grooming and dress. His dark olive complexion contrasted sharply with his almost white hair. He looked distinguished and as his most adoring fan Harry M. Daugherty said, "He looks like a President!"

Everyone agreed that Warren G. Harding had a fine speaking voice, but Daugherty, Penrose and other Republicans became nervous when Harding spoke without a written speech. Warren called it "bloviating" and he enjoyed it immensely. When Harding bloviated,

General Wood and Warren G. Harding. General Wood refused to go along with the Republican bosses and lost his bid to be President of the United States.
Credit: Ohio Historical Society

he spoke what was on his mind, often leaving his audience confused.

The senate cabal, headed by Boise Penrose, was the first to advise caution about allowing Harding to speak on his own. With characteristic biting sarcasm Penrose said, "Keep Warren at home. Don't let him make any speeches. If he goes on a tour, somebody's sure to ask him questions, and Warren's just the sort of damn fool that'll try to answer them."

The newspapers recognized Harding's nomination in Chicago as a victory for the Senate cabal. The day after the convention, the *New York Times* said the nomination of Harding was, "the fine and perfect flower of the cowardice and imbecility of the senatorial cabal." Others recognized Harding as the ideal candidate for the cabal. They said he would "stand without hitching and run without whipping." Senator Burton years earlier had called Harding, "that god-damned, honey fugling pussy footer."

Chancellor wrote: The Republican delegates went home, and going home, they expressed a fear that they were in for a licking at the polls. Judson C. Welliver and Will Hays, publicity mangers of the

Republicans told them not to be afraid, as victory was assured.

When the 300-strong Wayne, County, Ohio, commission of Republicans came back from Marion during the presidential campaign, they were strangely silent. The people asked them to tell what Warren was like. They flunked out on this question.

Republicans paused as the Democrats nominated their presidential candidate. Meanwhile, it took the country by surprise when the American Socialist Party nominated Eugene Debs as their Presidential candidate. He was still in jail at the time they nominated him. Woodrow Wilson had put Debs in jail for allegedly encouraging men to avoid the draft.

The Democratic convention started toward the end of June in San Francisco. Twenty-one names were presented at the convention. Unlike the Republican convention in Chicago, the divided Democrats took forty-four ballots to nominate James M. Cox for president and Franklin Delano Roosevelt for vice president.

Professor Chancellor wrote: On the Democratic side, the party showed three leading candidates and no dark horses anywhere on the horizon or in the woods. One candidate, William G. McAdoo, (also known as the Crown Prince), was the son-in-law of Woodrow Wilson. The politicians believed that Wilson would kill the chances of the Democrats with McAdoo at the head. McAdoo was "dry and pro suffrage." The Tammany outfit of New York had no use for him.

Attorney General Mitchell Palmer from Pennsylvania, called the handsomest man in politics and being in the Wilson Cabinet had a small chance too win. He was "impossible" according to the politicians, because he could not get any money for his campaign.

Jimmy Cox of Ohio, from Harding's own state and the best governor Ohio ever had, was worth millions and a great campaigner. Cox was "it." I have but two possible objections to him. He reputed to be "wet," and he had a divorced wife who was a cousin of Warren Harding. In all other regards, he filled the bill.

The Democrat's platform presented by Mr. Glass the chair, addressed the League of Nations issue and not much more. William Bryan wanted a plank against prohibition and universal training of the military. Doheny proposed Irish independence. Lyons brought up veterans' compensation. They dismissed these platforms because many democrats thought the battle was lost before it even began.

Senator Harding in a public statement said, "Governor Cox's nomination is an added consideration shown to our great state of Ohio. For this I am glad, as it gives assurance that finally a newspaperman will be the nation's chief executive." Warren predicted, "It is a great contest before us. Neither place of home nor personality will have any marked influence on the result."

Chancellor wrote: This will be the ugliest campaign in our

history since 1850. Whichever man is elected, he will serve no more than one term.

Cox and Harding are from the state of Ohio. Harding was a Senator and James M. Cox was the Governor of the State of Ohio. Harding published the *Marion Star* and James Cox published the *Dayton Daily News* and owned another newspaper in Ohio. The Democrat candidate was worth more than a million dollars and Harding, although comfortable, did not have much accumulated wealth. The rich man very seldom wins when pitted against the poor.

Harding married a divorced woman, Florence Kling De Wolf. Governor Cox was a divorced person but recently remarried. Both candidates have more common traits. Cox's first wife was a cousin to Warren G. Harding. When the race issue reared its ugly head Cox refused to join battle on this point. James Cox knew that Warren's great-grandmother was a Negro woman. The Democrat nominee did not want it known he had married a woman of Negro blood. Also, he thought he should protect the three children he had by his first wife. The word at the Democratic headquarters was not to bring the race issue up during the campaign.

Ned McLean, the owner of the Cincinnati *Enquirer,* became a close friend to the Hardings, but his newspaper was editorially Democratic. An editor of the newspaper stated, "The last thing the Republicans wished was the election of Governor Cox. As governor he had faced many new problems and worked them out successfully." The Columbus *Dispatch* remarked, "the people have a real affection for their governor."

A personal matter that would have influenced the outcome was that Warren fathered an illegitimate child, named Elizabeth. Nan Britton and Warren managed to keep this a secret. For the rest of his life the struggle to keep this a secret came at a great expense. Elizabeth Ann Britton (Harding), Warren Harding's child, was born October 22, 1919 in Asbury Park, New Jersey. Nan, the mother wrote, "exactly at two in the afternoon." As Nan held her newborn baby in her arms she said, "I saw Warren Harding. I saw him so strongly that it seemed I was holding a miniature sweetheart in my arms!" The baby had black hair that later disappeared to give way to a blond fuzz. As she grew, older Elizabeth took on the appearance of Warren's sister, Daisy. She had the dark olive skin color just like Daisy and Warren. Warren Harding always found an excuse not to see the baby.

Nan suffered from the effects of giving birth and Harding suggested that she seek rest in the Adirondacks at his expense. In mid summer James Sloan, a Secret Service agent, sought Nan at the Eagle Bay Hotel in Eagle Bay, New York. He handed her an envelope containing a note from Harding with cash amounting to eight hundred dollars to cover her expenses. Nan would stay in the mountain resort, until late August, then return to Chicago.

During the summer the Republicans concentrated on the issues of the campaign. A real issue was that economic effects of the World War had not worn off. Labor demands during the heated war-based marketplace, drove wages higher and higher. After the war, employers asked labor to reduce wages, which it refused to do. Instead of compromise, labor went on strike, with crippling effects all over the country. The effect of strikes put men out of work but prices remained high. In protest of high prices, the wearing of cover overalls became a fad. Those who did not wear overalls wore their oldest clothes. Department stores took notice and dropped the price of their clothes. These were part of the real issues ignored by the Democrats.

Also, the introduction of women into politics began at this time. August 1920 the ratification of the right for women to vote took affect and found most political campaign managers unprepared. They hurriedly established new ways for promoting a candidate from a woman's point of view. Most were ineffective.

Prohibition of liquor sales and consumption was a fact and the main topic of conversation across the country. They called those in favor of prohibition "drys" and those against "wets." This law tried to force the American people to stop drinking and bootleggers and amateur distillers ignored the law. They made huge fortunes selling contraband liquor. Federal Court dockets were overwhelmed with cases involving liquor sales. Harry Daugherty later said, "The only way to make America dry, is to drink it dry." James Cox said he would enforce the laws of the land, while the Republicans avoided the issue.

The social order at the turn of the century was in a hasty change. Men raised eyebrows as women's hemlines raised to a daring nine inches above the ankle. The automobile dramatically changed the social life of a new generation. In a short time young couples found they could go to the next town or city to find romance. No longer was courtship a hometown affair. The youth rebelled.

New outlooks of the young, economical changes, prohibition, and racial tensions faced the politician in 1920. Blacks who fought in the trenches of Europe returned home and demanded their rights as Americans. Democrats failed to give notice to these changes as Republicans began to rally all voters around Harding with his "America First" campaign speeches climaxed with a return to "normalcy."

Democrats had the biggest hurdle to over come which was the policies of Woodrow Wilson the incumbent president. Woodrow Wilson won a close reelection, four years earlier, on the promise that he would keep America out of the war in Europe. This was a promise he could not keep and America voters would not forget. Some felt Wilson lied as a ruse for reelection. Also, Woodrow Wilson became obsessed with creating a world order, within the League of Nations. He felt the country needed this world order to maintain peace on a global scale. Blindly he demanded that the Democratic party make the League of Nations the main issue in the presidential election. Cox, dogmatically, would follow this path and lose.

At Columbus, Ohio, the Democrat's National Committee convened. Cox introduced his running mate Franklin Delano Roosevelt from the state of New York. At this time FDR was well known only in New York. Wilson appointed him as Assistant to the Secretary of Navy. FDR pointed with pride to his writing of Haiti's constitution. In 1920, FDR was healthy and vigorous during the campaign. It would be the last year of his life that he could walk freely, before crippled by polio.

Chancellor wrote in his book. They made this election to order for the Republicans. The Democrats would capture the support of the progressives by naming Franklin D. Roosevelt, a cousin of Theodore Roosevelt. FDR's wife was also a cousin of Theodore Roosevelt. Cox and FDR made a fine-looking team. Many Democrats thought FDR was a lightweight and would not help the ticket at all.

Then the Democrats discovered the unpleasant fact that Harding's wife was a divorced woman. The Republicans responded truthfully enough that Mrs. Harding was not running for president and her first husband was dead. Democrats announced that Warren Harding owned brewery stock, but the sentimentalists swallowed this fact. The stocks numbered only three shares anyway and given to him for his newspaper influence.

James M. Cox, an owner of two newspapers and a line of Pure oil stocks, thought the American newspapers would treat him sympathetically. Both he and the Democratic party seriously miscalculated. Cox took credit for the working man's compensation act that had made Ohio famous in all the land. Big business thought Cox had been too good to labor.

Republicans discovered that Harding had a printer's union card, while Cox had none and they used this with great effect. The Republicans falsely asserted that Cox was worth twenty million and was trying to buy the presidency. Never does the richer man defeat the poorer when the people find out the comparative facts. In twenty out of twenty-three presidential campaigns since 1828, the poorer man had won.

In late July, Marion, Ohio, witnessed the arrival of the Republican National Committee. These members came to hear the formal acceptance speech of Warren G. Harding as the Republican presidential candidate. Harding read his acceptance speech but he did not write it, although some say he contributed to its content. With great attention Republicans listened, as did the press from all over the country. The *New York Times* felt that Harding scuttled the League of Nations in the speech. At times he agreed with the idea and other times he was set against it. The press soon dubbed him, "Mr. Wobble." All but one point of the acceptance speech, they printed in national newspapers. This Union newspaper printed the one point left out of other papers, which for the first time, Republicans introduced the issue of civil rights for Blacks into the campaign, a bold political move in 1920.

The *Union*, a black owned newspaper, in Cincinnati printed the story. Its headline read, "Harding said it! Harding said . . . I believe they should guarantee the Negro citizens of America the enjoyment of all their rights. That they have earned the full measure of citizenship on the battlefields of the republic. This entitles them to all the freedom and opportunity, all of sympathy and aid that the American spirit of fairness and justice demand."

Harry Daugherty, Harding's campaign manager knew about this newspaper. The *Union* certified it was a paper exclusively for Negroes and with a Negro editor. It used its influence in the primaries to defeat Harry Daugherty as a delegate-at-large of the Republican party in early spring. Its editor said in the spring, "D.D. or Dictator Daugherty, is down. As said by highbrows, he is persona non gratia." Daugherty learned a lesson from this defeat and would actively go after the Negro vote during the presidential campaign.

Harding's acceptance speech, on July 22, 1920 raised the emotionally charged issue of race. They would forever connect the issue of race with the Harding legacy. Cox would later say the contest was based on unfair accusations of race.

August 7, 1920 the fairgrounds in Dayton, Ohio, brimmed with one hundred thousand enthusiastic supporters of James M. Cox. The Democrats formed a parade downtown. Cox and Roosevelt led the crowd to the fairgrounds to hear James M. Cox's acceptance speech.

James M Cox accepted his nomination and spoke only of the League of Nations. He opened his acceptance speech, "We are in a time that calls for straight thinking, straight talking and straight acting. This is no time for wobbling." Cox began his bid for president the way he would end it, trying to get the dispassionate American people involved in world control and interest. He and the Democrats ignored the need for job security, lower prices and an adjustment from a war economy to a peace time economy. They also, ignored the underlaying race issue.

The race riots of 1919 were fierce and brutal. These riots were seen north of the Mason-Dixon line for the first time in Chicago and other cities. Washington, D.C. citizens saw Negroes' bodies swinging from telegram poles after a night of fighting and burning. The hanging of blacks became an issue.

Black Sam Albert Lewis wrote to the Executive "head elect," Harding. Black Sam wrote, "Ku Klux has taken place, White Caps have taken place and lynching and burnings have taken place and that has brought a disgrace upon the American Flag. This has caused me to grieve in my old days. We cannot depend upon the judges of the Counties, for they are lynchers and burners. Sheriffs are lynchers and burners. The Justices of peace are lynchers and burners. That is why I am making the appeal to the federal government."

The NAACP sent a delegation to Marion, Ohio to discuss lynching and their other concerns with Senator Harding. They presented him with questions about lynching, federal aid to education, the United States occupation of Haiti, the right to vote, and certain aspects of segregation. Harding told them that he agreed with them, but "from the point of view of practical politics, he could not make them the subject of specific and detailed statements in a public address." This answer did not satisfy the Black leaders. In an informal meeting they discussed the killing of Negroes in Haiti by American troops. Since FDR had been involved with writing the constitution of Haiti and its political control, Daugherty and others became very interested.

After this meeting the Republicans recognized the power of the Negro votes in the states where they allowed them to vote. In border states they could easily break a tie and swing the needed votes to give Harding a victory. So they established a Negro Republican club and designed special pamphlets, just for Negro voters. Also, they decided that on the tenth of September they would hold a Colored Voters day in Marion. C. R. Crissinger was placed in charge of organizing the Negro vote for Harding.

Republicans skillfully financed and prepared Colored Voters day to discourage militant Negroes from attending. Johnson the NAACP representative made sure no embarrassing questions or statements would come from those participating. Harry Daugherty was assured that only carefully selected, and moderate Negroes would attend Marion's event in September. Harry Lincoln Johnson told Harding and Daugherty the Negro voters were behind them.

The campaign continued as the attractive Nan Britton returned to Chicago after her Harding-sponsored vacation in the Adirondacks. Her health had improved and she had gained a few pounds. Nan immediately went to the Republican National Committee offices in Chicago to seek a secretarial job. Nan says, "Mr. Madden and I went to Victor Heinz's office. He introduced me as a friend of Mr. Harding. Mr. Heinz in turn took me to Mr. Frank Nimocks who hired me as his secretary."

Nan wrote, "Political fanatics roamed in and out of the headquarters." She kept a scrapbook and devoted one page to an Everett Harding. Everett claimed to be a cousin of Warren Harding. This disturbed those in the office, because Everett was a Negro. Just about this time Senator Howard Sutherland wrote to Will Hays. Sutherland in his letter told Hays that James Cox said, "that either the grandmother or great-grandmother of Senator Harding was a Black woman." They hid this letter from view.

Professor Chancellor returned to Ohio to his town of Wooster, Ohio where the College of Wooster was. They established the Wooster campus in an oak grove, near the Killbuck river and about a mile from the railroad station. The mile walk is all uphill. When formed they knew this college as the University of Wooster. In the south tower of the Memorial Chapel was a one ton bell. When they rang it, they could hear it all over the Killbuck river valley. This bell was presented to the college by Marcus A. Hanna, a Republican political boss from Cleveland Ohio. Hanna and his Republican political machine put McKinley in the presidency. Harry Daugherty was part of that team.

The summer following the death of his wife, Professor Chancellor gave lectures at the University of Wooster in Wooster, Ohio. That summer of 1909 William Estabrook Chancellor made a favorable impression on Mr. Dickerson who ran the University summer school. Dickerson invited Chancellor back every summer to lecture and teach. William in 1912 moved to New York City to manage and edit an educational magazine. In the summer he continued to teach at the University of Wooster, as it was known then. When the war broke out in Europe advertising for his and similar magazines dried up, forcing its closure. At this time royalties from his books exceeded all his other sources of income.

In 1914, they granted Chancellor a professorship in the Political Science department at Wooster University. This offer of a full professorship, his first, intrigued the successful author and he moved to Wooster, Ohio. The oldest daughter Louise Marie, attending Columbia University stayed in New York as the rest of Chancellor's family moved to the small college city in Ohio.

Lucy Lilian Notestein a noted historian in Wooster wrote, "President Holden hired as the new instructor of political science, William Estabrook Chancellor. He was enthusiastic and stimulating, sometimes erratic, however, and not always as tactful as one might wish. The professor was a graduate of Amherst with his Master's degree also from that institution. He had written several books on education and two others of which he was especially proud, for they had published them also in Braille. The books are, *Our Presidents and Their Offices* and *A History of the Government of the United States*. He will be teaching economics as well during the coming year. For several years past Mr. Dickerson had been using him as instructor, chapel speaker, and lecturer in the summer school. Chancellor had sixteen years of public school experience in Bloomfield, New Jersey, Norwalk, Connecticut, and Washington, D.C. William taught briefly or lectured at New York University, University of Chicago, Johns Hopkins and George Washington University. In 1919 the College gave him the life time Hoge tenure."

The College of Wooster said, "the Hoge professorship was an endowed chair. We established it through a gift by the Presbyterian Church, in honor of the Reverend Dr. James Hoge, prominently involved in the founding of the College of Wooster. We endow it in Economics, Morals and Sociology and Political Science."

In 1917 they decided that the University of Wooster should change its status and name to that of the College of Wooster. For many years the press and others would continue to call the school as Wooster University, much to the chagrin of the administration.

Chancellor wrote in his book. Standard Oil money established the College in its present condition. The President of its board of Trustees [Mr. Stone] was Chaplain of the Republican National Committee and the pastor of Senator Medill McCormick. Medill's wife, Ruth Hanna was the daughter of Mark Hanna, a great contributor to the College. It was not a municipal institution as its name surmises.

Chancellor's oldest daughter Louise Marie would graduate from Columbia and marry a Roy C. Miller. They held the wedding ceremonies in Wooster. Roy would become a successful attorney in Seattle, Washington. With Chancellor lived his other children, Catherine B, Susan B, Isabel B, and David B. The "B." in their names was in honor of Beecher, Mrs. Chancellor's lineage. In 1920 David, the youngest, was just twelve years old. David and only two daughters lived with Chancellor. Susan graduated from the College of Wooster in 1919 and had moved to Columbus, Ohio.

William noted with pride that he was a member of the New York Press club, a position he valued more than his professorship at the College of Wooster. In 1919 Chancellor ran for and was elected to the Wooster City Council. It was a very close race in the fourth Ward. This ward normally voted Republican, but William won his seat as a Democrat by four votes.

Chancellor's bid for a council seat in Wooster brought him in contact with the leading Democrats of Wooster. One leader was W. Howard Ross, aged 41, a noted criminal attorney in Wooster. Ross was also the head of the Wayne County Democrat Party. Ross practiced law with Judge W. E. Weygandt's law firm, *Symser, Weygandt and Weiser* in Wooster. His wife was a sister of Professor Howard Dickerson, who as head of College of Wooster's summer school had hired Chancellor. His son Ford would later become a trustee at the College of Wooster.

Chief Justice William E. Weygandt who was 62 years old at this time and a strong supporter and leader of the Democrat party. His sons were Carl, and Ross and he had a daughter named Ola. Ross operated a print shop in Wooster. Ola married John D. McKee whom we later connect with the College of Wooster.

Professor Chancellor every summer taught classes for the College of Wooster, except one year at Dennison University in Granville, Ohio. Also, he traveled extensively, giving paid lectures.

August 1920 the Democrats sent him to Marion, Ohio, to research Warren Harding. It was either W. Howard Ross or Judge Weygandt or both who asked Chancellor to look into the back ground of Harding.

The professor rerouted his travels while on the way to Circleville, Ohio and went to Harding's hometown. This investigation would dramatically change his life forever. The affable and friendly professor made inquiries about Harding for three days. While there, five highschool boys told him that they always called Harding a "nigger," and his sister [Daisy] also. Chancellor stated, "One of these boys was a Negro, and he was the only one among them who was not wearing a Cox button."

From Columbus, Ohio, the professor wrote a letter to W. Howard Ross from the Jefferson Hotel. In the upper left corner he wrote "or Judge Weygandt." The date of the letter was August 21, 1920.

Chancellor wrote in the letter, they baptized Harding as Warren Gamaliel Bancroft Winnipeg Harding, and he was an octoroon. An octoroon has one eighth racial mixture, and here the race is Negro. Republicans, both men and women, tell me they voted for Harding as Senator against Tim Hogan, who was Catholic. They thought that an octoroon was preferable to a Roman Catholic but they will never vote for Harding as President. They have also given to me a bill of particulars regarding all his martial affairs. His wife's birth name was Kling. For some years, Mrs. Harding was the wife of man named De Wolf. With De Wolf she had two children, a boy and a daughter. The boy died and the daughter, Esther married when very young. Florence provided a home for Warren but they quarreled constantly. After W.G.[Harding] got into politics, each traveled their own way. Mrs. Harding keeps her stranglehold on all the money and property. She was much richer than the Republicans admit and Warren had nothing. She gets into 'good society' because of her wealth. Chancellor ended the letter jubilantly, "Leave it to Marion to work the landslide to Cox!"

Governor James Cox and his counselors ignored this information. However, Ross and Judge Weygandt encouraged Professor Chancellor to look deeper into Harding and his ancestry.

During the presidential primaries the Republicans supporting General Wood brought up the race issue trying to defeat Harding. This tactic proved unsuccessful. Harry Daugherty realized the Blacks were becoming politically active and he decided to appeal to their voting power. Daugherty arranged with various Black people planning to come to Marion in September for the Colored Voter Day. He wrote to Manning of the Republican Committee for money to pay for the expense of two trains from Indianapolis. The campaign manager said in the letter he had already advanced James Johnson of the NAACP one thousand dollars to cover some expenses. He told Manning, when Johnson visited Marion, the locals did not allow him in any restaurants. They also denied Johnson access into a local drug store. Daugherty suggested something must be done to avoid such occurrences on Colored Voters Day in Marion.

Johnson, an invitee to Colored Voters Day wrote an article condemning the United States on the mistreatment of Negro inhabitants in Haiti. Stories about unarmed Negro citizens killed by armed Marines were featured highlights. Johnson would write three more articles and made sure Senator Harding got a copy of each. Warren gave the articles to Daugherty.

Word reached Professor Chancellor that Governor James M. Cox would not allow the use of Harding's ancestry in the campaign. Encouraged by other Democrats, Chancellor decided he would go to Marion, Ohio, and learn as much about Warren G Harding as time permitted. The professor also thought it was a good time to update his book on presidents. He felt it would be a long and impossible road for Cox to be elected and Harding had the best chance too win.

Professor Chancellor walked the streets of the quaint city and conversed with the local people. The more he talked and listened the more he learned about and became interested in Harding.

Chancellor wrote in his book, Republicans set out to prove to America that Marion was "all for Harding." They created a "Victory Way" from the Union railroad station to the front porch of Harding's house, on Mount Vernon Street. They decorated each building with bunting and signs. Every morning they arrived and marched along Victory Way that led through the business district. They decorated all the buildings except the one owned by Jim Phillips.

Some of Harding's biographers say he was a great speech giver and writer. Daugherty and others thought otherwise and they decided they would promote a front porch campaign and that would allow them more control over Harding speeches and movements. Some called him the "Mecca from Marion," but others called him the "Marionette from Marion."

Warren Harding had no program, he had no depth, he reflected what appealed to a very few primitive instincts. He is genial enough, and, in a light way, affable. Still, how can a man who had never studied American history or government beyond the elementary school converse on politics, law, and economics?

He can seem to listen. As his pastor, the Reverend Doctor McAfee, said in an interview in the *New York World*, he was an eloquent listener.

Harding announced his front porch campaign and his need to meet the people at his own home. Then began the most deliberate lying of a continued and planned kind that America ever saw in any presidential campaign. Republicans sent out many false "pen portraits" of Harding to familiarize the public. When a train full of visitors came to Marion, they credited it with more delegates then it had. One afternoon a delegation failed to show up, but the next day all the papers printed the speech and told about the applause of the nonexistent crowd.

As Harding did his front porch campaign, what did those who went to Marion see? The people saw a big office with a staff of secretaries writing the daily speeches for Harding. They saw him read speeches he had never before seen. Visitors saw Mrs. Warren Harding running about in the street at times to interview people, not once, but systematically stopping even the merely curious. They saw the great men of the Republican party in twos, sevens and at times with large organized delegations. However, they did not see any enthusiasm. Visitors saw a system at work. All the enthusiasm was Republican political bunk written to order by the paid prostitutes of the Republican press. Come to the prophet, as Oliver Herford put it, "see the Marionette of Marion, in his hometown."

As the professor gathered information about Harding, the Democrats watched with intense interest as the Colored Voter Day succeeded in Marion. On September tenth the black voters marched up victory way to Harding's front porch. Very few, if any, white delegates were present that warm September day. The Black people did not object to this obvious act of segregating them to a separate day. They were just glad to become a small part of the electoral process.

The delegates sang "*Old Time Religion*" with enthusiasm and "*My Country Tis of Thee*" immediately followed. Crissinger warned merchants to treat the Black people with respect if any came into their store. Many owners did not want a confrontation and simply closed their business for the day. At the American Methodist church a tent was set up to feed the throng of Black people.

The Indictment

Chairs and tables were set outside on the lawns.

Charles A. Cottrell, acted as chair of the delegation and introduced the speakers. Dr. Morris, Dr. Robinson, Dr. Taylor, Dr. Shaw and Mr. Lewis.

Lewis said, "We came here to renew our pledges of love, loyalty and devotion to the party of our fathers, the party of emancipation and of human progress. We notice the road to the White House leads through the great republican state of Ohio. The road comes through Marion, Ohio and not Dayton, Ohio."

Lewis addressed Harding, "In your own words, you said you will renew at Washington the great temple of liberty under law. You will enforce the constitution that contemplates no class and recognizes no group but by recognizing all groups. Our votes will be felt this year in the great pivotal states of New York, New Jersey, Connecticut, Ohio, Indiana and Illinois as never before. This will include Missouri, Maryland and Kentucky."

General Pershing, who happened to be visiting Marion that day spoke to the colored delegation. Then Warren Harding said, "I will center my interest upon the contribution of America to your people. Justice in America, must never relax vigilance. . . . Equality is worth nothing if we do not earn it, but an equal opportunity for all men and women to achieve."

Harding contrasted liberty in Russia with that in America. He talked about how the citizen should give to the government instead of taking. He then said, "I proclaim more. I assert to the world that America had not, and will not fail the American Negro."

Harding then used statistics to show the great progress the Negro had made in America. Near the end of his speech he said, "America has given you her great blessing of Justice. You have it and you will have it. If I have anything to do with it, it will also be good American obedience to law. True Americans can only deal with brutal and unlawful violence one way, whether they are of your blood or of mine."

Mrs. Robinson, Miss Brown, Dr. Lyon all spoke after Senator Harding. The high yellow skinned and attractive Mrs. Fleming caught the eye of Harding as he listened to her short speech. Warren would later write her a letter that was three times longer than her speech telling how he admired her "ideals."

National press releases named the organizations that were present that warm fall day in Marion. They did not quote the speeches of Harding or any of the colored delegates. Nor did any of the national papers mention that William Monroe Trotter of the National Race Conference was in Marion or that he held a "private" conference with Warren G. Harding. Only the *Sentinel Press* in Wellston, Ohio, and a newspaper in Bucyrus, Ohio, wrote truthfully about the Colored Voters Day in Marion. The *Sentinel Press* headlines read, "Harding appeals to the Black Voters."

William Trotter, considered a radical, because he spoke out for the civil rights of Negroes, agreed not to speak publically in Marion. They gave him a special conference with Harding and Daugherty. He spoke, "On the very night of the day they nominated you, a delegation of this National Equal Rights League secured a minute of your attention. We asked you whether you, if elected, would abolish Federal segregation at Washington. With only a moment to reply you said, 'I am for Democracy in its fullness.' This was in June."

William Trotter continued, "In your speech of acceptance in July you amplified this in strong words of your political creed. You said, 'I believe the Federal Government should stamp out lynching and abolish that stain from the fair name of America.' You also said, 'I believe we should guarantee the Negro citizens of America the enjoyment of all their rights. The Negro had earned this full measure of measure of citizenship as they sacrificed blood on the battlefields of the Republic. This entitles them to all of freedom and opportunity, all of sympathy and aid that the American spirit of fairness and justice demands."

"Today we come, a delegation of this League, to present to you the specific complaints of the fourteen million colored Americans about abuses suffered under the government of the United States of America. A National Race Conference had formulated this and called for the purpose at Chicago in April and the specific redress justly demanded, as the race believes."

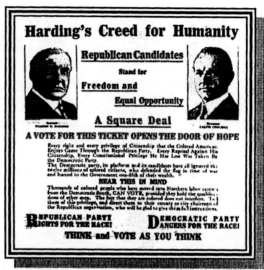

The Republicans placed this ad in the Union and other Black owned newspapers. This ad aroused white supremacists and the ever growing KKK. This ad would start an avalanche of flyers during the campaign in retaliation.

"America denies," continued Trotter, "Colored Americans' protection from the lawless mob without federal interference. They deny us the right of suffrage because of race in federal elections without federal interventions. We are subjected to exclusion, denial of service, or segregation for race in public places. The national government in federal employment, executive departments and in public facilities where the federal government has jurisdiction denies us"

"We demand Congress enact a law making lynching a crime against the federal government. Congress must enact a law enforcing the right to vote without any colored restrictions. Congress must enact a law, forbidding the separation of interstate passengers for race or color. We want the Chief executive to recommend said measures to Congress. Especially to abolish and forbid segregation in any department, branch, or any feature in the federal service in the Executive branch."

Senator Harding promised to Trotter a careful study of the Congressional measures to end and correct these abuses. He declared, "If the United States cannot prevent race segregation in its own service we are not in any sense a Democracy."

So ended the segregated Color Voters Day in Marion, Ohio. Daugherty with the help of Lasker had ads created to be placed in various Negro owned papers. Racist Democrats watched Harding very closely after the Colored Voter's day in Marion. They waited for the right time to unleash their hatred for Blacks.

Chancellor wrote in his book, D. R. Crissinger, a local attorney, was placed in charge of organizing the color vote in and around Ohio. Attorney Crissinger and Warren Harding were born in the town of Blooming Grove. The played together as youths and Crissinger like his boy hood friends called Warren, his given nickname, "Nig." Daniel Crissinger sent information to various colored organizations hinting that Harding was one of them.

Congenial Chancellor asked everyone in Marion about Warren Harding. It did not take long before he discovered Carrie Phillips and Warren had a love affair going for more than fourteen years.

Professor Arthur Hirsch, the head of the History Department at the Ohio Wesleyan University, saw Carrie Phillips in action. Professor Hirsch wrote, "I stood some distance back one forenoon when Mrs. Phillips was standing a few feet away, on the Harding front lawn. She was talking to Mr. Harding who sat on the porch corner that he used as a campaign headquarters. With one eye on him and the other on the front door, she would take a cautious step, then another, toward the porch. Suddenly, Mrs. Harding appeared. A feather duster came sailing out at Mrs. Phillips, then a wastebasket. Mrs. Phillips did not retreat. Next came a piano stool, one of those old four legged things with a swivel seat by which it could be lowered or raised. Not until then was there a retreat. Mrs. Phillips tossed him a kiss and left quietly."

Chancellor wrote, the Republicans had to quiet the threat of Carrie Phillips. The Phillips case illustrates Hardings sex instincts. Mrs. Phillips very showy and vain, was the wife of a dry-goods man in Marion, with a passion for men. Jim Phillips, her husband, was a poor little fellow who was a part owner of a store in Marion. This woman had made herself useful to men of a kind. She got in with Warren, who as usual, paid no attention to his own wife who was "passee" through the years. Often, even after the nomination, he and Mrs. Phillips visited together at Upper Sandusky.

The scandal was too open for the Republican National Committee to tolerate. Hays sent Albert Lasker to deal with Carrie Phillips. Lasker had his own opinion about Harding. At their first meeting Harding asked Lasker to agree not to quit if they should disagree. That was not the way Lasker saw life. Harding, he felt, was

Carrie Phillips

soft. As the campaign's publicity director, his job was to humanize Harding as an old-fashioned, sage, honest-to-the-core Middle Westerner whom they could trust never to rock the boat. Lasker thought that would be easy.

Lasker was the son of a German-Jewish peddler who had come to Texas and established himself as a merchant and trader. His father's bitter memories of Europe had left the son a fanatic isolationist. At the age of eighteen, Lasker had gone to work as an office worker in the Chicago advertising firm of *Lord & Thomas*. One of his first duties was cleaning the cuspidors. In five years he was making $52,000 a year, and before he was forty he owned the firm and was taking a million a year from it. Besides *Pepsodent,* he created *Puffed Wheat* from *Puffed Berries*, gave *Palmolive* its school child complexion, and set women to smoking *Lucky Strikes*. He had the advertising man's sixth sense for the popular mood.

With massive use of all the modern advertising techniques he was going to streamline Hanna's methods to replace the image of 'wobble and wiggle' with Harding and Coolidge. With a dozen picked advertising specialists, he set up headquarters in New York. His secret concern was that Harding was not an isolationist. With Carrie Phillips, Lasker was blunt. In his one interview he agreed to pay her twenty thousand plus a monthly sum of two thousand dollars if Harding held public office. In addition, she and her husband were to take an expense-paid trip round the world via the Orient where Jim would investigate the raw silk trade. The stipulation was that they must leave Marion before the election and stay away. Jim and Carrie left for Japan at the summer's end.

Warren married Florence Kling De Wolfe when he was twenty-six years old and Florence was thirty-one. Her father Amos Kling was considered the richest man in Marion and did not care for Warren. Amos refused to attend the wedding and he openly called Warren a "nigger." Never fully explained by any biographer was the fact that Warren soon had to enter a sanatorium because of mental and nervous breakdowns. His first visit was right after his marriage to the domineering Florence Kling.

The sanatorium, he attended and would return repeatedly, is found in Battle Creek, Michigan and known as the Kellogg Sanatorium. Dr. John Kellogg established the institution that became recognized around the world for it's "health building and training." John Kellogg believed in hydrotherapy, exercise and a vegetarian diet.

The Doctor's brother Will Kellogg conducted research to find a digestible bread substitute. One night Will left a pot of boiled wheat to stand and it became tempered. They put the contents through a rolling process, turning each grain of wheat into a large thin flake. They served this flake and it was an immediate favorite of all the patients. With just a sixth grade education, William would develop *Kellogg Flakes* into a successful and nationally known business.

Jim Phillips suffered mental strain in 1905 and it was the Kellogg Sanatorium that Warren Harding recommended to his neighbor and friend. Almost simultaneously Warren had to send his wife, Florence to Grant Hospital in Columbus, Ohio, for a kidney removal. Warren went over to Phillips South Main Street home in Marion to see Jim's wife Carrie.

Carrie a redhead, a head taller than her husband Jim had once taught school in a town just north of Marion, called Bucyrus. Her birth name was Fulton and in her linage was the famous inventor of the steam boat. Warren and Carrie became attracted to each other and made love in Jim Phillips bed. As much as Warren needed sex, he found in Carrie a woman to love and care for. As Jim Phillip recovered from his nervous breakdown in the Kellogg sanatorium and Florence recovered from her kidney aliment in Columbus, Warren and Carrie made love. It was not long before the town people realized that Harding was having a love affair.

Their respective mates returned home. Warren purchased a touring car and hired a Black friend from his former town of Blooming Grove to be his chauffeur. Florence, Warren, Carrie and Jim Phillips made it a point on sundays to get together on a drive in the country. Phillips entertained the Hardings at their home and the Hardings reciprocated. The town people shook their heads in disbelief. They were in for more of a shock when the Phillips and Hardings traveled to Europe together in 1909. On this trip Carrie Phillips fell in love with Germany and entertained the idea of moving there with her daughter. Warren's refused to divorce his wife and marry her, was reason enough for Carrie to pack up, take her daughter and move to Germany. This was in 1912.

A year later Jim Phillips went to Germany to convince Carrie to return. The red head wanted to stay, as she knew that marriage to Warren was out of the question and she loathed Marion. She rebuffed Jim's efforts until Germany declared war. Jim Phillip returned to Marion with his wife in tow.

For many years Warren wrote letters to Carrie. Some were short letters and others more than forty pages long. He called her "Sis" and his code name was "Constant." Carrie, after reading and answering the letters secreted them in a box. By this time Warren was a Senator and lived in Washington in a house Florence had purchased.

Warren's letters to Carrie-darling, Carrie-sweetheart, Carrie-adorable, continued while he was in Washington. He wrote many letters with the heading of his Senate office on top and sent most in blue envelopes. Those who read them felt Harding's proses remained them of a love sick high school boy writing to his sweetheart. When war with Germany raised its grotesque head Carrie threaten to expose his love affair with her if he voted for war in Congress. Warren voted for war but Carrie did not expose him.

About this time Warren started his love affair with Nan Britton and the letters to Carrie became fewer and not so long. It took sometime, but Carrie finally figured out who Harding was having an affair with and in 1919 threatened to expose him. Warren did not take this as an idle threat. On a trip to Marion Warren managed to make up with Carrie, holding off exposure.

While in Marion in 1919, he talked to investors, who wanted to purchase his newspaper the *Marion Star* but, they agreed upon nothing. Warren returned to Washington after he gave more control for running of the newspaper to his employees. He told them he liked Washington and being in the Senate. In 1920 he planned to run for another six-year term.

The letters between Carrie and Warren would stop after he became the nominee for president. One last letter stated the terms between the star-crossed lovers. Harding wrote, "I will if you demand it as the price, return to Marion to reside. If you think, I can be more helpful by having a public position and influence I will pay you five thousand per year, in March of each year, while I am in that public service."

This letter was in response to Carrie's fury after Warren refused again to divorce Florence and marry her. The volatile red head then told her husband Jim Phillips about the long affair she had with Warren G. Harding. The dry-goods merchant could not comprehend the betrayal of his wife with his best friend Warren. Lasker's move to send Carrie away, took from the Democrats a sex-expose on the Republican candidate.

Republicans were concerned about Harding's love affairs but not enough to be worried. With prohibition came a dramatic change of morals in the country. Causal sex affairs by married couples almost became passe. Unheard of sex before marriage they openly discussed at parties. Lasker and others knew this and easily played down any reference to Harding and Carrie Phillips.

The Negro issue was another matter. Within a week after the Colored Voters' day in a speech Harding described the rape of Haiti. He overstated "American Marines killed thousands of native Haitians." He also stated "they have sacrificed many of our gallant men." In reality Harding paraphrased the articles written by Johnson, which they had sent to him. Harding blamed the rape of Haiti upon James Cox's running mate Franklin Delano Roosevelt. Harding stated in his speech that FDR had publically boasted that he had written the constitution on Haiti.

FDR's response called the accusations mere dribble and demanded an apology from Harding, which he got. Harding in his apology said, "This does not in any way abate my opinion as to the policy of your Administration in dealing with Haiti and Santo Domingo."

The NAACP rejoiced with Hardings tactics and Johnson wrote, "I see you have finally gotten under the skin of the Wilson administration. You have smoked them out and got them on the run and I hope you will keep them running."

The Indictment

The day after the Colored Voters Day advertisements appeared in most Negro newspapers. Republicans appealed to Negro voters to register and of course vote for their party. Some issues of the black owned papers would get into the hands of white supremacists who would use any tool to down grade the Negro.

White supremacy rhetoric increased as colored populations in cities spread. Writers and speakers proclaimed that dark skinned races are a worse threat to Western civilization than Germans or Bolsheviks. It was in this era that the Klan or the Ku Klux Klan grew in stature and power. The KKK already five years old was small and insignificant under the influence of Colonel William Simmons. In 1920 Simmons put his organization in the hands of Edward Y. Clarke who knew the time was ripe for the Klan. He recruited from small Protestant towns who with anonymity of hooded robes, flaming crosses and secrecy brought fear to Blacks, Jews and Catholics. Sales agents called Kleagles divided into Realms headed by King Kleagles. Realms made up Domains and put under the control of Grand Goblins. Clarke gave himself the title of Imperial Wizard. Membership cost just ten dollars of which four dollars went into the pocket of the Kleagle that made the sale. King Kleagles kept a part of the fee before passing it onto the Grand Goblins. The Imperial Wizard got just part of the membership fee but after they signed four million members into the organization, Clarke became very rich.

Franklin Delano Roosevelt was considered a political light weight in the year 1920.

The Klan on the march at night with torches, instilled fear into all who witnessed. Sheriffs soon refused to investigate if they saw "KKK" scribbled on a fence or door. In a matter of time the KKK gained tremendous political power.

CHAPTER THREE
OCTOBERFEST

The Republicans nervous when the roorbacks started to appear, and counter maned, their impact anyway they could. This rally in Marion, Ohio, clearly demonstrates the race issue.

Credit: Ohio Historical Society

Just northeast of Marion, Ohio lays Bucyrus, Ohio, a farm community known for its Bratwurst festival. This small town once supported two newspapers that chronicled the 1920 presidential election. The *News-Forum* favored the Democratic party and the *Bucyrus Telegram* was decidedly Republican in its editorials and news presentation. In its September 28, 1920-edition the *News-Forum*, headlined an article, "Dr. William E. Chancellor Makes Instructive Speech on The League of Nations."

Most authors said that Chancellor concentrated only on the Negro issue during the Harding election campaign. One writer claimed that Chancellor would always say prejudice remarks about Negroes in his speeches. This was not true. Chancellor always said, "race was NOT an issue, he was FOR the league and FOR Cox because Cox supported the League."

Friday, September 24, 1920 Chancellor made a speech at the Opera Hall in Bucyrus, to more than two hundred and fifty people. Dr. William E. Chancellor opened his speech by saying, "The American people at this fall's election will write an outstanding chapter for our future school histories. The League of

Nations should never have been a political issue in this campaign and would not have been except a bitter fight caused by scheming politicians."

A *Bucyrus News-Forum* reporter stated, "Chancellor showed by illustration many important issues that are being kept in the background in this political campaign. These issues would have furnished plenty of material on which to conduct a campaign. Decisions in these unspoken matters, the future welfare of our country depends upon."

The *News-Forum* reporter stated that Chancellor was well informed on subjects of the day and an able speaker. The professor drew a verbal picture of Senator Lodge and President Wilson and struck home at what he termed the real cause for bringing the League of Nations into politics. He stated that President Wilson was born of foreign lineage. They educated him at a Presbyterian college, became a college professor, president of Princeton University, governor of the state of New Jersey and finally the president of the United States. President Wilson wrote several books, and prominent among them was his series of histories.

Chancellor said that Senator Lodge on the other hand was of native New England stock, wealthy, educated at Harvard, a rival of Princeton. Senator Lodge was a close friend of Theodore Roosevelt when he was president and he spent a great deal of time in the company of the past president. He had staked his all to defeat what he terms the "Wilson League." He successfully waged a battle in the senate that prevented a ratification of the treaty and the league covenant. Senator Lodge was fighting to the last ditch to carry this election to defeat the League.

The professor explained the Republicans have misunderstood and misrepresented conditional provisions of the parts of League of Nations. "Quoting one of Senator Harding's front porch speeches, in which the candidate termed the League a fraud," the professor dramatically brought his arguments to a climax. Dr. Chancellor stated, "they should include as a provision in the covenants of League, to guard against international traffic in drugs and women. Then considering the League would be more worthwhile."

The Republican paper, Bucyrus *Telegram* editorially rebuffed Chancellor's speech given at the opera house. They pointed out that Woodrow Wilson was a professor from New Jersey (Princeton) and "we have had enough of the 'Little Schoolmaster' in the presidential chair, and the people this year want something more practical." The editor goes on to suggest that Chancellor, the professor, should get away from high-minded views and back to American standards. This editor said, "the public did not need another professor telling them how to vote."

In rebuttal the Democratic, Bucyrus *News-Forum* pointed out that Frank B. Willis was a college professor and was "running on the Republican ticket for a Senator from Ohio." This editor said, "Aside its attack upon college professors and teachers, no one need have any serious doubt that this organ will support the candidacy of Mr. Willis."

Not once in his speech did the professor mention the issue of race that evening in Bucyrus. The Republican party started this issue during the spring primaries. They said Harry M. Daugherty was furious when he heard that General Wood and his campaigners brought up the Negro ancestry of Harding. Harry had fought this issue when Warren Harding ran for the Governor of Ohio, and thought this single factor cost them that election. Warren lost that contest by a count of one hundred thousand votes. Knowledge of Harding's Negro ancestry was not new in Ohio. A popular and well written black oriented magazine noted this fact.

Author A. N. Fields wrote in the black-owned *Abbot Magazine*, "In Harding's battle for governorship against Patterson of Cincinnati, they brought the race issue into the campaign. It had gained such strides that Harding's campaign manager held conferences with his faithful colored supporters to discuss the matter. He stated that he had put the question direct to Harding who would neither affirm nor deny the accusation, treating it, however, as too ridiculous to warrant any serious thought."

Professor Chancellor would become personally entangled in the race issue. The Bucyrus speech was one of forty given by Professor Chancellor during the election campaign. Despite his full schedule at the College of Wooster he made time to give these speeches and continue his research on Warren G. Harding. Someone, found the key research paper of General Wood's people and Chancellor got a copy of it. This "research" paper is worthwhile to note because later they will accuse the professor of being its author.

No one knows who the author was, and we quote it with original miss spellings and grammar errors.

This is the linage of Warren Gamiel [sic] Winnipeg Bancroft Harding. His father was George Tyron Harding, obviously a mulatto. He had thick lips, rolling eyes, chocolate skin.

His mother was Phoebe Dickerson, a mid wife by trade. She died several years ago. They had two sons and three daughters, and W. G. W.B. was born when G. T. was only twenty-one years old. We know nothing about the ancestry, or of this Phoebe Dickerson.

One daughter was black with kinky hair. Only one ever married. Their names were Abigail, Carrie and Mary.

The parents of G. T. Harding were Amos Harding, of whom we know about nothing. He was a white man from New York State and Mary Ann Dixon or Discon Harding, a black woman, but when they were married, if ever, one knows.

They had this son in the year 1844. Another son of Amos and Mary Ann was Mordecai Dixon or Dickson, of whom and his children all Bucyrus have made a tale. He sat in the corner of the Baptist Church reserved for Negroes, was often on his feet in prayer meeting, etc.

He was a cooper by trade and had a large and wild family. Mordecai was born in 1818 and died in 1901.

The professor kept the "research" paper and forwarded a copy of it to the Democratic Headquarters in Columbus, Ohio. Before mailing it he put the notation on the bottom, "Just a choice bit of fact I found in the files of an actual investigation." Democratic party leaders told Chancellor that it was their policy not to use the Negro issue in the campaign.

James Cox, the Democratic President candidate, returned from his western tour at the beginning of October. His long journey covered twenty-four states west of the Mississippi river. It was estimated James M. Cox traveled more than ten thousand miles and spoke two-hundred-thirty-eight times. Cox said after awhile he could detect the political leaning of the railroad switching engineers. If the yards were quiet, the operator was a Democratic, while the Republican engineer made all the noise he could as Cox spoke.

Chancellor wrote in his book. Cox made three moves that look like serious mistakes. First, he campaigned in Washington, Oregon, and California. He imagined that he could carry the Coast. This took him away from the East, where Harding was doing the front porch work. The trip around the circuit, getting out to see the people, looks good, but few future candidates will try it. Cox made votes out on the coast, but he lost more votes in the East by leaving the battleground.

Second, he relied upon the one issue in his speeches, the League of Nations. No candidate ever wins with one issue. It was true that the League of Nations covenant was worth all the time he gave to it, but the voters did not see this. The country was trying to recover from wartime and feared the lack of jobs. They cared less about solving problems in Europe. Factories created for war production stood empty. Tavern owners and citizens become criminals as the Volstead Act went into effect. The Democratic candidate ignored these conditions.

Third, Cox asked the Democratic publicity men not to mention the colored blood of Harding because it would involve his three children by his first wife. He thought of his posterity rather than of his country. The Republicans falsely charged that the Democrats were secretly using this story, but the truth was that the Democrats frowned upon it.

Fall semesters at the College of Wooster commenced late September with an enrollment of five hundred and seventy students. Professor Chancellor taught twenty-three classes in Economics, Political Science and Social Psychology. Because of his methods, he often had the largest classes and attracted the best students. Lucy Lilian Notestein author and a professor, thought Chancellor was, "erratic and lacking in judgment at times." Lucy Notestein never reveled why she thought Chancellor was erratic or lacked in judgement. She did write that Chancellor did not follow the well-beaten path but instead stimulated his student's thinking.

Lucy said, "He encouraged currant-event discussion and aided in introducing the Republican and Democratic clubs on the campus. Chancellor was active in community service, student publications, publicity and served on the library committee. In the town of Wooster he spoke on occasions, served on the town council and wrote letters to newspapers all over the country as the spirit moved him. Although the elections took much of his time, the professor maintained his dedication to the College."

Chancellor also served as president of the College Republican Club. He followed Roosevelt out of the Republican party in 1912, and later became a Democrat. He wrote thirty-nine different books on education and history. On the campus at the College of Wooster his nickname was Chancy, and others called him the "Mark Twain of Wooster." His friends called him Bill.

The professor was a member of the New York Press Club for many years. Among his literary credits were articles for the *New York Times*, the *New York Tribune*, the *Cleveland Plain Dealer*, and other newspapers. As a political analyst, he was nearly unequaled in the world. He was so engaging in reputation that six Ohio cities had him deliver the Roosevelt memorial funeral oration.

When speaking he would, without benefit of notes, lean against the podium, not behind it, and with a clear melodious voice deliver his speech. The professor knew his audience and never spoke down to them but, always at them. He was in great demand as a speaker and gave paid public addresses in many different states more than 4,500 occasions. When he delivered his speech called *Rivers of Life, the* audience always gave him a standing ovation.

Professor Chancellor had given lecture courses in the states of Washington and Iowa. His lectures reached every state in the Union, including every county in Vermont and fourteen counties in Pennsylvania. His income from lectures and book royalties kept his revenue well above average. Most of the time, this income exceeded his salary as a full time professor. On an average day, he would receive more than twenty letters. That was more than six-thousand a year!

Chancellor wrote about the election. Democrats made other errors. One may have been the failure of Cox to declare himself on the wet question unconditionally. He said meekly that he would "enforce the laws." If he had declared he disliked prohibition, as Wilson had done, or that he firmly believed in it, he would have kept more votes.

The Democratic management at headquarters was incompetent. It had no policy, it had no faith in victory, and it would spend no money beyond what was in sight. Management was loyal to Cox, used too few speakers and too little ink and paper. Cox had the loyalty of very conservative and rich businesspeople who would not risk too much.

The plutocracy wanted their man Harding in control. They need to control the public press, the larger banks, the larger business enterprises, and the government to gain even more control. Oil, steel, railroads, and banks are the main interests of the plutocracy that began to form in the days of McKinley. Then they went under the names of syndicates, pools, and trusts. The Rockefellers, George Baker, the Guggenheims, Judge Gary, and the Noyeses of Washington are plutocrats. They want a man in the white house they can control. These plutocrats knew that Harding would do their bidding, and as a president would have no other ambitions or goals other than comfort. Cox was too much of his own man to suit them.

It was after James Cox returned, that Chancellor began his earnest research on Harding's ancestry, education and background. Accompanied by newspaper people professor Chancellor searched archives, Court house records and talked to anyone who had anything to say about Harding. The team went through Bucyrus, Iberia, Steams Corner, Mt. Gilead and of course Harding's place of birth Blooming Grove.

As early as 1911, A. J. Baughman, published the book *The History of Morrow County*. Baughman wrote about Harding's birth town and his ancestors. Warren Harding was born in Blooming Grove, Ohio, which to this day is a small farm town. Baughman's unbiased account is important because he wrote and published it before Warren Harding became famous.

A. J. Baughman wrote, "Grain of all kind was extensively grown, while they pay considerable attention to stock raising. Fine timber, consisting of oak, walnut beech, hickory, elm ash and other species once covered the township. Stephen Borham, who settled about four miles south of the village of Blooming Grove, came to the vicinity before 1820. His daughter, Mrs. Eckler, was perhaps the first white child born in Bloomfield Township. William Harris came about the year 1820."

"A Mr. Maxwell came from Pennsylvania and settled in the area and then sold out to the Hardings. Amos Harding, the patriarch of the Harding family, settled first in what is now Richland County about 1819. Ebenezer, one of Amos's sons, arrived with Maxwell in 1821. Then the following year his two brothers, George Tyron and Salmon E. came and settled near him. While the elder Harding settled north of the village, his two sons moved south of it. Salmon laid out the village of Blooming Grove, but afterwards sold his property and removed to Galion, where he died. They brought back and buried his remains in the village cemetery in ground he had donated for cemetery purposes. Ebenezer did not remain too long, removing to the west. They buried George Tyron a short distance where his father had settled when he came to the township."

"The pioneers found an unbroken forest, marked only by Indian trails. Now the historian finds well-cultivated farms, beautiful homes, churches and school houses, where once the woods stood dark and dismal. It was 1835, in March of that year, that Salmon recorded his plat. That same year they built the Methodist Episcopal Church and William Johnson built his home. Carl and Dunlap Johnson were the first merchants. Later, a Mr. Whitaker operated a store for some years. William Wallace opened the first post office in his home three miles south of Blooming Grove and called it Barcelona. Wallace moved to Blooming Grove and changed the post office's name to Corsica. Soon,

I.G. Baker became the post master. John Johns kept the first tavern and a J. C. Johnston was the first blacksmith in 1836."

"Blooming Grove was very pleasantly situated, an ideal little hometown, not a business center, but a place of rural domesticity. Not more than one hundred citizens lived in the town and it had a post office still named Corsica and two general stores. Corsica was moral town, a religious one, and of the size where everyone knew each other."

At this time they published only one biographical book about Harding and Joe Mitchell Chapple, a newspaper reporter, wrote it. Chapple self-published from Boston and called his company Chapple Publishing Company Limited. The title of his book is *Warren G. Harding the Man* copyrighted in 1920.

Chancellor purchased a copy of Chapple's book and in the inside cover he wrote a very terse review of the book, "All wind, signifying nothing." On page margins Chancellor wrote observations or his thoughts about the text. On page fifty-one Chapple is discussing the brothers and sisters of Warren Harding. Chancellor noted on this page that Mrs. Votaw of Washington, D.C. was a sister to Warren. Chancellor wrote on the bottom of the page, "I appointed a Mrs. Votaw as a colored woman to the colored schools. Suppose to be a colored woman in Washington? Was she a Teacher there? Truant Officer?"

Another interesting observation Chancellor made is on page sixty-four. They characterize two photographs as Charles Harding and Mary Ann Crawford Harding. The heading reads "The grandparents of Warren G. Harding from old daguerreotype." The photos show two Caucasians, with no Negroid features at all. Chancellor writes on the left page, "Are these fake pictures? In a point of truth, are not these the brother and sister-in-law of Amos Harding and his wife? Was not her real name Elizabeth instead of Mary Ann? The Crawford's of Bucyrus told me this." He continues, "Text says Amos and picture says Charles. Text says nothing, and pictures say Mary Ann Crawford and the people say Mary Ann Dixon."

Chapple's book is one hundred twenty-eight pages with eight full-page photographs that are part of the page count. In his foreword Joe Chapple the author prints the reason he published, "When a friend appeared and offered to stand as sponsor for a book, I could not resist." Joe Chapple mentions the book is not a political book and that it is not. At best it is a very sketchy biography of Harding published after he became nominated by the Republican party. Today, 1999, used book stores' sell copies for two to five dollars.

The professor continued his research in Marion, before Harding closed his front porch campaign. With a piece of information here and there, the background of Warren G. Harding began to appear. The professor walked the "Victory Way" from the Union Station to Hardings' Mt. Vernon street home. He stood just fifteen feet from Harding's wife, Florence, as she conversed with a couple who were sitting in an automobile. Professor William Estabrook Chancellor heard Mrs. Harding tell the couple that she was "afraid that those dreadful stories, about Mr. and Mrs. Wilson were true." Florence turned and saw the professor standing there, smiled, and returned to her conversation with the visitors.

The professor listened to Senator Harding read a speech from his front porch. For a moment the Senator stopped reading and looked up to the crowd. He said, "I did not write this and I do not believe what I am reading!" A chuckle came from the crowd and the affable Harding finished reading the speech. As he completed the speech, a photographer took a picture of Harding looking directly at the camera. They seated the crowd to his right on folding chairs placed on the lawn. In the back on the extreme right row there sat Chancellor.

Chancellor viewed Harding's home from the street and then made his way to downtown Marion again. He had noted that one store, the Uhler-Phillips dry goods store, had no bunting or had pictures of Harding displayed on it. The professor wanted to find out why.

Chancellor wrote about his observations in Marion. I found that Jim Phillips owned the undecorated building. In early spring of that year Phillips learned that Warren Harding and Carrie, Jim's wife, was having a love affair. The Phillips-Harding romance had been going on for years. More than once Harding had sex with Carrie in Phillip's home. Jim, unsuspecting, had often motored in the countryside with Warren Harding and his wife.

Jim Phillips sent his wife to Sandusky, Ohio, during the election campaign, but this did not stop Harding from seeing her. The lack of bunting and pictures on his store was Jim Phillips way of telling the world that he did not support Harding.

Daniel Crissinger was one man that Chancellor wanted to visit while he was in Marion. Daniel thought to be a staunch Democrat had fruitlessly run twice for Congress as a Democrat. Chancellor thought he could trust Crissinger. He told Crissinger about his plan to get more information on Harding's background. Crissinger would report this to Harding and his campaign group.

Crissinger knew the Harding family exceptionally well as he was also born and once lived in Blooming Grove. Warren and Daniel had gone to school together and rollicked together as youths. Stories abound of how they robbed watermelons from neighbors gardens. It was through the effort of this attorney that the "Victory Way," and the "Harding for President Club" became organized. He became the driving force to get the town's cooperation to help with Hardings election. Daniel gave only sketchy information to Chancellor.

Chancellor wrote about the attorney. Crissinger practiced law and once was a member of the board directors at the Marion County Bank. The attorney ran for Congress twice under the Democratic banner and lost both times.

When he discovered Harding had won the Republican nomination, his civic pride for Marion swelled. He organized a bipartisan "Harding for President" club. The attorney insisted that merchants, especially restaurants and hotels were not to charge outlandish prices to visitors to his city. The Marion Civic Association also encouraged the making of Victory Way. Later, at Isabel Island, Texas, Harding appointed Crissinger Comptroller of the Currency. Harding came under heavy censorship from his Secretary of Treasury when he made Crissinger a governor of the Federal Reserve system.

Democrats liked to think that the return of James M. Cox from the west drove Harding off the front porch and out on the circuit. In part this may be true but it had become more difficult to get delegates to come to Marion, Ohio. Daugherty, and Lasker sent Harding out to make speeches.

Oklahoma the home state of Jake Hamon wanted Harding to speak in that state. With care and dedication Hamon worked to make Harding's visit a success. On the ninth of October 1920 the city was ready for Harding.

A civil war veteran, Jonathan Neff, starred in the opening ceremonies, and he had difficulty getting the straps of his drum over his shoulders. The civil war veteran added new and unusual flourishes while keeping time with the drum corps in the pit. Jonathan proudly told anyone who wanted to listen that he had beat the drums for Abraham Lincoln when he visited Dayton, Ohio, in 1860. Jonathan played to the enjoyment of the large crowd packed into the Auditorium in Oklahoma City, Oklahoma. The great crowd gave him a standing ovation.

Jake Hamon, the oil magnate, then took the podium, and introduced Florence Harding. Next he introduced Mrs. Hilliman, as the first women's elector in the United States and the head of the Women's Christian Temperance Union of Oklahoma.

Mrs. Hilliman in her speech said, "We have given twenty seven-million women the right to vote. These women are looking for a man who will give them a clean administration. We are looking for a man who will stand above accusations. We want a man who stands for America first!" Great applause and cries of "Hurrah for Harding!" prolonged the short introductory speech by Mrs. Hilliman.

Harding gave this speech October ninth. The day before, the Oklahoma press challenged him on his stand about the Negro vote and the race question. Boise Penrose had warned against allowing Warren off the front porch, because "the fool will start answering questions." Neither Daugherty nor Lasker knew what Harding had in mind in Oklahoma. They heard, with dismay, Harding's answer to the Oklahoma press.

The partisan crowd applauded his opening statement. Individuals yelled, "Hurrah for Harding!", "That is fine" and "bless your heart." The crowd became quiet when Harding continued, "The only difference between the North and the South in the last two decades have been that incident to a lack of intimate understanding. For more than a quarter of a century we have been getting away from the old wounds of conflict. Men in government have been seeking to bring old divisions into complete harmony and concord of purpose. . . . I have not come into this section to preach new doctrine to you. Although, I am just bringing to you an old doctrine that we adapted to the making of America. . . . I have not come from older Ohio to tell you how to solve your peculiar problems of the South."

"Somebody asked me what I would do about the racial question. I cannot answer that for you. That is too serious a problem for some of us to solve who do not know it as you do in your daily lives. It would not be fit to be President of the United States if I did not tell you in the south precisely the same I would say in the north. You cannot give one right to a white man and deny the same right to a black man. This does not mean I intend to have the white man and the black man to experience the enjoyment in each others company."

"Someone asked me," said Harding, "if I am to revive the Force Bill when I am elected President of the United States. I do not know that they said it that-a-way, but let me tell you. The Force Bill had been dead for a quarter of a century. I am a normal American citizen and a normal man could not resurrect the dead."

For the first time the quiet crowd applauded. They said that Daugherty covered his head with his hands and slowly shook his head. Daugherty thought Harding just negated all his hard work getting the black vote over to the Republican side. Then Harding said, almost sarcastically, "I want you to bear with me for a little while and I will restrict myself to the manuscript. I would not be worthwhile to you if I did not bring a special message."

The manuscript Harding referred to was a written speech the Senator grew to dislike as the campaign continued. He loved to "bloviate" and say what was on his mind and disliked the written manuscripts the party gave him. Lasker and Daugherty knew that keeping him under strict control was best. The *New York Times* printed Harding's speech in entirety, except the part he added about the race problem. Editors represented the speech was about the issues of oil and the League of Nations. Harding's "bloviating" opening speech would start a series of events that is typical of politics. Without the help of the press his message about the Negroes got around.

That same day, back in Ohio, Calvin Keifer agreed to meet with professor Chancellor in Marion. Calvin gave his address as 315 West Railroad Street, Galion, Ohio. Galion is north of Marion at some distance.

Chancellor wrote about Keifer. Keifer told me, "I am fifty-eight and I have lived in and around Galion for about fifty-five years. Often I heard the report that George T. Harding, the father of Warren G. Harding had Negro blood in his veins. I believe this and other people believe this to be true."

The Galion resident continued, "None of the Harding family had ever denied the report there was Negro blood in his family. Also, my mother, Mrs. Hannah Keifer, was a second cousin to a Starnes. Starnes lived in Blooming Grove and they murdered him there. David Butler killed Starnes because he had called Butler's wife a 'nigger.' A sister of George T. Harding was married to Butler. They tried Butler for murder, convicted him and sent him to the Ohio State penitentiary."

Chancellor had Keifer tender an affidavit and Homer Johnson of Marion County, Ohio, notarized it, on the ninth day of October 1920, the same day Harding gave his Oklahoma speech. The professor knew he had something exciting and all he needed to do was to investigate the records at the court house in Galion to find proof of the murder trail. This was not that easy. Much later the professor would find out that Butler's attorney tried to say Butler was justified in killing Starnes because he called Butler's wife a "nigger." The jury said no, because they knew Mrs. Butler as a member of the Harding family and that they always knew the Hardings were of the Negro race.

George Cook of Marion, Ohio, had befriended Chancellor and told the professor he knew of a Montgomery Lindsay who lived in Marion. "Mr. Lindsay," said Cook, "was a very old gent and he was willing to talk, I will get in touch with you." Chancellor said he had to go to Akron but if Mr. Lindsay wanted to talk he would come back to Marion.

The next day professor Chancellor went to Akron, Ohio, to the home of Elias Shaffer. Elias, seventy three years old, who lived on Holloway Street and stated he had the politics as Harding.

Shaffer told the professor, "My dad bought a farm south of Blooming Grove. I lived there most of my life. In fact I was born there. I went to school with Warren Harding's father George and I have known that man for about fifty years. The school was in Bellsville."

"Warren's grandfather was Charles Mordecai Harding, who was the father of George. I have seen his brothers, Perry and Ebicaness-er often over the years. They are of Negro blood. They have dark skin, the features and hair of that race and looked like Negroes."

"The sisters of George Tyron Harding, I have met," continued Shaffer. "One was very dark in color, more so than the rest. She taught school at Halfacre, which was about two miles from Blooming Grove. Phoebe Harding, the aunt of Warren Harding was decidedly of Negro appearance."

"As a carpenter I worked on the Blooming Grove church. A mason, by the name of Dickerson worked with us. He was the brother-in-law of George Tyron Harding. Dickerson talked to me about his sister who had married George. We opposed the marriage because George was a decedent of a Negro. He said George, Warren's father, had colored blood in his veins."

Shaffer signed an affidavit for the professor. In the affidavit Shaffer mentioned Charles Harding, the father of George T., had married a miss Crawford. The Akronite said he fought in the civil war and belonged to the Carpenters Union. This was signed Sunday, October 10, 1920. Upon his return to Wooster, the professor found that George Cook had called and they arranged for the professor to return to Marion in the middle of the week.

Harding's speech in Oklahoma surprised everyone. The southerners were pleased to hear the candidate would not resurrect the Force Bill. They established the Force Bill during the "reconstruction era" after the civil war and the southerners hated it. It gave the Federal government power to regulate voting booths and use military force if they denied Negroes the right to vote. Southern states quietly ignored this law and northern states looked the other way. The Negroes and whites from the northern states marked Harding's statements as a shift in his stated policy.

William Monroe Trotter of the Equal Rights League demanded to know where Harding really stood on the race question. He remembered the words Harding had said in Marion. "If the United States cannot prevent race segregation in its own service, we are not in any sense a Democracy." The black leader sent a telegram to Harding stating that the Oklahoma speech had "altered your statements in Marion to the Equal Rights League, or now interprets their true meaning." Thirteen Negro rights advocates telegraphed the Marion Republican headquarters saying clearly that Negroes' disappointment was general.

Senator New of Indiana, a close friend of Harding, received negative phone calls about Harding's Negro stand in Oklahoma. Senator New, in charge of the Chicago Republican publicity bureau, notified Harding's secretary. New said, "They have created too much excitement today with the Oklahoma City answer. Avoid any reference of any kind to it if possible." Senator New realized a shift had taken place in the campaign. The League of Nations as the key issue waned as the race issue took over as the main topic.

The *Union* newspaper editor failed to mention what Harding said at Oklahoma. In his paper he told his readers to back the Republican party. He urged his black readers to vote for Harding, Davis, Willis and the entire Republican ticket. He wrote, "Republicans will put an end to the segregation policies that has disgraced a land consecrated to LIBERTY." This *Union* editor continued by saying Harding was anti segregation, and anti Jim Crow and the "volleys fired by him against racial discrimination and its condonation by some of our people will bear good results." The NAACP voiced no opinion because they knew the Republican party had given them their only progress in race relations over the years.

In the middle of the week, October 13, 1920, Chancellor went to Montgomery Lindsay's home at North State Street in Marion. He took his friend George W. Cook who witnessed Keifer's affidavit and Homer Johnson the Notary. Montgomery at the time was ninety three years old, a retired farmer living in Marion, Ohio.

Montgomery Lindsay told Chancellor, "I know of three Harding families. One lived three miles southwest of Blooming Grove and two of the families lived near Blooming Grove. I have known George T. Harding, the father of Warren for sixty-two years now."

Lindsay continued, "The Hardings we know, are 'niggers.' I knew George T's father. The men of the other two families were his uncles. Rosalindy Harding taught at the school to which I went. She was a cousin of George T. She had the features, colors and resembled a Negro. Rosalindy's brother was of very high coloring and came to take his sister home one day. The children were very scared of him, because that was the first Negro many had ever seen. The school was on the James Miller farm in Scott Township, just two miles east of Kirkpatrick. I was twenty-one when Washington Sickel came running home. He had seen Rosalindy's brother and was frightened."

Lindsay told how when he was age nine, "My mother and I sought shelter with a Harding family during a storm. This was either the home of the father or uncle of George T. Harding. We colored the father and so were the rest of the family. I can still picture the one-half story home today. One year when Warren was sixteen or eighteen years old I offered to pay him two cents more each shock then the rest harvesting corn for me. I did this because the Harding family was very much in need of help at the time. He started cutting one shock and quit, saying the work was too hard."

Oliver Perry Harding, the son of David G. Harding the great-grand uncle of Warren G. Harding.

Source A.N. Fields
Abbots Magazine

Continuing the elderly Lindsay said, "When Amos Kling, the father of Mrs. Warren G. Harding, said to other people his daughter had married a Negro, I was present. Amos said his daughter disgraced all of her family connections. No one had ever denied the Harding families had Negro blood in their veins. We always assumed and referred it as a fact." This affidavit was signed Wednesday the thirteenth, October 1920.

Chancellor added another affidavit to his research papers. His historian friend Cook signed the affidavit. It read, "People of Marion told Professor Chancellor that they had reported and often stated that the family and ancestry of Warren G. Harding were of colored blood. The Hardings, to his knowledge, never denied this report and statement. We repeatedly talked about it. Montgomery Lindsay, 93, of North State Street, Marion, swore that he had always known the Harding families as the 'Nigger' Hardings." The 63-year-old, George W. Cook signed the affidavit, dated October thirteenth, 1920 and in Marion.

Chancellor thought all the affidavits were of tremendous value to his research. After making copies he placed the originals in a safety deposit box in the local bank in Wooster. Most likely he told his Democratic attorney friends

The Indictment

Ross and Judge Welliver of his discoveries. Armed with written information, the professor now had names and places to help him in his research. He met, took pictures of and talked with Harding's ancestors. Only a one of theses photographs have survived over the years and none of the original affidavits can be found. The **bold** highlighted names are ancestors of Warren Harding.

Chancellor wrote about the Harding lineage. **Amos Harding** married **Phoebe Tripp** in 1794. He married a second woman but her name is unknown. Amos and Phoebe had 17 children. They were Abigail, **George Tyron (I),** William Tripp, Solomon, Mordecai, Rice, Wealthy, Ebenezer S., Benjamin F, Huldah Jane, John, Chauncy, and four others who are unknown.

George Tyron (I) had two wives. His first wife, **Mary Ann Roberts** had two daughters, Huldah and Phoebe Ann, before she passed away. The second wife of George T., **Elizabeth Madison** was Negro, as told by the people living in and around Blooming Grove. She gave birth to Oliver Perry, **Charles A**. and Miranda. Oliver Perry, had distinguished Negro features. A neighbor, Elias Shafer, said, "George's father's name was Charles. I knew and met two of Charles's brothers. They were men of color or Negro. Dark skinned, features of the hair and looked like men of the Negro race." **Charles A.** married Mary Ann Crawford.

George Tyron (II) was the son of Charles and Mary Ann Crawford Harding, and he married **Phoebe Dickerson**. George T. would later marry Eudora Adella Kelley and, in 1921 a Mary Alice Severns. Phoebe and George Tyron had ten children. **Warren G. Harding** was the oldest and neighbors described him as having a swarthy (dark) complexion.

A good researcher follows up and confirms his findings. In the process papers accumulated and most never see print, but authors need many documents to confirm the written word. These papers are gone as they had destroyed most of Chancellor's research papers.

Chancellor wrote more about Harding's family. Warren's brothers and sisters were Mary, Clarissa, Eleanor, and Priscilla who died before reaching her fourth year. Charles A. (II) died as a youth. George Tyron (III), Abigail Victoria, Charity Malvina and Phoebe Caroline were the names of his surviving brother and sisters. I cannot account for two other children.

Phoebe Caroline would marry a Heber Herbert Votaw. I remembered her when I had hired her as a teacher. Senator Joseph B. Foraker, who took very great interest in the black people, had sent a letter of introduction to me. He requested the appointment of Phoebe to a position in the schools. Foraker stated that she was a quadroon (eighth black) and wanted to teach in the colored schools.

The Indictment

The professor wrote a letter to the Democratic National Headquarters. In this letter he said, "Warren Gamaliel Harding was not a white man, he was not Creole, he was not a mulatto, he was a mestizo, as his physical features show. Anyone who hears or reads his public utterance is free to judge his intellectual and moral traits. Anyone who knows the quality of his public record in various offices was free to judge his character. I might cite the names of scores of persons who have always considered Warren Gamaliel Harding a black man. They resent his present masquerade as a white candidate upon the ticket of a previously honorable and dignified party. Of hundreds of persons interviewed,

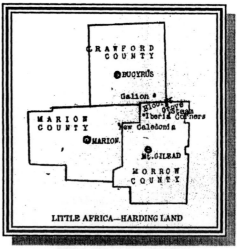

LITTLE AFRICA—HARDING LAND

This drawing was created by William Estabrook Chancellor.

they knew him as a rural school boy and as 'college' student. Everyone without exception says that Warren Gamaliel Harding was always considered a black boy and nicknamed accordingly."

Parts of this letter would be incorporated into a letter the professor would title "Open Letter." He never gave authorization or permission of any kind to the Democratic party to use his material.

Chancellor wrote more about his findings. Little Africa consists of three counties, where for a hundred years had raged the feud between the whites and the mestizoes. In it live almost one thousand descendants of Amos Harding and 10,000 other hybrids.

Warren was born at Blooming Grove, Ohio. At Steam Corners lives the mother of Warren's chauffeur, and she remembers Warren as a baby. Here also live other people who knew all the history of Harding Corners.

At Iberia was the seat of a teacher's school. Warren attended this school to train for rural work for just two years. They called it a college, but it did not require even a rural elementary school diploma for admission.

In Galion, Ohio, lives a man who went to school with him and roomed with him at Iberia. In New Caledonia lives the banker who remembers Warren as one of his school mates and always called him *Nig*. They said that Warren was either number one or two in Iberia College the year he graduated. The reason was that year, only two students graduated.

The Indictment

Old William Chancellor, of Mount Gilead, a Negro, told the truth to the Negroes of America. He said in their church pulpits that Warren Gamaliel Bancroft Harding was a Negro in part, himself. He was perfectly willing to admit this until political ambition to rise in politics got the better of what little sense of truthfulness he had. Here we propose to take up a few points from the various articles printed about Harding in Republican and Baptist organs.

The aged Abie Gunn Baker in an article published by *The Christian Herald,* told a story of Phoebe. She said that, Abigail Dickerson discovered that her daughter, Phoebe, was deeply interested in George Tryon Harding. It appears that their youngest child failed to enter the church with her parents, but lingered outside. Right in the midst of the service, her daughter walked in on the arm of her soldier mate. After church Mrs. Dickerson asked the young woman what was the meaning of the affair. She replied that, so Mrs. Baker says, George was already her husband. This makes a perfectly good story, for Mrs. Baker does not neglect to say that this young woman was a full year older than her mate. Which, of course, was the truth.

Let us look into the civil war dates to get the truth itself from these conflicting yarns, and from certain facts that are indisputable. The army released Harding's father from the service in March 1865. It was a furlough, and he went back in the service. Nine months later Warren Harding was born on November 2, 1865. This credibly establishes the paternity of the boy, which no one doubts. Nevertheless, when did the marriage take place?

Old George Tryon Harding says that they had a long courtship and often went out together. If so, when did he have time for this so-called long courtship? George served three years in the army. Now the truth was that these two persons never agreed as to dates, places, or persons variously reported by them to have celebrated their wedding for them. Nor did Mrs. Harding ever have a marriage certificate, nor was a license ever issued by any court officer. This does not concern the legitimacy of the ten children. It happens to concern the fact that one was white and the other was not. It explains why the Dickersons made her move out.

The true story of George Tryon Harding was he got his white wife without the courtesy of asking her parents. They got a piece of land for him and made him work it. They got Doctor McFarland, the only white physician in the place, to allow George to study with him privately. In time George Tryon became first a veterinary, then a country doctor. When Warren was fifteen years old, the father returned to Marion, where he got a practice with servants, black people, and cattle and horses, the highest he ever rose.

Mrs. Phoebe Dickerson Harding.
The mother of Warren Harding.

In these same two articles, according to Doctor George, he never had any other love other than his wife, Elizabeth Dickerson. Yet the records of Marion County, Ohio, show indisputably that no sooner was the old lady laid in her grave in 1907, then the old man married a widow. She was living in Muncie. Three years after the marriage, she got a divorce from George T. because he had been trying to cheat her out of her money. The court allowed her to take as her alimony a small house that belonged to the Hardings.

She signed an affidavit that her real reason for wanting a divorce was that George T. was too much a "Nigger" for her to endure him. Republican and Democratic reporters interviewed her, but telling the story had seemed too delicate for their newspapers. Of course, her last name was Harding, her first name was Endora, and anyone who care to find her in Muncie can see her.

So much for the testimony of George T. Harding, who said he had never loved but one woman. This bears out the story that he tried to cheat the second Mrs. Harding. Still, it makes him out to be a deceiver of women again in his old age. Of course, he deceived his real mate, Phoebe Dickerson, by proposing to support her.

The old man and the writer of the Harding story have tried to make out that George was a good provider for his large family. Unfortunately, for the beauty of this story, it happens that the very naive Warren had himself spoiled it by spilling some facts. Warren had said that whenever the children got hungry they went either down the road to Grandmother Dickerson or up the road to Grandfather Harding. Another of these immature statements was that they always ate at their grandparents on sundays and feast days. Still another was that the children all worked at the neighbors when they were big enough to do anything at all. Still another statement was that their only real poverty was in respect to clothes.

Now, to get the whole situation pictured, I have but three facts to present. One fact was that Mrs. Phoebe Dickerson Harding, mother of Warren, went out as a midwife and a nurse and even as a servant frequently. A second was that the George Tryon family got their little farm from their blood kin as tenants. A third was that all the children had little education. In other words, the father, mother and children were drifters protected from poverty by the good nature of all their neighbors, and the pity that they felt for a white woman with a black husband. Of course, this was usual, as many Negroes were about. Mixed unions were the common thing. Fifty years ago, more than half the Blooming Grove people had Negro or Indian blood, or both.

Another one pleasant fiction in which the Republicans have indulged was the printing of the alleged birthplace of Warren. The house they claim was the place of his birth is only 30 years old. They burned his original log cabin shack down long ago. The family occupied it only a few months. The truth was that his mother gave birth to Warren in her own bed chamber at the Dickerson house. At this time the two were not yet living in their own home.

I have the affidavit from the present Dickerson family that they allowed this marriage solely because their sister was pregnant. Phoebe Harding often said that she "married" George T. only because he wore soldier stripes and blue. Taking the picture of her may be worthwhile as portrayed, first, by the Republicans, second, by her neighbors, third, by the photographer.

Mrs. Baker says that she was tall and willowy, with a lovely singing voice, and very industrious. She had light brown hair and was pale. The neighbors report that they always overwork her. She was not interested in anything except babies and sick people and always penniless. They say that she was very agreeable. The picture of her shows her at 40 years of age, with very dark hair, a thin, anxious face and poorly dressed. On the other hand, her children are fat and cheerful in their early pictures.

Of course, Mrs. Phoebe Dickerson Harding was a very good woman, but having poor judgment, else she would not have taken up with this imposter. She had ten children and was as good a mother to them as any woman in poverty can be. Phoebe was the youngest of all her family, their pet. The Dickersons were among the good people of the neighborhood, far above the Hardings. Her union with this George Tryon was a heavy blow to her old parents. It came when she was 21 years old, and she had only elementary schooling. Her parents and her mate never cared for books. Nor did she make a reading man of her son, Warren. Professor Chancellor told some of his friends about the compiled history he had of Warren G. Harding and these friends would soon use this information without permission.

Chapter Four
The Roorbacks and the White Backlash.

Harding's Family Tree

Amos Harding (Black)   Wife-Huldah Tryon (Colored)
West India Negro

    Issue

George Tryon Harding 1st   Wife-Anna Roberts (Colored)
(Mulatto)

    Issue
Charles A. Harding   Wife Marry Ann Crawford
(Colored)   (Pass for White)

    Issue
Geo. Tryon Harding 2nd   Wife-Phoebe Dickerson
(White)

This marriage was objected to by the brother of Phoebe Dickerson for the reason that George Tryon Harding the second (the father of Warren G. Harding) had negro blood.
The above is verified by Elias Shaffer, 804 Hollaway St., Akron

Ohio, who has known Mr. Harding for fifty years. He went to school with Dr. George Tryon Harding, the second (father of Warren G. Harding,) he knew his father Charles Harding and Charles Harding's two brothers who were uncles of George T. Harding, the second, (father of Warren G. Harding) and says that they had the color, features and hair of negroes and were so considered and accepted in the community. Mr. Shaffer is 75 years old, is a member of the Grand Army Post at Marion, and the republican in politics.

    Issue
WARREN GAMALIEL HARDING   Wife-FLORENCE KLING (WHITE)
(Colored)

This marriage was objected to by the father-in-law, Mr. Amos H. Kling of Marion, Ohio, a prominent Republican and one of the wealthiest men in Marion, who spoke out publicly and openly denouncing the marriage

and said his daughter had disgraced herself and family by marrying a man who had negro blood in his veins. This statement can be verified by a hundred people in Marion, Ohio.
Senator Harding has not publicly or privately denied the statement. All denials have been made by unofficial announcement.
Sister of Warren G. Harding, Mrs. Carrie Harding Votaw, Washington, D. C., formerly in 1908 under Roosevelt taught in colored schools; was also missionary in Murrwah.
Authority: Prof. William E. Chancellor, Wooster University, Wooster, O.

The Indictment

Within three weeks of election day the Democrats knew they had no chance of winning. Most newspapers predicted Harding as the winner in the upcoming election. The odds ran ten to four in favor of Harding.

Harry Daugherty possessing a distrustful personality had a great fear about Harding being identified as a Negro. The campaign manager remembered vividly the sudden turn of the Ohio Governors' election when he thought Harding was in the lead. Within days after the opposition sent out flyers about Harding's ancestry his winning chances slipped and he lost. Daugherty believed this was the reason Harding lost his bid to be the Governor of Ohio. Opposition thought he did not qualify for the job.

In the 1920 spring primaries Harding won his Ohio delegates by the narrow margin of just fifteen thousand votes. The Negro voters backed General Wood. Most Negro owned newspapers editorially condemned Harding in the spring. They said his lily-white Republican connections marked Harding as a man opposed to equal Justice for the race. Daugherty thought the narrow margin of victory was due to the slur campaign of his fellow Republicans against Harding. General Wood who ran against Harding allowed the race issue used in hopes of defeating his opposition.

As the presidential campaign continued, white supremacy groups, especially the Ku Klux Klan, were afraid that Harding would favor Negro issues. Some voters thought he would give control of the government over to the blacks. Democrats felt a slap at Harding's ancestry could turn the election to their favor. Republicans who did not like Harding joined in the racial attack on the candidate.

More flyers began to appear about Harding's Negro ancestry. These flyers' sudden appearance galvanized Daugherty into action. The Presidents' manager Daugherty set into motion every measure to naturalize their efforts. He said, "As the closing week approached, a boomerang was sprung, destined to have a sensational ending." Daugherty never mentioned who tossed the boomerang. Since Professor Chancellor's name was associated with the roorbacks, Daugherty aimed his attack directly at him.

The backlash and sending of flyers or roorbacks about Harding's ancestors appeared to have started in Cleveland, Ohio, right after Harding's October ninth Oklahoma speech.

Six Negroes running for office wanted to ride the winning shirt tail of Harding as it became more obvious about his winning chances. They created a handbill focused at Negro voters in the Cleveland area. This handbill, in full support of Harding, consisted of nine pictures and some text. The handbill had a picture of Harding as the presidential candidate and a second photograph depicted Frank B. Willis for the Senate, the third picture was of Harry L. Davis as the Republican choice for the Ohio Governor. Six other photographs exhibited Republican Negro candidates running for various Ohio offices. The heading for the handbill in capital letters said, "EQUALITY FOR ALL." A partial quotation of Harding's Oklahoma speech was on the bottom of the flyer. It quoted Harding as saying, "I want you to know that I believe in equality before the law. That is the guarantee of the American Constitution. You cannot give one right to a white man and deny the same right to a black man."

White supremacy Democrats from the north and south attacked the Republicans with massive reprints of this "EQUALITY FOR ALL" leaflet. Within this reprint of the Cleveland handout they added "Harding is for integration of the races." Variations of the roorback cropped up in Ohio, Oklahoma and North Carolina among other states. The black candidates' bid for the Ohio legislature received notoriety all over the country at no cost to them.

Voters responded to this back handed political advertising by writing letters to Harding and the Republican headquarters. A Mrs. Taylor of Ohio begged senator Harding in a letter "to tell her this was not true."

Soon flyers appeared that depicted the White House with headlines on it saying, "Keep it white!" Another handout showed a picture of the White House and Harding together. Blazoned across the roorback were the words, "Uncle Tom's Cabin!". We could contribute none of these flyers to Chancellor, directly or indirectly.

In California the postmaster confiscated two-hundred-fifty thousand flyers. These flyers graphically stated that Harding was a "nigger." No author's name appeared on the handbill, although Daugherty and others thought it was the work of the professor. Daugherty estimated the cost of the mailing would exceed five thousand dollars. The senders objected when the United States post office refused to deliver their mail. The post master appealed to higher authorities and President Wilson gave the order to have the handbills destroyed. President Wilson, a Democrat, suppressed freedom of speech, because he thought the flyers were a contemptuous reflection of the Democratic party. These roorbacks began to appear all over the country with a heavy concentration in the Midwest states.

A roorback is a political handbill, often scandalous in nature. Only imagination limited the designers of the flyers, handbills or roorbacks. These roorbacks suddenly appeared in small and large cities. Some listed an alleged Harding ancestry claiming his family members were all Negroes. Others described Harding's father as having chocolate lips with big rolling eyes. The Republicans described them as printed on the cheapest of paper. It was interesting these flyers made their sudden appearance after James Cox returned from his western campaign tour in early October.

James Cox changed his campaign tactics after arriving from the west, by attacking Harding. In Columbus, Ohio, the Democratic candidate said, "They did not nominate me at any 2:11 A. M. conference in the smoky back room of a hotel suite, by a boss controlled Senatorial cabal. My nomination came in an open convention as the result of free choice by the delegates. I am willing to say, that we have examined and compared forces endorsing my candidacy with those behind the reactionary candidate, as part of the issues of this campaign. The senatorial ring has the most motley array of questionable groups and influences that are behind a candidate for president. We believe they did this to evade the great issue such as the League of Nations. Their huge expenditure, necessary too secure support was unthinkable, and brings the crimson blush of shame to

Americans."

The Democratic candidate brought the Negro issue to the public's attention. Governor Cox said in this speech said that Harding was making special appeals to racial groups by falsely claiming a belief in social equality. Cox said, "The Afro-American party was behind Senator Harding, whose activity has attempted to stir up troubles among the Negroes upon false claims that it can bring social equality. This was subjecting unsuspecting Negro people to counter attacks of those fomenting racial prejudices and endangering them to bloody riots. Senator Harding through this appeal to prejudice in a Negro invasion of doubtful states and was inviting loss of progress made by the Black people." Cox made this Columbus speech addressing the racial issue on October 14, 1920, just five days after Harding made his Oklahoma speech.

James M. Cox Taken in 1920 by Lucas A. Weeks

In Cleveland, Ohio, Walter L. Brown published another four-page handout designed for the Negro population and voters. Under the heading of "Now is the time for all Colored Citizens to stand together" were pictures of three black candidates. Those depicted are W.R. Green, Harry E. Dave and S. E. Woods. In bold capital letters Brown said, "We have three candidates for the legislature in Cuyahoga County on the Republican Ticket. Vote for them." On the same page he stated, "The Democratic party never does anything for our people while the Republican party is the party of the Black man. If the influx of Black men and women from the south keeps up it won't be long until the Negroes will hold the balance of power in Republican politics in Cleveland. That will be a glorious day. We are twenty-five thousand strong in Cleveland and if we vote as a unit there will be no question what will happen."

Mr. Woods, in his handout, quotes the black newspaper, the *Toledo Pioneer*. The pioneer stated its position in its September 11, 1920, issue. It read, "If the Colored voters, men and women, stands together in the coming November election we can secure in this state the full fruition of the rights guaranteed us as people. We have nominated six members of our own race as candidates for membership in the Ohio General Assembly, three in Cuyahoga County, two in Franklin and one in Hamilton County. If these men are elected to the Legislature, one of them can introduce a duplicate of the Beatty bill passed in the house two years ago and defeated by the Senate. The Beatty bill had teeth in it. It imposed penalties upon those who discriminated against Negro people. Especially those seeking admissions to hotels, theaters, places of public resort and amusement, ice cream parlors, bathhouses, . . . and would soon put a stop to this injustice to the Black people."

The handout printed by Woods ends, "We have the moral support of our candidate for the Presidency, Senator Warren G. Harding. His words are an eloquent endorsement of the spirit and letter of the Beatty bill. Its purpose of which was to insure civil rights to Black people by imposing heavy penalties upon those who would deny them these rights. . . . The Beatty bill provided penalties of one hundred to five hundred dollar fine, and thirty to ninety days imprisonment, or both."

If Mr. Woods had checked the voting of the senate records, he would have found that Warren G. Harding did not vote for the Beatty Bill. Then again Senator Harding, dubbed "Mr. Wobble," had voted against prohibition thirty times and voted for it twice. He also voted to accept the League of Nations but as a candidate debated against it. These actions galvanized his nickname of "Wobble."

The handouts, including the one titled EQUALITY FOR ALL, incited the racists', bigots' and white supremacy groups. They believed that blacks wanted to dominate government but in fact they only wanted enjoyment of civil rights. New racist roorbacks appeared everywhere almost at once. They mailed them to homes or stuffed many into the doors of voters. The intensity of flyers increased daily.

Harding made an issue, in the later part of September, about the Haiti crisis and claimed that American Marines in that country killed thousands of Negroes. About mid October the press picked up the story that General Barnett had investigated the Haiti problem over a year ago. This shocked the General who insisted on a full senatorial investigation of the matter. His report revealed that two marines had confessed to the killing of some natives. Press releases of this story made Harding's claim of thousands upon thousands of Negroes killed, appear false. The Republicans ignored the press but the Democrats pushed this allegation in their papers.

The flood of roorbacks and the Haiti news release affected the election rhetoric. Over night Negro civil rights became a lost issue and it suddenly became a black versus white race issue. Republican handbills from Cleveland and the truth about Haiti, triggered the desire to make race the issue in the closing weeks of the election.

Suddenly, William Estabrook Chancellor became throughly enmeshed with the racist muckfest of the Democratic and Republican parties. The professor's research into Harding's ancestry, background and political records became known. Chancellor's mail increased with inquiries about the family of Harding. A sheriff from Paris, Kentucky, called on the telephone and wanted to know if the professor was black and asked if "Wooster University" was a black school. Politely, the professor answered every letter and telephone inquiry.

Because of his research Chancellor would encounter the fury of this storm that would change his life forever.

Chancellor wrote subsequently that the local Democratic newspapers printed 10,000 copies of the true photo of George Tyron Harding, and they needed more. In this picture George Harding, the father of Warren, showed the traits of his heritage. The Democrats thought this picture would get their message across to the public that Warren Harding's father was black. Republicans stole the original photo from the office of the rival newspaper when it was by mistake sent to a wrong address.

Doctor George Tryon Harding, Warren's father, buttonholed all neighbors and many others, begging them to, "Help elect my boy." Occasionally, Democrats protested that the "boy" was a Negro, but the old man nevertheless persisted in his appeal.

The banks in Marion, Ohio, sent out letters to other banks to back Harding. Inquiries regarding the colored bloodline of Harding, the banks either ignored the inquiry or denied the truth.

New roorbacks appeared first in Ohio then other states. Six of these roorbacks varied in title and makeup but had many distinguishing points in common. They titled one *"This is the lineage of Warren Gamaliel Winnipeg Bancroft Harding."* Another, written on a typewriter had the heading of *"Lineage of Warren Gamaliel Bancroft Harding."* One simply stated *"Warren Gamaliel Winnipeg Bancroft Harding."* They titled A duplicate roorback *"This is the Lineage of Warren Gamaliel Winnipeg Bancroft Harding."* The *"Below is the Genealogy of Warren G. Harding"* roorbuck appeared. Another announced the *"Harding Family Tree."* These different roorbacks, had many similar traits. Their language and content originated from the "research" paper that Chancellor had found and sent to the Democrat headquarters. On the research paper he had written on the bottom of the page, "look at what I found," and signed his name. Ever who wrote the roorbacks used this "research" paper and thought it was the work of William E. Chancellor. The original author of this "research" paper was unknown.

All the roorbacks using the "research" paper information mentioned that Harding's father was a mulatto and that he had thick lips, chocolate skin and rolling eyes. In one flyer, someone misspelled rolling and said he had "reeling" eyes. These hastily written flyers had many errors in them. One roorback said Warren Harding had three brothers, another said two, but all say he had three sisters. Chancellor's research showed that Warren was one of ten children.

Six examples stated that Warren's father had chocolate skin. The roorbucks varied in size, kind of paper, the color of paper and printing. They typewrote, mimeographed them or printed them on a press. Three made no mention about whom the author was. Two noted the author as "Professor William Chancellor, Professor of Political Economics of Wooster University." They use "Professor Chancellor, Wooster University, Wooster, Ohio" as the source of information. Other flyers or handouts used the signatory of "Authority: Prof William E. Chancellor, Wooster University."

If in fact William Estabrook Chancellor was the originator of these six roorbacks, he would have signed his name properly. The professor's correct endorsement was Professor of Economics, Politics and Sociology at the College of Wooster. The original designation of the school being a University ceased in the year 1917 when it became the College of Wooster. It boggles the mind that an author of thirty-nine books would have allowed these errors to stand and that he wrote the roorbacks. A cursory investigation would have shown that Chancellor did not write any of these roorbacks. Yet he would get blamed for them.

Chancellor wrote in his book. There was set in operation a system of spies, informers, and agents. They were troublemakers of the like of which we have known but twice before in the history of humankind. Once in Rome, and once in France, a system that was still in operation and was part of the "overhead cost" of operating their present plutocratic social order.

We have no qualms about telling the American people the stories invented by those paid agents of Satan. They had to conceal their own candidate, to send up a very dense smoke screen to hide their own cloud.

The Republicans took keen notice of Chancellor and the roorbacks in the state of Ohio. As Daugherty had feared, the Negro issue began to claim too much attention. George Hill wrote to Charles Hard at the Marion Republican Headquarters stating, "You have no conception of how the thing is flying over the state. It is everywhere. It is affecting the woman vote. We cannot get Hays and the National Committee fixed on any question of the policy with respect to the matter. I wired Hays this morning demanding the fixing of policy. They do not alarm me about the matter, but it is incident in the campaign. We must take care of it. We have fought this thing before, and we must fight it out again."

Hill in the same letter wrote, "We have had Chancellor of Wooster interviewed. Chancellor backs water quite handsomely. He admits that he knew absolutely nothing and said that the typewritten propaganda being circulated was absolutely false. He thinks that the color stain if anywhere was in the paternal side. The typewritten copy circulated fixes' it on the maternal side. He thinks something may be to it, but that the admixture of blood was so far back that they could prove nothing."

Page two of this letter had the following hand written notation. "The Negro blood story did much harm to Harding all over the country. One morning Harding wanted to go over to Wooster and beat Chancellor up. It took sometime to cool him off!"

Kathleen Lawler, the personal secretary of Mrs. Harding, remembers how angry Harding became about Chancellor and the roorbucks. The senator came into her office ranting and raving, "if you just let me see this fellow

Chancellor, I will make him a subject for 'Niggers' to look at." It took time to calm Harding. Kathleen said, "Mrs. Harding told the presidential candidate he would not do and say anything."

John C. Harding, a cousin of Warren Harding, sent a book containing Harding's genealogy to Warren. "It was fortunate," the Senator responded, "that you can furnish the data requested. Although I do not know what use it will be. I have always been averse to dignifying this talk with attention or denial. If finally deemed necessary, we will stamp it out as the unmitigated lie, it is."

Warren's letter to his cousin argued for the first time in writing that Harding was sensitive about the Negro issue. Also, he conveyed his true feelings to staff members that he would stamp it out and if given the chance beat Chancellor. All of Harding's biographers claim that Harding acted unconcerned about the race issue and the professor. His hatred for and his fear of William Estabrook Chancellor would continue even after he became president.

At first the Republicans decided not to reply to the charge of Harding having Negro blood. As the flyers or roorbacks continued, the Republicans finally reacted to the issue. Lasker, the campaign promoter, sent out an elaborate Harding history to the press. He also issued a lily-white Harding family tree prepared in part by Pennsylvania's Wyoming Historical and Geological Society. Republicans did this to counter the effect they thought the broadcasts were creating. Henry Cabot Lodge suggested that Harding should speak three words about this accusation. Senator Lodge suggested that Harding say, "It is a lie. Why does not Harding speak them?" Publically Harding never did. Privately, he had told a reporter that it was possible someone in the past jumped over the fence.

Republican voters sent more letters to Harding about their concern of the circulating flyers. Dan Cox of Coshocton, Ohio wrote to Harding, "no matter how anxious they might be to vote for you they positively would not do so because you have nigger blood in you." Dan Cox implored, "For God's sakes get busy stamping it out." Franklin Williams of Cambridge, Ohio, reported, "they will not vote for a 'nigger' President. Also, reports say you are chasing around with another woman!" S. A. Ringer of Ada, Ohio, wrote, "they may cause thousands of voters, especially the women's voters, to vote against you." James Curren of Cincinnati begged, "why don't you protest. If not, you will lose many votes." To these letters and others, the Republican headquarters officially answered that the accusations were baseless lies and slanders.

Chancellor wrote about the issue. Republicans sent out men among the farmers to tell them that Wilson was the cause of the low price of their wool. At this very time, they were sending light-colored Negroes to every part of Ohio, Indiana, and Illinois to tell the Negro people that Warren was one of them. In many Negro churches they preached this.

They discussed stories of George Tryon Harding from Blooming Grove to Steam Corners. The very aged mother of his motor car chauffeur, Mrs. Blacksten, lives as a widow with an old man who was a widower. This old woman was a chair-bound invalid of large size with many stories to tell of Warren, whom she tended as a baby.

The Republicans diligently circulated a story that their candidate was born in Pennsylvania and was not a Blooming Grove man at all. Old Mrs. Blacksten was furious at this denial of his birthplace. She said that this man, for whom her son worked, made her upset because he as the Republican candidate for the presidency and he lied about his birth. She also insisted that she had often seen him naked and that he was dark skinned like all the Hardings. On this point, the testimony of all her neighbors was unanimous.

At first, the Republicans sent telegrams asking me to deny that I investigated Harding and I refused to do. I said nothing for weeks. Then they offered me ten thousand dollars to make a denial. This I refused. Then they went out and reported that I was in the pay of the Democrats. Even this did not smoke me out. I stood pat and silent.

It would be sometime before I discovered the Republicans prepared an attack upon me. They filed an indemnity bond of $500,000 with the Newspaper Association in Chicago to protect themselves against any libel suit by me.

Harry M Daugherty sheepishly said in his memoirs, "As the campaign swept toward its conclusion, something like a panic gripped the Democratic Headquarters. With no announcement from the Democratic Headquarters, a vicious and outrageous personal attack on Harding began. They suddenly flooded the nation with millions of offensive circulars of anonymous authorship declaring that the Hardings had in their family a trace of Negro blood. A ridiculous fake family tree always accompanied these circulars. They printed it on cheap pulp paper about five by seven inches wide and bore the signature of no authority whatever. This fake tree alleged that Warren Harding's grandfather was Amos Harding and that his grandmother, Mary Ann Dixon, a black woman." Daugherty would single out Chancellor to discredit the story.

The professor not aware of the pending attack upon him concentrated on his teachings at the college. Within a week and a half before the election professor Chancellor sent a letter to the editor of the *Voice*, a College of Wooster newspaper. He wrote, "Kindly say in the *Voice* that we invite all students and neighbors on the hill to visit the home of Professor William E. Chancellor on the evening of the election. Here we will receive the election returns in a special *Western Union Telegraph Service* like four years ago. Service will be beginning at 9:00 P.M. and last until 4:00 P. M." The professor also planned for the same announcement to be placed in the Wooster newspaper, the *Daily Record*.

Many individuals wrote to the professor asking about Harding. Sherwood P. Synder of Dayton, Ohio, asked about the Negro family with the name of Hardin. They date the reply October 22 and Chancellor states, "I know nothing of the question you ask and think what you have heard was quite false. Another family with the name of Hardin [not Harding] who lives in Marion was of mixed blood. I find no connection between the two families of Harding and

Hardin."

The original intent of the blacks was to alert the public about their civil rights, but this was lost in the battle that settled on race, caused by the roorbacks. Mr. Trotter of the Equal Rights League, Johnson of the NAACP and other Negro promoters for the rights of blacks found it difficult to get press on civil rights as the muckfest intensely grew.

Despite increasing mail that professor Chancellor received every day he made a point to answer everyone. On certain days his mail delivery went as high as two hundred letters. The Wooster post office delivered the mail in card board boxes to the professor's home. From Middletown, Ohio, Homer U. Eaton sent a copy of a typewritten flyer received in the mail. At the bottom of the flyer it said, "Authority: Prof. William E. Chancellor, Wooster University, Wooster, Ohio." It was entitled "Harding's Family Tree"with many typing errors in it. When the typist made an error, he used the $$$$$ key to type over the error. In all of his manuscripts if Chancellor made such a correction he used WWWW. This flyer closely follows the information gathered by Chancellor when he talked to Elias Shaffer in Akron, Ohio. On the bottom of the flyer they note in a script, "*Correct copy, J. L Hopley, Bucyrus, Ohio,*" the owner of the Bucyrus *Telegram*. How he got a copy of the flyer or who wrote it was unknown but it was not the work effort of Chancellor. Mr. Eaton received a reply from professor Chancellor.

The letter reads, I am not especially interested in the race question of the Presidential candidate Harding, though I do prefer to take my politics from white leaders, if possible. I am FOR the League of Nations, and FOR Cox on this ground. I have spent twenty-two days investigating the ancestry of Warren Gamaliel Bancroft Harding and since you as one of hundreds who ask me the question, I answer.

Warren Gamaliel Bancroft Harding was born the oldest child of TEN children of George Tyron Harding II, mulatto-creole and Phoebe Dickerson who passed for white. His Grandfather was Charles Amos Harding, mulatto-creole, and Ann Crawford, Creole, wife. Harding's great-grandfather was, George Tyron Harding I, mulatto-creole and great-grandmother Ann Roberts of whom little was know.

His Great Grandparents come from Virginia and spoke French. They were Amos Harding, a West Indian creole and Huldah Tyron, a Black Negro. They had seventeen children and ninety-eight grandchildren and immigrated to Blooming Grove, as it was a main station in the underground railroad. Blooming Grove is five miles south of Galion. This was closed and signed,

Very respectfully yours, William Estabrook Chancellor.

We repeat, in the hundreds of letters sent by professor Chancellor he stated. "I am not especially interested in this race question about the Presidential candidates though I do prefer to take my politics from white leaders, if possible. I am FOR the League of Nations, and FOR Cox on this ground." Yet, everyone believed it was the professor who was behind the racist like slanders of Harding.

On October 25, 1920, a reporter from the *News-Forum* of Bucyrus traveled by train to Wooster to interview Professor Chancellor in his home. A New York Times reporter remembers Chancellor having grey hair and a pencil thin mustaches. He described the professor as a tall man, about six-feet tall, weighing about two hundred pounds but spare. The reporter noticed he had a slight stoop in his posture. Chancellor's home was a yellow frame house on the corner of Beall and Pearl Street in a residential area that was walking distance from the College of Wooster campus. (This home still exists.) Other homes in the area are more prestigious than the professor's home. Posters of the Democratic candidate James Cox were placed on the ground floor windows of the two-story home. One got the feeling, said the reporter, it was a campaign headquarters for the Democrats.

The reporter from the *News-Forum* explained to the professor that the Editor of his paper really did not want to get involved with the race discussion. However, a slanderous article in the Bucyrus *Telegram,* a local competitor, prompted the newspaper's editor to get the facts. He handed the *Telegram* article to Chancellor to read.

"Before going into the matter," said Chancellor. "Permit me to make it plain to you that, I have never printed, had printed or authorized the printing or distribution of any circular regarding my investigation of the Harding family. These were all prepared and distributed by other parties. This was information that was not the result of my investigation."

The professor read the *Telegram* article. He paused a minute and told the *News-Forum* reporter, "For the third time in so many weeks the Republicans have tried to bribe me into silence. Recently a man representing himself as a representative of a large metropolitan newspaper came to my home. The newspaper he was associated with was hostile to James Cox. Sitting in this very room he offered to pay me ten thousand in cash to make a statement that my investigation of the lineage of Senator Harding had revealed nothing but white blood. I could not do this and I asked him to leave my home."

Professor Chancellor said, "These hand bills are false not only in content but in the way they are trying to associate me with them. At least they could have done some research. They print that I am a professor from Wooster University. This is false. The College of Wooster dropped its status of University more than three years ago. You would think they would get my name correct. I sign my name as William Estabrook Chancellor, not W. E. Chancellor or William Chancellor as they have on all of their flyers."

Chancellor read the *Telegram* article. It stated "that he did not authorize the circulars, and that during the past week they took them from inside pockets and read in confidence to friends. The circulars are derogatory to Senator Harding and have made their appearance in Bucyrus." Certain men, "stated the *Telegram* article, "are secretly giving publicity to these false and scurrilous circulars. These same men become highly indignant that they have connected their names with its circulation. These men are more contemptible than the circular stated the *Telegram*. They become highly indignant and this alone ought to be proof to its slanderous falsity."

The article stated, "An Bucyrus friend sent one of those circulars to Wooster to ask if professor Chancellor was responsible for it." His reply was, "this was not correct. I never authorized or promulgated it." Bucyrus *Telegram* stated, "and Chancellor signed the reply."

The *Telegram* continued its story line, "It seemed surprising that some people who are supposed to have higher ideas of decency would be responsible for putting out this defamatory circular. We now prove that it was a forgery because Chancellor denied writing it, although his name appears on it. Those who have circulated it are guilty of circulating a forged document. This matter should not have had serious consideration at the start. We now absolutely revoke it, as unauthorized and therefore worthless!"

Chancellor smiled after reading the article, "This is true. I did not authorize the use of my name and anyone who uses it are in fact creating a forgery. The newspaper was correct in saying this."

"The friend mentioned in the article was Rawlins L. Todd," explained Chancellor. "He was a school teacher in Bucyrus and he graduated from the College of Wooster. Mr. Todd sent to me a copy of a circular and asked about its validity. He was a strong Republican partisan and most likely enjoyed doing this. Elias Compton, Dean of the College of Wooster had sent this typewritten flyer to Todd, who in turn sent it back to me."

The Forum reporter told Chancellor, "I interviewed Dean Compton and he told me that he sent a roorback to Mr. Todd." Chancellor now knew the Dean and Mr. Todd were in close contact with each other.

"I replied to Mr. Todd with a letter, explaining my research," stated Chancellor, "and signed by initials W. E. C. at the bottom of the letter. I told Mr. Todd that race was not an issue and I was for the League of Nations. Mr. Todd was not the only man in Bucyrus whom I have written to on this subject. I told this other man the same thing I told Mr. Todd about the results of my investigation. These replies I write in long hand and I always endorse my name."

"Everyone who writes to me gets a reply from me. These replies number into the hundreds. Most of my inquiries come from the Midwestern states. These circulars they have accused me of authorizing are in part distributed by Black people. That I know to be a fact. They have told me they handed them out on the Pennsylvania railroad to passengers. Someone recently told me that in Chicago the Black people passing the circulars were beaten and tossed off the train."

Chancellor showed the reporter the pile of circulars he had collected. "Look," he said, "they vary the names of Harding's ancestors. Most are incorrect about Harding's lineage. Yet, everyone said that I authorized or wrote the flyer. Like the *Telegram* reported in their article that these flyers are a forgery!"

As the *News-Forum* reporter headed back to Bucyrus, the book makers had changed their odds within ten days of the election. The ten to four odds of Harding wining went to seven to one. A few people wanted ten to one odd's but could find no takers.

Republicans and Harding became even more paranoid about the race issue. To protect their big lead they had a lily-white lineage sent to all the Newspapers. Some lineage rosters went to the mid 1600's and they differed from newspaper to newspaper. In the Chicago office where Nan Britton worked, all kind of excitement was felt as printed flyers arrived. Hallways and offices became full as they delivered the flyers to the headquarters. Nan placed one in her purse to take home with her. The headquarters became busy as the last minute mailing was prepared.

Chancellor wrote about the impending personal attack upon him. The Republicans paid $500,000 with a certified check from a well-known Chicago millionaire to publish articles throughout the country. This transfer of funds happened on October 25, 1920. The millionaire was, Medill McCormack, the husband of a woman whom I had angered by refusing to agree with on an issue when on the District Architectural Commission in Washington, D.C. Also, by order of President Theodore Roosevelt, I had insulted him by removing his mistress from the schools.

October 26, Senator Harding traveled to Cleveland by train. They planned to have him speak in Cleveland, stop at Akron then go to Cincinnati. After the Queen City he would finish his speaking tour and end the campaign at the Memorial hall in Columbus, Ohio. This last campaign tour was to be finished Saturday the thirtieth. Harding would then retire to Marion, Ohio and wait for the election returns in his home on Mt. Vernon St.

Before Cleveland, Harding made a speech in Birmingham, Alabama. In this speech he made the statement that it was his duty to see they give the Negro the right to vote. He said qualified Negroes should vote and they should not give unqualified whites the right to vote. This offhand statement by Harding incited many people.

Of every form and description, thousands upon thousands of roorbacks appeared in Cleveland. They told about Harding's family tree, his education and of course his Negro blood line. All had the name of William Chancellor and the typically wrong designation of Wooster University on them. They could not contain Daugherty' and Hardings' fury. Harding wanted to smash and destroy Chancellor.

The campaign manager got on the phone and made phone calls near and far. Harry M. Daugherty learned politics from Mark Hanna. Daugherty they acknowledged as the present boss of the Republicans in Ohio and knew how to control like a master.

Chancellor wrote that Hanna was a Cleveland steamboat and steel man, who made a great fortune and was amazingly energetic. He put William McKinley into the White House, lent to him enough money to pay his unfortunate business debts. They owned him fully, body-soul and breeches. McKinley never named a man to office until Hanna had told him to do it. Hanna finally bribed his way through the Ohio Legislature and became a Senator of the United States. He was a bitter, violent enemy of Theodore Roosevelt, and a warm friend to many vile men and women in that part of the United States. Fortunately, he died at a comparatively early age, in 1904.

Mark Hanna was the father of Dan R. Hanna, who owns the *Cleveland News*. Dan had just divorced his fourth wife. Mark Hanna's daughter, Ruth Hanna McCormick, was the wife of United States Senator Medill McCormick, of Illinois. McCormick was an owner of the *Chicago Tribune*, said by itself to be the greatest newspaper in the world.

Who was the Hanna of Harding? He was a bulldozer, he was corrupt to the center, but he has intelligence, foresight and vigor. This man was Harry M. Daugherty, who was the Columbus part of the Hanna machine. Harry was a man who knows the State Capital, and works hard for the party. He spent Hanna's money skillfully and hid the work well enough.

Here it was enough to say that Daugherty was a business-getting lawyer. He knows how to go out and get suits and clients while his partners furnish the law service. During the World War, he and others built an envelope factory and got a contract to make envelopes for the Post Office Department. Daugherty made a profit of $300,000 selling this contract too some Dayton envelope makers for twice what the factory cost him. How much of that he kept for himself was unknown. No one ever accused him of being a book-learned lawyer. He has been a very shrewd party politician all these years. Warren Harding became a Senator, and Lt. Governor and now President because of him. Daugherty has long been Harding's political Mentor.

Author Russell Francis wrote about Daugherty. "The political battle pitted and toughened Daugherty. The struggle made him morally ambiguous. A good judge of men and their weaknesses, he knew when to flatter, when to threaten, when to bluff. They feared him but he was liked, but even in his own party, they did not trust him."

Newspaper reporter Mark Sullivan says about Daugherty. ". . . Always he knew what wire to pull, always he kept a web of wires running from his office out to all sorts of men who occupied places of leverage. Always he knew how to get results."

Daugherty knew Mark Hanna contributed to the College of Wooster. Also, he knew the McCormicks had donated to the College of Wooster. Harding's campaign manager put together his plan to stop and embarrass the professor.

In Chicago Reverend Timothy Stone was the pastor at McCormick's Presbyterian Church. Senator Medill McCormick remembered William Estabrook Chancellor when he was on the Architectural Committee in Washington, D.C.

McCormick would be a man Daugherty would call and use.

Chancellor wrote that Standard Oil money established the college in its present condition. The President of its board of trustees (Reverend Stone) was Chaplain of the Republican National Committee and the pastor of Senator Medill McCormick and his wife Ruth Hanna McCormick. This explains the willingness of the trustees to play the republican game and why a million dollars was added to the endowment soon after.

President Wishart would state many years later, "The day of the individual angel in the program of the college is over. Endowment has increased from a million and quarter to its present three and half million. It is better that one thousand men should give one hundred dollars that one man should give one hundred thousand dollars."

Dr. Elias Compton,
Dean: College of Wooster

Reverend John Timothy Stone was the president on the Trustees Board at the College of Wooster. Stone got Reverend Charles F. Wishart his job as president of the College. Reverend Stone thought he was a natural for the job. Author Lucy Notestein wrote, "Dr. Wishart was already familiar with many problems of a small church-related college. He had been the director of the Presbyterian Hospital in Chicago. The youngest of twelve children, he had early learned the art of surviving while getting along with others." Within the next few weeks Dr. Wishart, president of the College of Wooster, would have to muster all his ability to just get along.

Chancellor wrote, Charles Frederick Wishart, pastor of the Second Presbyterian Church of Chicago, was the choice of the trustees that June. In 1921 Mrs. Cyrus McCormick of Chicago pledged $10,000 to the College of Wooster.

Doctor Elias Compton was an author, teacher, a professor and in 1920 held the position as Dean of the College, a position he enjoyed for more than twenty years. About sixty-nine years old at the time, he was well respected by students, faculty and members of the board of trustees. Dean Compton fathered three brilliant sons, Karl, Arthur and Wilson. Arthur would strongly influence the development of the first atomic bomb and became a Nobel Prize winner in Physics. In 1920 Dean

The Indictment

Compton was a professor of Ethics.

Dean Elias Compton and Chancellor met in the afternoon, October 28, 1920. Dr. Compton already knew that Chancellor had signed a denial of the roorback sent to R. L Todd of Bucyrus but he wanted another admission from professor Chancellor. Dean Compton, asked Chancellor if he would sign a paper to the effect that Senator Harding ancestors were all white. He wanted Chancellor to put this in writing.

Chancellor wrote that on October 28 Elias Compton the dean told me the Presbyterian Church at Kenton, Ohio, wanted an affidavit. Compton asked me to sign a statement that Warren Harding was all white. This I declined to do for the professor of ethics, since I believed it was a lie. I signed a truthful statement that I had not circulated any papers whatever about Harding. In letter and spirit this was the exact fact.

They would never send this affidavit to the minister as promised by the dean. Instead it would become the center piece of the attack on Chancellor.

The professor continues, I offered to take Dean Compton, at my own expense, to Blooming Grove and show him the brothers, sisters and cousins of Charles A. Harding and of his brother Oliver Perry Harding. This way he could see for himself these people were Negroid. Dean Compton preferred to publish his statement that I had circulated nothing on the subject and let the country believe that I had "retracted" what I denied having done. [Compton resigned as Dean in March of 1921.]

Before leaving Elias's office Chancellor wrote and signed the affidavit for the Dean of the College. This affidavit read, "As to the Harding ancestry, I hereby certify that I am in no way responsible for, never wrote, never authorized anyone to write, and know nothing whatever about the circular bearing my name." . . . William Estabrook Chancellor October 28, 1920. Dean Elias Compton witnessed Chancellor's statement and signature. A James McLaughlin notarized it.

The roorbacks distributed in Cleveland included *Harding's Lineage* and other variations. For the first time a new roorback appeared titled the "*Open Letter*." The open letter roorback was a copy of the letter professor Chancellor used to respond to those who wrote inquiries to him. Instead of writing each response, the professor had made copies to save time when answering. All of sudden his letter became a flyer and poster and it appeared in Cleveland while Senator Harding was there. Denials from the Democrats and the Republicans were about the same. "We did not do that. We do not know who printed it and we do not who sent it out." As in all the other roorbacks they printed professor Chancellor's name on the poster incorrectly and listed him as a professor at the University of Wooster, Wooster, Ohio. This was a misstatement of the facts. Except the heading and the signature lines this would be the only flyer, poster, roorback or broadcast that they quoted Chancellor's actual words. If one cleaved off the headline of the Open Letter flyer and the signature line, it would read, word for word the preprinted letter Chancellor sent out to many people. William Estabrook Chancellor did not know that the Open Letter roorback existed on the October 28, the day it appeared for the first time in Cleveland.

The Professor went over his notes preparing for his last speech of the forty he gave during the campaign. He would give this speech in the town of Shreve, Ohio, just seven miles southeast of Wooster. While writing, a Mr. West from Dayton, Ohio, called him on the telephone. West identified himself as the sales manger of Dayton Steel company and said an employee had received a copy of the roorback titled, "Harding Family Tree."

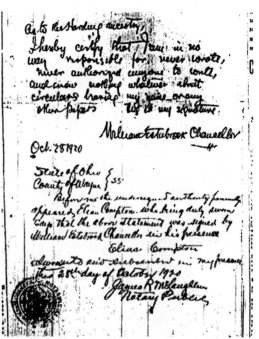

Facsimile of the affidavit signed by Professor Chancellor for the Dean of the College of Wooster.

L. V. West wanted to know if the professor knew anything about it. As he had said often before, the professor repeated he had nothing do with the circular and knew nothing about it. West asked, "Then you know nothing about the Harding lineage." With patience Chancellor tried to explain to the Dayton caller "that is not true. I know nothing about the broadcast flyers, and I did not authorize them. Nor did I print them or send any to the public." After a prolonged conversation Mr. West finally hung up and Chancellor went back to writing his speech.

Chapter Five
The Trial and the Train.

The Chairman of the National Republican Committee, attends a rally at Marion, Ohio.
Ohio Historical Society

Late Thursday afternoon, October 28, 1920, Senator Harding's train arrived in Akron, Ohio. That evening Harding spoke for more than ninety minutes to a packed house at the Akron armory. Harding told his audience, "I want an America that does not take orders, industrially nor economically from anybody in the world. The United States is not going to submit to dictation by diplomats sitting around a table at Geneva. The United States will decide what our foreign obligations will be." This brought intense cheering.

As Harding spoke, Daugherty kept in touch with those in Wooster. He also contacted Myron T. Herrick of the Dayton *Journal* because he needed the services of Herrick's newspaper. It was Herrick who had walked arm in arm with Warren Harding the night of the smoke-filled room nomination in Chicago. Myron and Harding were boyhood friends and Myron when he spoke with Warren, never dropped the nickname of "Nig." Harding's manager also informed Mr. Todd, an attorney in his law firm, to go to Wooster. Before the Republican train left Akron, Ohio, the next morning, Harry M. Daugherty would have his plan in place.

The roorbacks, broadcasts or flyers sent out did not refer to the College of Wooster as we officially know it. All the flyers, referred to the "University of Wooster" or "Wooster University" not the College of Wooster. Despite this obvious error, telephone calls from newspaper reporters and alumni disrupted

The Indictment

Doctor Charles Wishart's administration of the College of Wooster for many weeks, according to some historians. No documents exist that say this bothered the president of the college enough for him to put a stop to the interruptions. Chancellor mentions that Dr. Wishart wanted the professor to send some of his collected information to some friends.

The only evidence that President Wishart may have executed anything was that Dean Compton had R. L. Todd of Bucyrus sent a flyer to Chancellor. Information to support this allegation is non existent. The professor responded by writing a letter to Todd denying he had anything to do with the flyer. Dean Compton interviewed Chancellor and had an affidavit signed by the professor denying he had anything to do with the flyers. Compton's involvement may have been the only contact the professor had with any official of the college.

Howard Lowry, a future president of the college, wrote that letters and telegrams came to the college from fourteen different states and newspapers called the college from many cities and states. He wrote "Wooster was clearly the storm center of the return to normalcy." Howard Lowry in twenty-two years later would replace Dr. Wishart as the president of the college. The future college president claimed Wishart called a trustee meeting to solve this vexing problem. Lowry does not offer, College records do not offer, nor does any other source offers evidence that Dr. Wishart tried to do anything about the Chancellor Affair. No records exist that the president ever interviewed one of his best professors to get his side of the story.

No records exist that Dr. Wishart was even remotely concerned about the problem that he must have known would end in days. Yet, Howard Lowry states, "Dr. Wishart kept his head and practically lived by the telephone." Lowry claims Wishart summoned at least a quorum of the Board of Trustees to the meeting on the campus. Trustee records contradict this statement.

When the College of Wooster converted from being a University, they shifted the control of policy making over to the Board of Trustees. This happened because the politics within the faculty threatened the well being of the college. They made the president responsible for administrative duties rather than policy making. In theory only the Board of Trustees had the power to call special meetings. Dr. Wishart possessed the wisdom to know this storm would soon pass. Dr. John Timothy Stone called this meeting from Chicago Thursday evening, October 28, 1920.

Howard Lowry dramatically states, "the president of the college called all over the country." Out of the thirty trustees, only seven lived out of the state of Ohio. Four trustees lived in the state of New York, and two lived in Illinois and one in Pennsylvania. The majority lived in the State of Ohio. Chicago trustees were the only out of state trustees who responded to the call of the special meeting. They never told many trustees about the meeting.

"Trustees of Wooster college were reaching the city on every train," reports the Wooster *Daily Record.* "They come to the city in response to summons issued at Chicago last evening and sent to Wooster trustees all over the country. They called the meeting, officials of the trustees stated, to investigate charges that Dr. Wm. E. Chancellor had sent out what claimed to be the lineage of Warren G. Harding."

The vigilant reporter for the *Record* interviewed strangers debarking from the train. He talked to Mr. Todd who had several books that he stated, "showed a complete linage of Senator Harding with a family tree." John Todd, from Columbus, Ohio, was a law partner of Harry M. Daugherty. He came to Wooster to protect the interests of the Republican party.

They called another man as a witness who carried a stack of letters and telegrams. He stated to the reporter that he had gathered this correspondence from various parts of the country. Another attorney refusing to give his name, stated the meeting was not so much concerning the circular that Dr. Chancellor had disavowed, but it was concerning the four affidavits that he had about Harding's ancestry.

Dr. Chancellor asked by the *Record* about these affidavits answered the reporter's question. The professor stated, "I have investigated Senator Harding by walking about Marion and many other towns. I have four original affidavits but I never sent out copies of them as alleged. I have received many inquiries from persons interested in this investigation and have answered them."

The reporter from the *Record* checked to find out if any other newspapers had information about Chancellor and the circulars. He stated, "They have published nothing concerning this lineage, as far as the *Record* could learn. An exception was the Bucyrus *Telegram*. That weekly paper stated that a Bucyrus friend of Chancellor sent one of these circulars to a Wooster man and he received the copy of the slip back." Chancellor had written on the slip, "This was not correct. I never authorized or promulgated it."

The same reporter wrote, "I have gathered that a special meeting was taking place in the morning at the College of Wooster. At this meeting they discussed the activities of Dr. Chancellor in sending out statements concerning the Republican candidate for President. The witnesses or visitors say they have copies of the matter." Dr. Chancellor told me, "He had not sent out the circulars or the affidavits."

From Marion, Ohio, came D. R. Crissinger along with J F Prendergast a lumber dealer and a close friend of Warren Harding. Prendergast arrived with a lily-white history of the Harding family. Crissinger carried the genealogy book sent to Warren by his cousin in Chicago. These men headed for the law office of Ross W. Funk on West Liberty, where they held the trustee meeting, off the campus of the college.

Attorney Ross W. Funk represented the College of Wooster in its legal matters. Attorney Ross Funk was a Republican and had recommended Chancellor to the local Mason lodge. Later Ross would later gain a judgeship directly from the newly elected Republican governor of Ohio.

Chancellor wrote about the special trustee meeting. D. R. Crissinger with a half dozen other Republicans went to a secret Trustee's meeting for the College of Wooster. At this meeting they disowned the family history of Harding they had written and circulated in millions of issue paper slips. They rejected what they said in Sunday sermons of churches for Black people in several states.

Friday morning, Senator Harding's campaign party left Akron before breakfast. The president made a press release. "They are quite satisfied that this section of Ohio was amenable this year to Republican persuasion," said the press release. From Akron the train was supposed to go directly to Cincinnati where Harding would give his next to last speech for the campaign. His last speech would be in Columbus, Ohio. However, a series of impromptu rear platform deliveries delayed its progress across the State.

That same day, the Democratic candidate James Cox spoke in Youngstown, Ohio. Cox's final campaign plans were to make platform speeches across Ohio then go to Gary, Indiana. From Indiana, Cox would return to his hometown Sunday then go to Toledo, Ohio, to give his last speech in his "battle for ballots." In Youngstown, Cox said, "I predict dire things will happen if Senator Harding is elected president. They are steeping in a creed of poisonous hate. They are sinking to a very low standard to continue a propaganda of hate, a creed of poisonous hate." Events of that day would prove Cox was correct.

As Senator Harding and Governor Cox were making their last bids to the electorate, the Board of Trustees at the College of Wooster decided to have a formal meeting. They document this meeting started at two in the afternoon. The local paper reported the time as one thirty.

Members of the Board of Trustees were elected to their position by the Ohio Synod of the Presbyterian church. The school's year book, titled the *Index*, shows for 1920 thirty people made up the board of Trustees. Page ten lists their names as elected for the class of 1919, 1920 and 1921. We list John Timothy Stone's name as President of the board and his name appears again in the Class of 1920. No one lists Charles Wishart as president, as they listed his predecessor J. Campbell White instead. A photo of Elias Compton shows the Dean of the College when he was a much younger man then his sixty-nine years.

Official trustee meeting minutes listed just ten members present, including Reverend John Timothy Stone. The ten members were not enough for a quorum. In the meeting's minutes they list Charles F. Wishart, but Dean Compton's name was noticeably absent. Of the twenty absent trustees three were from Wooster. Six of the absentees were from out of state while the rest lived in Ohio. Those absent were not contacted or were unable to attend.

The *Record* reporter states, "The trustees meeting took place in the office of Judge Funk and Harry R. Smith. In all my life I had never seen such an intent assemblage for any cause gathered at once. Those present were detectives, investigators, statisticians, and some just plain, honest to goodness, but astute politicians."

Chancellor wrote later, but one absent Trustee told me he had never received any notice of the meeting. Besides the trustees at the meeting five Republican lawyers who were not members were present and one National Committee Member of the Republican party.

The minutes listed the nine Trustees at the meeting not counting Dr. Stone. They were "Reverend Palmer, Judge Krichman [Kirchbaum], Mr. Woodard, Mr. Woods, Mr. West, Judge Cameron, Doctor Wishard, Reverend Higley and Judge Bigger."

Mr. Robert Woods, a trustee, lived in Wooster and was a close friend of the Chancellor's family. He was a teller and owner of the Wayne County Bank. He was a democrat, went to the same church and belonged to the same Masonic lodge as the professor.

Reverend Stone opened the meeting with a prayer and the first order of business was to elect Judge Bigger, from Columbus, Ohio, as Secretary pro-temp. Judge

Reverend Timothy Stone

Bigger wrote in the minutes about the reason for the special Trustee meeting. He wrote, "to investigate the connection of Professor Chancellor's name with the authorship of certain circulars. These circulars concern Senator Harding, the nominee of the Republican Party for president."

Without apparent concern for the truth or falsity of the accusation, it seemed the Trustees felt the College faced an extreme situation. This the trustees, or more pointedly John Timothy Stone, felt it was important to the College. Reverend Stones said, "I deemed it advisable to call the Board together when it came to my attention." This entry into the minutes conclusively proves Reverend Stone called this special meeting not President Wishart.

Board minutes acknowledge the presence of the committee on Tenure of Office was present. The Tenure of Office committee consisted of faculty members of the College. The minutes are silent about how many members from the faculty were present and who they were. Reverend Stone thought it necessary they were there to have "the benefit of the advice and guidance of the Trustees."

An informal discussion took place after Reverend Stone described the purpose of the special meeting before they decided to call in Professor Chancellor. This discussion took more than two hours. Led by Robert Woods, half the trustees present felt Chancellor had every right to investigate Warren Harding.

While the special trustee meeting took place at Attorney Funk's office, Senator Harding continued his train ride across Ohio. A *Daily Record* reporter said the Senator Harding's train made several impromptu stops on the way to Cincinnati. By early forenoon the train went through Wayne county heading west. Harding made rear platform stops at Ashland, Green Camp and Hamilton, Ohio. At Urbana, Ohio, Harding spoke for fifteen minutes from a shipping platform, next to the railroad. The stop at Dayton caught Senator Harding by surprise.

Harding had told the reporters aboard his train he really did not want to stop at the Union Station in Dayton as this was the hometown of his opponent. Instead of making a speech Senator Harding got off the train and shook hands with the sparse crowd. Local partisans said they would have had a larger reception if they had made an announcement ahead of time. They promised a large turnout if Harding would stop on the way back to Columbus the next day. Harding then boarded the train after promising he would stop on his way back to Columbus.

Harry M. Daugherty wrote about the train passing through Dayton although he failed to say it was an unscheduled stop. Daugherty said that they widely distributed copies of the *Dayton Journal* on the train. The front page"was screaming about a denial of slander." Senator Harding's campaign manager sheepishly wrote, "When Harding saw the paper, he was wild with rage. Daugherty claims Harding was a man slow to anger, and I had never seen him in such a fury. He had jumped immediately at the conclusion that I, as his manger, had ordered this denial printed." Senator Harding was extremely sensitive about any statements of his ancestry. The senator went to the car forward of his to confront Daugherty. Daugherty said, "He annoyed me." Then the attorney claimed to have calmed Harding down by saying he had nothing to do with giving the paper any instructions. Attorney Daugherty and Harding discussed the implications of the *Journal's* headline story.

This edition of the *Journal* never mentioned the word denial or stated there was a denial of slander as claimed by Daugherty. The headlines of the Dayton Journal claimed that before the sun is set, the slanders will seek their skunk hole. Editor E. Burkam states, "I say that over my name because I believe that truth and right and justice will prevail. Before today's sun is set, this great nation will know the truth." He goes on to say, "the *Journal* will send the degrading, shameless and unthinkable perpetrators of this cowardly assault upon the family of Warren G. Harding to oblivion and merited disgrace."

Burkam never stated what could happen after the sun set in Dayton or the world for that matter. Burkam said that they had distributed enough circulars in cowardly secrecy about Dayton and Montgomery County to supply every man and woman with several. He dramatically states, "innocent children have them!" They never mention the author of the circular. He does not explain who the skunk was or how he was going to put this skunk in his hole before the sun sets.

Burkam's secondary headline screamed, "The Most Damnable Conspiracy in History of American Politics. The time has come for plain language," Burkam wrote. "These vile circulars declare Warren G. Harding has Negro blood in his veins. These statements come from the flyer known as *Harding Family Tree*." Those who had a copy of the Harding Family Tree flyer would know he was talking about William Estabrook Chancellor. With guarded newspaper language Burkam, an owner, of the Dayton *Journal* was telling his readers clairvoyantly what will happen to Chancellor, as if it were a fact.

When they distributed the Dayton *Journal* aboard Harding's train, the sun had not yet set. Chancellor most likely was answering, or trying to answer the harsh, direct questions of the College of Wooster trustee John Timothy Stone. Yet, more than some hundred-thirty miles to the south west of this college campus, Harding and Daugherty were reading the predicted story of Chancellor's end. He would be "Sent to oblivion and merited disgrace by American public sentiment," before it even happened!

"The trustees summoned Chancellor and he was quite willing to answer questions," wrote Lowry. "He denied authorship of all these pamphlets. He confessed that he had studied the Harding ancestry and had supplied the genealogical facts, but he denied having ever put material into the printed forms that were under contests."

Lucy Notestein wrote, "Chancellor denied writing the tracts and pointed to their crude language and he steadfastly denied connection to them."

Chancellor wrote about the meeting. At 4:00 P.M. the Trustees asked me to come and see them. At this raid were five Republican lawyers, not members of the board, and one Republican National Committee Member. Most board members were absent. One trustee later told me he never received notice of the meeting. This trustee said I had a perfect right to investigation.

The President of the Board of Trustees began by telling me that he did not wish to know the truth whether Warren Harding was white or colored. What he wished was a denial by me that Warren was not a Negro. I absolutely refused to make this denial. The interview lasted fifteen minutes. In fifteen minutes, I had perhaps three minutes to make a plea of my defense. I offered to prove that only an illiterate person could have conceived this campaign. They refused to look at my written evidence of misspelling, etc. The meeting then adjourned.

The Indictment

Trustee minutes said the board voted to dismiss Chancellor after hearing his defense. Minutes of the meeting, also stated the retention of the professor at the college was impossible.

The board selected a committee of three to draft a resolution expressing the views of the Board according to the minutes. These three men who made up the committee were John West from Columbus, Judge Cameron of Wooster and Judge Bigger of Columbus. Judge Cameron told the board he did not want on the committee. They increased the committee to four adding President Charles Wishart and Judge Kirchbaum.

Later they appointed a committee of two to go to Chancellor's home and to have him tender his resignation. Judge Kirchbaum of Canton, Ohio, and Reverend John Timothy Stone left the meeting to see Chancellor. The board then took a recess.

The board of trustees had voted ten to five. Ten voted for dismissal and five votes were against letting Chancellor go without first having a proper investigation. Actual members of the board present numbered just ten. One can only surmise the first vote for dismissal was in a deadlock, five for and five against his dismissal, and they then took a recess. Dayton *Journal's* prediction of putting the skunk in its hole before sundown, missed its mark.

Chancellor later wrote to a student. When Reverend Doctor John Timothy Stone led his "lynching bee," as you call it, he was exercising for the College of Wooster his undoubted legal right to govern the institution. The only questions are two. Did he act according to law and order, or not? In the end will the denial of the right of academic freedom serve the nation and serve this school? He denied my right not to sign a lie that he needed signed for the advancement of the Republican party. Stone invaded my citizenship. He denied all the rules and regulations between man and man. He denied to me the ordinary rights of the Anglo-Saxon law, being himself a red Kelt. The Reverend conducted himself like an angry chief of a clan offended by the unwillingness of a clansman to accept his feudal overlordship. Reverend Stone said. "I was his man." I replied, I am a American citizen.

Judge Kirchbaum and Reverend Stone went to the professor's home. Reverend Stone attempted to be friendly with Chancellor but his natural disposition would not allow him to be other then overbearing. Reverend Stone told Chancellor the board voted to have him dismissed from the college. If he agreed to simply disappear, they would take no formal action against him. The College would have nothing published against him if he left, provided Chancellor would not write anything against the College. The professor asked what the vote for his dismissal was. He found fifteen members voted and ten voted for his discharge. Chancellor asked at what time the other five new members arrived because he counted only ten in the meeting at four o'clock. Stone told him they had called absent members on the telephone and asked for their votes.

The Indictment

Chancellor then informed the Judge and Reverend Stone the board lacked enough members present to make a quorum according to their own rules. They had violated the College rules and regulations, and they had violated rules of legal evidence. The three men talked this over. Before Judge Kirchbaum and Reverend Stone left the professor's house Chancellor thought, he had an understanding.

Chancellor wrote about the agreement. I thought I would have ninety days to prepare my defense, after all charges were presented to me in writing. I would have a hearing, first before the faculty and second before the trustees with legal council present. Then if the faculty and Trustees agreed I did wrong, they could discharge me with a full year pay in advance.

Judge Kirchbaum and Reverend Stone returned from Chancellor's home. The trustees reconvened, after a prayer led by Stone. First order of business was to make it official that Judge Cameron of Wooster wished removed from the committee of resolutions.

They do not record the agreement reached between Judge Kirchbaum, Reverend Stone and Chancellor. What the record said was, "Reverend Stone reported to the Board of Chancellor's willingness that he would sever his relation as a professor in the College, at once." Stone led the board to believe that Chancellor said "while conscious of embarrassment occasioned to the College, he felt in his breast that he had done nothing wrong or improper." Reverend Stone stated, "The professor will continue to have the kindest feeling toward the College and the board."

They do not record that a very vigorous discussion took place at the trustee meeting before it adjourned. Trustee Robert R. Woods, cashier and owner of Wayne County National Bank, argued to retain Chancellor. Woods, the Democratic banker, felt the professor had every right to investigate into the background of Warren G. Harding. Despite his gallant stand the affable banker lost to the so-called majority of ten. Mr. Woods and four other members who voted not to release Chancellor lost their argument to keep him.

Chancellor wrote later, when the meeting reconvened the Republican majority rejected the agreement I had with Stone and Kirchbaum. They called Warren Harding on the telephone and asked him to deny that he had colored blood, but he refused, saying that it would cost him the colored votes. Then they wired him, asking him to deny this, but he did not answer. After a late session, the President of the Board of Trustees, with a vote of ten to five, revoked my full faculty membership for life.

The board moved and carried to fire professor Chancellor, and they eliminated his Hoge professorship of Political Science. The dismissal of professor Chancellor was strictly along political lines as attested by Secretary Bigger. He wrote into the minutes of trustees, "Circulars concerning Senator Harding was the work of professor Chancellor. The Trustees concluded the circulars manifest the purpose was to appeal to prejudice." Bigger also states, "they distributed the circulars to influence the electorate in the up coming election. Therefore, be it resolved that we, the Boards of Trustees of the College of Wooster, disown and denounce such political methods as utterly unworthy of our College and country. Indignantly, the College of Wooster disclaims all connection with, knowledge of, or authority for making and issuing of any such circular letters." Graciously, in the minds of the Trustees, they moved to vote Professor Chancellor "the equivalent of his salary to the first of January."

Chancellor wrote, they sent a telegram to Judson C. Welliver, head of the publicity for the Republican National Committee. They sent identical telegrams to Will Hays and H.M. Daugherty, explaining that they had ousted me after a full hearing. Stone also, sent a telegram to the New York Press Club advising the Club that I had confessed libeling Harding and had both lied and broke promises. Ten members of thirty on the Trustee Board ousted me. Later one trustee told me that the others had deceived him, but this availed nothing.

The *Wooster Daily Record* reporter wrote, "They won! Dr. Chancellor, one of the most personally charming people I have ever met, a man with unusually large classes was free to go elsewhere."

October 29, 1920, marks the darkest page in the history of the College of Wooster. Ten trustee members, two where ministers and three were Judges tried, condemned and ousted William Estabrook Chancellor from his life time tenure as a professor, without a fair trail. On this dark day, they ignored freedom of speech, equity of law and good sense for exigencies of politics. He had no hearing, no written charges, no time to prepare, no legal representation and no salary. Later they only gave him a few hundred dollars to move away.

After meeting with Dr. Stone and Kirchbaum, William E. Chancellor drove to Shreve, Ohio, to give his last speech of the campaign. By this time the Harding campaign train had arrived in Cincinnati where the Senator would speak. Daugherty wrote, "The train arrived in Cincinnati and I spent most of the evening over the long distance telephone. I called Will Hays, who was in New York, and many others over the country and discussed the situation."

During the evening E. B. McLean, owner of the Cincinnati *Enquirer* came into Daugherty's room. McLean was in a rage and he drew from his pocket the proof sheet of an editorial denouncing the Democratic party. The *Enquirer* was a Democratic newspaper founded by McLean's father. "I told McLean," wrote Daugherty, "This will turn out to be the worst boomerang in the history of American politics. Harding's election is as safe as if we counted the votes. You must not sacrifice your father's memory as it is not necessary."

Chancellor wrote that the Republicans paid, $500,000 in cash for flyers and newspaper articles and released these on October 27, 1920. Senator Medill McCormick wrote the certified check to pay for

The Indictment

the publishing costs. The flyers stated that on October 28, 1920, they had ousted me from my chair, by the College Trustees, for libeling Warren Harding. (They ousted Chancellor on October 29.) This announcement predated my actual dismissal and printed a full day ahead of the trustee meeting. The spirit of prophecies rested upon the Chicago millionaire and the Republican party.

Republicans soon received surprise contribution of twenty five-thousand dollars, from Doheny the oil magnate and a Democrat, to pay for full page portraits of Harding's mother and father. The fact Doheny was a Democrat got the attention of Hays, Harding and Daugherty. Republicans would not forget this donation. Doheny would later harvest the oil fields out west.

Early in the evening Columbus found itself inundated with circulars. Democrats freely distributed the reprint of Chancellor's Open Letter. Frank Linny of Greensboro, North Carolina had telegraphed the Republican headquarters "the Democrats were about to distribute the EQUALITY FOR ALL leaflet." Two Oklahoma Republicans sent in copies of the leaflet being distributed in their area. The leaflet, roorback, or broadcast crusades increased in distribution after the Republicans ousted professor Chancellor.

James J. Davis wrote to Senator Harding, "It's very seldom I go off on a tangent. If I could have gotten a hold of that professor, who was circulating that stuff on you, I'm sure I'd have punched his snout and punched it hard. However, I guess it's best that we have never met."

The reporter from the Wooster *Daily Record* tried to find professor Chancellor but he discovered that the professor went to Shreve to address a Democratic rally. The speech in Shreve marked the fortieth time Chancellor spoke for the Democrats. Following his return to Wooster, the reporter interviewed Chancellor. When asked who sent the flyers out, Chancellor answered, "I do not know who sent out the flyers. In any letter that I sent out as a reply to an inquiry I told only the truth. They fired me on a strict party vote. The vote was ten to five."

President Wishart asked about the ten-to-five vote replied, "the vote was unanimous." When asked about the number of trustees at the meeting, Dr. Wishart told the press a dozen trustees were present. This reporter pointed out that Chancellor said only ten trustees were present. President Wishart replied, "They called members not present on the telephone and consulted them before we decided."

They asked Chancellor if he resigned. He said, "I will leave the matter to the pleasure of the trustees. I did not write a resignation nor did I give an oral resignation and I do not know what I will do in the future. Persons still unknown to me circulated alleged pedigrees, falsely assigning me as authority. I do know I will stay in Wooster and serve out my term as member of the city council. The primary reason for under taking the investigation was to add a chapter to my

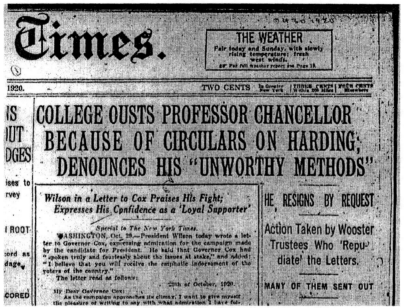

Chancellor's dismissal made the front page of the New York Times.

book, *The Lives of Our Presidents.* I hope to have this out not long after the election." The *Record* reporter added, "Talk on the streets of Wooster was that they might try to oust professor Chancellor from his the city council chair. City council members said they did not know whether they could take any such action."

Some College of Wooster trustees discussed Chancellor's dismal with the *Record's* reporter. They prefaced their remarks with "poor Chancellor!" One trustee remarked the discussion at the meeting did not take on "any political meaning." However, one trustee told the reporter about Judge Kreichbaum. "The judge was from Canton, Ohio, and was a prominent Democrat. Kreichbaum was very determined to see Chancellor dismissed. The discussion became very warm after the Judge and Reverend Stone returned from Chancellor's house. A member of the Republican National Committee arrived at the meeting in the evening."

Saturday, October 30, 1920, Chancellor made the front page of the *New York Times.* The *Times* headlines read, "COLLEGE OUSTS PROFESSOR CHANCELLOR BECAUSE OF CIRCULARS ON HARDING; DENOUNCES HIS UNWORTHY METHODS." A few of the sub-headlines read, "He Resigns by Request! Action Taken by Wooster Trustees! Who Repudiate the Letters! Many of Them Sent Out! Admitted his Authorship! Dr. Chancellor Said to Have Declared, However, He Felt He Had Done Nothing."

The *Times* goes on to say, "It was not until ten days ago that Republican leaders in Ohio became aware of the extent, intensity and seeming effectiveness of the circularized attacks on Senator Harding. They freely admit that since they made this discovery it has given them more worry than any other feature of the campaign."

The article in the *New York Times* continues, "The circular propaganda had been in progress for some time before the Republican leaders in Ohio became aware of its existence. They have conducted it in Ohio, Indiana, borders States and even to States south of the Mason and Dixon line where the Republicans have been making a campaign. They have heard echoes of the crusade from Virginia, North Carolina, Tennessee and Georgia and even as far south as Alabama. It was not until yesterday that an 'Open Letter' addressed to the men and women of America appeared over the signature of professor William Estabrook Chancellor."

Harvey L Bausher in Reading, Pennsylvania, stood on a corner handing out circulars when a police officer put him under arrest. The circular Bausher was circulating was one that had Chancellor's and the University of Wooster names in it. Alderman Charles A. High had signed the warrant to place Bausher under arrest. Bausher learned he would have to post one thousand dollars for bail. Word got out about Bausher, and people arrived at the police station donating money until they made his bail. Bausher a prominent Democrat in Reading would soon learn that Thomas C. Seidel of the Republican party filed a libel action against him. Harvey Bausher said that Seidel could not legally sue him.

Headline banners of most Saturday newspapers in the country told about the firing of Chancellor, except the Dayton *Journal*. The Editor, E G Burkam declared in bold letters a headline that stated, "Whole Vile Structure of Slanders Crumbles Under the Avalanche of Evidence." The second headline in the article read. "Two Distinguished Ohioans, Both Democrats, Utterly Shatter and Destroy the Slanders Upon the Family of Warren G. Harding! With the Searchlight of Direct Intimate and Personal Knowledge and After Complete Investigation!" A minor headline blared, "Professor Chancellor, First With Pen, Again in Direct Conversation and finally by the Due Processes of Law Repudiates and Denies the Statements Attributed to him."

Burkam wrote his story line. "Right and justice has prevailed, and before yesterday's sun went down the *Journal* had in its possession the absolute refutation of the unthinkable assault made upon Warren G. Harding and his family. Evidence shows what the truth was, what was the fact. Evidence not only indicts the cowardly campaign of vilification, but it declares that this low and indefensible assault upon the Harding family was a lie."

The editor Burkam reveals on his front page that his two distinguished Ohio Democrats experts are D. R. Crissinger and James F Prendergast. Crissinger was a Republican according to a *New York Times* article. This article stated, "Since Crissinger's defeat, in his Democratic candidate bid to congress in 1912 and his support for Taft as president, he did not care to be a Democrat. This article said they have never identified Prendergast with Democratic politics."

James F Prendergast, a lumber dealer from Marion of Ohio, reaped the biggest exposure in Burkam's front page story. Prendergast claimed in the *Journal,* as he did for the College of Wooster, he investigated Harding's family back to the year 1534. Later, they would prove that most of the information stated by Prendergast was wrong.

The editor wrote, "Mr. Prendergast's evidence absolutely and completely refutes the vile falsehoods to which Warren G. Harding and his family have been subjected." Then Burkam informs the reader about his next "witness" over a column headed, "Nailing it again!"

Burkam says, "The other distinguished Ohio Democrat is D. R. Crissinger." *The Journal* quotes Crissinger, "I have been a friend of Senator Harding for more than fifty years. Never has such a cruel, outrageous, contemptible and malicious political lie, ever sent by any party in the history of the country as this was. It was done to influence the voters to vote against Senator Harding." The Dayton *Journal* now comes down to the basics of its self-proclaimed grand exposure of "vile skunks." It states, "We now take up Professor William E. Chancellor. His name was in all the circulars spread broadcast over the country in this contemptible assault upon Senator Harding's family name. We present the evidence of his denial and repudiation, first by his own letter, second by his own spoken word and third by a sworn affidavit!"

The *Journal* editor states, "Sherwood P. Synder of Dayton Ohio has a letter of response addressed to him by Professor Chancellor." On October 22, 1920, Chancellor wrote in his reply to Synder, "I know nothing of the question you ask and think what you have heard was quite false. Another family of the name of Hardin lives in Marion, which was of mixed blood. I have found no connection between the two families of Hardin and Harding." One has to wonder what the Editor Burkam had in mind by printing this letter. Chancellor's answer clearly establishes his was familiar with Marion and the background of Harding.

The second point that Editor Burkam pursues to "prove" his avalanche of information that will destroy all "vile structures" was a phone conversation. Burkam stretched the limitation of fair play, by saying, "Professor Chancellor's spoke these words over the long distance telephone Friday afternoon, October 29 to Mr. L V West."

This conversation took place before they had called the professor into the trustee meeting around 4:00 just the day before at Wooster. Also, the Editor wanted the reader to believe the words he printed were the words spoken by Chancellor, when he only quotes Mr. West. The editor continues, "Mr. L. V. West, sales manager, of the Dayton Steel Foundry yesterday authorized the *Journal* to repeat his version of the long distance telephone conversation with Professor Chancellor. He said that one of my employees received a copy of the fictitious Harding Family Tree, to which they attached Professor Chancellor's name, sent through the mail. He showed it to me. I immediately called up Professor Chancellor on the long distance telephone and talked to him. In his conversation with me over the telephone he assured me he knew nothing whatever about the circulars entitled 'the Harding Family Tree.' I then asked him in particular if he knew anything about Senator Harding's pedigree and he replied emphatically and positively that he knew nothing whatever about it."

In fact what Chancellor told Mr. West was that he knew nothing of the circular. West or Burkam interpreted the answer the way he printed it.

Item three of the Dayton Journal "evidence" he saved for last. Burkam wrote, "And finally the sworn statement signed by Professor Chancellor in the presence of Elias Compton, dean of Wooster university, and attested and subscribed to law." Burkam in his paper now quotes the affidavit taken by Dean Compton of the College of Wooster. This affidavit was the one Chancellor had signed for the scholarly Dean Elias Compton. Dean Compton had told Chancellor the affidavit was for the pastor of a church in Kenton, Ohio. This affidavit was never presented at the trustee meeting. If it went to the Kenton minister, who requested it, it somehow ended in Dayton, Ohio. This full page story attracted attention all over the country.

Dayton's *Daily News,* a decided Democratic paper, owned by presidential candidate James Cox, did print the story of Chancellor's dismissal as written by the Associated Press. The *Daily News* also ran a story headlined, "UGLY RUMORS WERE CIRCULATED DURING FIGHT IN PRIMARIES." The *Daily News* states, "Chair Clarence N. Greer of the local Democratic executive committee entered denial to the insinuations carried in the local Republican newspaper the past two days. General Wood originally circulated these charges in the Republican primaries. Bars of justice are open and they can bring Chancellor to answer these questions."

In a rare front page Editorial the Dayton *Daily News* prints under the title of "The *Journal* and the Chancellor's Statement." This article stated, "The Dayton *Journal* was the recognized blackguard of American journalism. Besides, its editor, in his wrath may prove the Barnard of this campaign. He has brought in the open, a story that the anti Harding Republican forces in the presidential primary campaign quietly used. Now the *Journal* editor stews in his own juice, while Republican leaders regard him everywhere as a stupid blunderer. He deliberately falsified a statement from professor Chancellor. The telegram Chancellor sent the *Journal* was a matter of a public record. They deliberately said that in the office of that newspaper."

The news of the firing of professor Chancellor had spread rapidly through the small college city. Over the weekend some College of Wooster students suggested a revolt because of Chancellor's dismissal. President Wishart decided that telling the students of what transpired Friday at the trustee meeting would be best. Wishart's audience with the student body lasted just a half hour. Howard Lowry remembered how bright the sun was that Monday morning as he and other students made their way to the Chapel.

Susan Chancellor when she heard of the problems in Wooster immediately boarded a train in Columbus and went to Wooster. Susan, the professor's daughter, sat in the audience at the Chapel and listened to the president of the College speak.

He said, "While I have not been a supporter of Senator Harding I do not approve the attacks that they have made against him. These attacks have been purporting to emanate from a professor of the College of Wooster. For three weeks the storm has been brewing in every state in the union. The attack on the Harding lineage was a last-minute campaign attack, the kind known to hit below the belt. The circulars were five to six in variety. They connect the name of William E. Chancellor as a professor at the College of Wooster with them. The storm of indignation of the whole United States involved Wooster College. Many people assumed it was the action of the college itself and not the individual."

"Action by the board," continued Wishart, "was done to preserve the college from ruin, because of indignation by people everywhere. Anybody would resent an attack on his ancestry."

Susan Chancellor stood up and in a loud voice said, "Yes, President Wishart and any young woman would, too. It is unfair . . ." Students sitting near her, forced Susan back into her chair.

Dr. Wishart addressed Susan, "I'm coming to that side of the proposition in a minute, Miss Chancellor." The president of the college continued, "We never entered the subject matter of the proposition at all. We merely knew that they were scattering thousands of circulars over the country bearing the name of a professor at Wooster College. Men were present at the trustee meeting who had copious evidence to show the real lineage of Senator Harding."

"Professor Chancellor was one of the most brilliant men ever connected with the college, but along some lines he was temperamental. The interests of the college are greater than the interests of one man. If one man's actions are detrimental to the college, we will remove him."

Susan would remember forever the final part of the statement made by President Wishart, which at the time numbed her senses. Wishart said, "It was probably not Chancellor's fault that we linked his name to all this matter." The president then invited anyone whose mind was not clear in the matter to come and discuss it with him.

Susan would marry a successful business man and raise a large family. She would carry her bitterness of the action taken by President Wishart for the rest of her life. She refused to allow her children to become Presbyterians.

Chapter Six
Its Not Over Yet!

Harry M. Daugherty, a Columbus Ohio, attorney led the battle to get
Harding elected. He made as many enemies as he made friends.
Credit: Ohio Historical Society

Judge Spencer walked outside the cigar store into a small crowd in downtown Marion, Ohio. George T Harding, Warren Harding's father, spotted the judge and pushed through the crowd. Judge Spencer with one wooden leg balanced himself on his walking cane. George yelled, "You circulated false stories about my ancestors!" The Judge denied George T's accusations and said, "I will be very happy to sign an affidavit to that effect."

Herman Irey saw the confrontation between the two men. Irey, a hired hand on Crissinger's farm, shouted, "You are a liar!" Irey struck the Judge in the face. "Hit him again," someone in the crowd shouted. Irey smacked the Judge hard enough to drive him to the ground. The crowd held Irey back as the sixty-year-old Judge struggled to his feet. George T helped the wooden legged Judge up and took him into the cigar store.

In Hudson, New York, Franklin Delano Roosevelt commented on the ending campaign. He said, "Looking over the last eleven weeks one thought is uppermost in my mind and it gives me deep and lasting satisfaction. We have fought a clean fight. I have not resorted to mud-throwing, given no misrepresentations, did not attempt to mislead or deceive any issue. In direct contrast to the more than questionable campaign methods of our opponents we have fought fair, waging a campaign worthy of the great moral issue for which we stand."

Scott Bone, publicity director of the Republican party spoke about Chancellor's dismissal. "The whispering campaign so insidiously and wickedly carried on by the conscienceless Democratic party is now out in the light and condemned by the press of the country. Originating in Ohio," continued Scott Bone, "with no other foundation for it than the vapors of a miserable person of unbalanced mind, it spread from state to state. They designed it at the cost of many thousands of dollars. The author of the calumny, professor Chancellor, has now borne this expense."

Saturday evening at the Memorial Hall in Columbus, Ohio, Senator Harding gave his last speech of the campaign. A huge crowd numbering more than two thousand greeted the Senator at Union Station. This crowd, far more than the capacity of the Memorial Hall tried to storm it's way into the building. Inside Warren Harding told the enthusiastic crowd, "I am unpledged! I am unowned! I am unbossed!" The candidate went on to say, "I am the most unbound, unpledged, and untrammeled candidate ever offered by the Republicans for president!"

At the *Telegram* window in Bucyrus, Ohio, a poster made from Dayton *Journal's* Friday headlines drew attention and comment all weekend. The newspaper *News-Forum* of the same town ran a front page story explaining how during the campaign they were not interested in Harding's race. They said, "Professor Chancellor offered them a copy of his Open Letter but they refused to print it. In this Open Letter the professor comments on the accuracy of the flyer titled *Harding Family History*. He denied writing this flyer and told the reader he was not interested in the race issue. He also stated in the Open Letter he was for Cox because the governor was for the League of Nations. The professor had told us at the *News-Forum* he would make his statements good. It was interesting the immediate action taken by Dr. Chancellor to counteract the alleged denial by the *Dayton Journal*. Dr. Chancellor in an action today sued for one hundred thousand dollars in the court of common pleas against Burkam and Herrick Company, publishers of the *Dayton Journal*."

Headlines of the Wooster *Daily Record* read, "The Chancellor Storm is Still Raging." The *Record* states, "Dr. William Estabrook Chancellor, who has become the storm center of an under currant of the presidential campaign, declared today he has authorized a libel suit against the Dayton *Journal*. He may be contemplating at least half a dozen suits for libel, probably more than that."

"I was informed today over the long distance telephone that we sued the Dayton paper this morning," said the professor. "I asked for a judgement of one hundred thousand dollars. This was based on my earning capacity as a lecturer and writer over a twenty-year period. Two newspapers and individuals who I may also sue have slandered me. Their statements have libeled me and will decrease my earning capacity as a lecturer and writer." He added, "I will not sue the *New York Times* over the libelous statements made about me on their front page, because their editorial satisfied me. Still, I may include the *New York World* and the *Oklahoma City Times Star*. Bill Hays has libeled me and so has Scott C. Bone!"

E. G. Burkam, editor and part owner of The Dayton *Journal* headlined another front page story on William E. Chancellor, "THE JOURNAL AND THE CHANCELLOR STATEMENT." The article said, "Yesterday Chancellor sued The *Journal*. James M. Cox, candidate for president was in Dayton yesterday and cannot, as usual, disclaim responsibility. He made a charge in his newspaper the Dayton *News*. The charge is the statement the *Journal* published made up stories."

E. G. Burkam's anger was obvious in his article. In bold headlines he states, "The Journal answers! Here is our answer!" On the front page he prints a photocopy of the affidavit signed by Chancellor in Elias Compton's office. The article said, "Above is a photographic reproduction of the statement taken from the original document that is with the *Journal*. They executed it in Wooster, Wayne County, Ohio, October 28, 1920, two days before we published it in the *Journal*." Burkam continues, "Compare word for word, letter for letter, the printed statement and the photographic reproduction. See for yourself Chancellor's handwriting and that Chancellor signed the statement." Elias Compton Dean of Wooster University witnessed the affidavit, and "note the signature of the notary public," pointed out the editor.

This affidavit was Chancellor's denial that he did not send out any propaganda about Harding's ancestors. We know the dean told Chancellor the affidavit was for people in the Kenton church. We know Chancellor just lost his life time tenure as a professor, at the College of Wooster, by refusing to deny Harding was not Black and sign a statement stating that. Burkam in his front page story prints the only defense Chancellor gave at the board of Trustee's inquisition and the trustees refused to listen. The *Journal* states that Chancellor wrote, "I certify that I am in no way responsible for, never wrote, never authorized anyone to write, and know nothing whatever about circulars or other papers, bearing my name."

E G. Burkam said in the Saturday article that the professor denied this denial. The professor said he never denied the contents of the affidavit and Burkam had libeled him. Professor Chancellor felt the Dayton *Journal* was deliberately trying to embarrass him.

Burkam ran this article November 2, 1920. On this day, H. J. Thompson, deputy sheriff handed E. G. Burkam a true copy of the summons to Montgomery County Pleas Court. The summons stated William Estabrook Chancellor has sued for judgement for one hundred thousand dollars against the Burkam-Herrick publishing company.

Dayton *Journal* publically proved this affidavit, taken by dean Elias Compton under false pretenses, made it to Dayton, Ohio, Friday evening while the trustees' inquest was still in progress. College of Wooster trustees never saw the affidavit, although they heard its contents verbally from Chancellor.

Harry M. Daugherty said he tossed a "boomerang" and it reaped a curious harvest. One has to ask, was this in error or was this in fact exactly what the campaign manger of Warren G. Harding really wanted all along? The Bucyrus *News-Forum* editor answers this question.

News-Forum of Bucyrus, Ohio headlines its story, "The Negro Question Alarms Republicans. When caught in their own Dragnet."

"The Republicans attempt to secure the Negro votes of Ohio and carry the election has worked a boomerang. At the last primary, Republicans nominated six colored voters for our lawmakers. This, of course, was done largely to secure the entire colored vote of Ohio for the Republican national ticket and state ticket. The white people of the state soon noticed this fact and were not slow to comment on it. So general has it become, that we alarm the Republican organization in its attempts to charge the Democrats with bringing on the great agitation throughout the state. Let's understand on the eve of the election that the Democrats had nothing to do with making up the Republican ticket. Republicans nominated these men and they must retire to the bed of their own making. Another matter of great concern to the Republicans was the question of Senator Harding's lineage. Republicans brought forth this, too, in their primary fight in the contest between Senator Harding and Major General Leonard Wood. As this matter would not disappear during the campaign, the Republican organization charges this was also the work of Democrats. Democrats did not bring on this condition. Republicans themselves first circulated it. The Democrats are not interested in the lineage of Senator Harding. It does not concern them, as Democrats do not intend to vote for Senator Harding, lineage or no lineage. The Republicans alone are concerned and so the great excitement in the Republican organization."

That evening twelve-year-old David, Chancellor's youngest son, sat with his father listening to the election returns coming over the *Western Union Telegraph* in the parlor of their Wooster home. Isabel and Catherine came downstairs at times to learn that Senator Harding took an early lead, an advance he would not relinquish the rest of the evening. Unlike the election of Wilson years earlier, no students came that November night to the home of Bill Chancellor. An upheaval on the Wooster campus the past weekend cooled any ardor they had.

A small crowd grew in front of the Wooster *Western Union's* telegraph office to hear the returns of the election results. The Senator from Marion, Ohio, was evidently going to be the twenty-ninth president of the United States. Obviously, the Republicans were going to sweep Congress and most state elections. As the news came over the wire, a few drunks in the crowd blurted that they should tar and feather "that snotty professor Chancellor." Five or six men jumped into a car and said they would get the tar boiling just out of town. The cry to penalize the professor grew louder as the effects of liquor took control of their senses.

Howard Lowry heard about the crowd shouting for the tarring and feathering of Chancellor and he solicited three other students to help him. Four young men drove to Chancellor's house to convince him he should leave before the crowd arrived. Every few minutes the ex-professor answered the phone to listen to another threatening call. Lowry's plea for the safety of the children won over the reluctance of Chancellor to leave his home. The Wooster students took David, Isabel and Catherine to friends' houses and they took Chancellor to the Kenarden hall on the campus.

Lowry said they stopped at some friends homes and borrowed every shotgun and rifle that they could get in their hands. When they returned to Chancellor's house, they turned on every light. From various windows they stuck their shotguns and rifles out so anyone could easily see them.

A street light illuminated the corner and part of Chancellor's porch. A few more students arrived and took a station. Lowry and his vanguard could see the drunken crowd approaching the house. He said, "Many men in the crowd were drunk with mean dispositions. They marched in a phalanx up Bever Street and stopped just a few yards from the house."

Armed men in the unruly crowd brandished their weapons. They wanted Chancellor to come outside or they were going inside to get him. Lowry pleaded for them to settle their differences another way, but the drunk men jeered and came closer to the porch. Lowry ran inside and "braced himself for the onslaught." At this very moment the Wooster police drove up in two cars. The police "collared" whoever looked like leaders of the mob. With revolvers drawn the police shined their flashlights on those in the crowd. After some threats the crowd scattered. As Lowry later said, "It was good the police arrived. If any of the students had fired their guns, they most likely would have shot themselves first."

The students guarded the house in case the crowd decided to return. They took turns as guards as the others slept. At daybreak a man approached the house with a large black metal box under his arm. The guard woke up the rest of the students and said someone was returning with a bomb. As the Wooster man tiptoed across the porch, six students tackled him. It did not take long to find out the intruder was just taking a short cut to read the results of the election posted near Chancellor's house. They sheepishly grinned when they found out the black metal box, alleged to be a bomb, turned out to be a lunch pail.

Nan Britton's employment was finished at the Republican's National Headquarters in Chicago and she caught the midnight train to Marion in hopes of seeing and being near Warren. Nan boarded the train and headed to Ohio. About six thirty she awoke and called the porter. She asked who was elected. "Harding's the man, Miss," he replied grinning from ear to ear. Nan jumped out of her bunk and dressed for the day.

Bill Chancellor woke up in Howard Lowry's Kenarden Hall dormitory room. As he walked home, people in the street informed him that Harding won the election. Bill would learn that it was by a landslide margin of eight million votes. If all the Negroes voted for Harding as they said they would, their votes would have amounted to fifteen million. The Republican play for the Negro vote gave them a decided edge. Bill Chancellor thought of this as he walked through the Oak treed campus at the College of Wooster toward his home.

During the day Nan Britton got word to Warren that she was in town, and they met in a little house on Mount Vernon Street. The shades were drawn and the house was very dark. A secret service agent, James Sloan, held the door open for the President elect. Once inside Nan and Warren groped their way to the kitchen where he found a chair to sit with Nan on his lap. They kissed passionately. Warren told her, "Nan, your being here is the best thing that happened to me in days."

The couple after embracing talked about Elizabeth Ann, who Harding called, "Our baby." Nan showed him all the pictures she had of the baby. Before Warren left he gave Nan three new five hundred dollar bills. He warned her to be extra careful about seeing him because now the Secret Service would be watching him day and night. Nan told her lover she planned to return to New York City and try to get her old job back. Harding told Nan that he was planning a trip to Port Isabel, Texas and would be gone for an undetermined time.

Crawford County lies directly north of Marion County where Harding lived. The *News-Forum* reported, "Harding swept every county in the State of Ohio except Crawford County. Crawford voted Democratic on National, State and County tickets. Twenty-one precincts went strictly Democratic in its votes." It was the one bright spot in the election returns for Chancellor and other Democrats. The people of Crawford County knew Warren G Harding and refused to elect him.

Governor James Cox formerly congratulated Warren Harding. Franklin Delano Roosevelt said about the defeat, "It is a good thing, I am young enough to survive this disaster."

At the College of Wooster, President Wishart agonized over the replacement of professor Chancellor. Mrs. Notestein notes, "He started his students thinking of political, economic and sociological problems and to enjoy that thinking. No one in the field at Wooster could step at once into his shoes." By mid term Chancellor had carried more than twenty-three classes and they were in limbo until Wishart selected Charles West. Mrs. Notestein states, "Of all those around, Mr. West, may be the best qualified." The College of Wooster adjusted to the dismissal of its most popular professor.

Chancellor prepared for the Wooster Council Meeting. In this position he advocated more sidewalks, patching, repaired and wanted an overpass at the railroad crossing. Chancellor pushed for the overpass because of the danger of speeding trains passing through town.

Word passed around town that they should dismiss William Chancellor from his position as council member. Bill Chancellor braced himself for this new insult on his integrity. At the meeting council member Newman said he had talked with Mr. Gessner about the expected completion of his company laying pipes. The contractor promised the council he would have his work done before winter set in. Council member Clark reported the safety director was purchasing a motorcycle for the police department. The meeting ended without any mention of Chancellor. Following the meeting Dr. Chancellor in a sarcastic tone said, "I am grateful that no member of the council had made a motion to remove him from this body." That evening he received a telegram informing him it was official he was no longer a member of the New York Press club.

Chancellor wrote to a fellow member of the New York Press Club. I received your letter and thanked you for being plain with me. You regret that they expelled me without a hearing and without notice from the club of which both of us have been so long members. Yet, you see no way to straighten the matter out.

You ask me to try to forget that I was ever a member and say that "the Club is now in bad ardor anyway." Perhaps so, but the public regards me as properly blacklisted. I propose to pursue my policy of letting the public know the truth.

You tell me that my income from writing was not very important and that probably I can get another teaching position anyway. Evidently, you know nothing about my financial affairs, except that I have written many articles published in newspapers and magazines. First and last, I am a writer and in the middle, I have done other things. The Republican trustees at the College of Wooster have undertaken to destroy a writer. That was some undertaking, even for millionaires who own the present government. Writers live by what overthrows other men. Their troubles are their assets. They sell their books and articles because others are interested in their lives and opinion. The more trouble they have, the better their writings sell. Only God Himself can over-throw a writer!

God needs to do just three things to keep me alive. First, keep my brains at work. Second, keep me human. Third, see that I have food and shelter and necessaries of life. After doing this, God can trust me to do the rest. Nevertheless, He must keep my mind going, keep me inter-ested in humanity, and see that I have the means of mere life. Then I will write and write.

The Indictment

I have published thirty-eight books and have edited more than a hundred other books for publishers. One of my students once undertook to list all my signed published articles but gave up after tracing three thousand. The College of Wooster employed me because I am a writer, and for no other reason. Because I was a writer, they fired me, and for no other reason.

Very soon it will be a crime to own a home, because then one can probably laugh at the Lords of Land. Still, then the plutocrats will find a way to steal a man's home just as they stole my professorship and my membership in the New York Press Club.

You say that such things are the ordinary conditions of human life. They are. Newspapers should be superior to ordinary methods and conduct. The world needs truth. It needs truth far more than it needs shoes, oatmeal and coal.

In the present situation with slaves for writers, the newspapers are not telling the truth to us Americans. "First the truth" they put on the corner of their front pages, but the truth itself was not in them. What is the remedy? We need an enlightened public opinion to back up the writers.

You will say that the country newspapers are so owned. Possibly, the country newspaper can be truthful but only in the "hay fields," where they operate for the "hay" facts.

America is an empire of great cities. Forget the state lines. What counts is what New York, Chicago, San Francisco, and Washington tells us. You can test a great civilization by its great cities, and nowhere else. The farmers cannot save the nation. The cities rule us. To them the farmers send their best, their sons and daughters included.

I now ask the merchants of the obvious who run most of our newspapers to observe and consider that Harding was like a cloud that looks like mass and substance. Nevertheless, it floats and is lighter than air, for it floats high. Aviators can fly through it.

The excitement and intensity of the election died down. Republicans led in the popular vote and the electoral vote. James M. Cox won only eleven states and Harding received 404 electoral votes out of 531. Victory was more thorough than Harry Daugherty and other Republicans dared even to dream about. Later, it would be found that the voting was not heavy at all. The women did not exercise their franchise to vote. Most Americans, believing the newspapers, thought it was a dead issue and decided not to vote. The Negro vote estimated to be just three million, far from its potential of fifteen million. Eugene Debs, the Socialist candidate, although in prison, received almost one million votes.

Chancellor wrote about the election. Harding, a pawn upon the chess board of Ohio politics, advanced to the "King's Row" in Washington. Like a balloon, he has floated again into the National Capitol itself. After Harding and Taft, will America ever again tolerate an Ohio

President? Nevertheless, a far greater political crime was the rejection of peace for the world. The injury for the present is irreparable.

Therefore, bad as Polk was, bad as Taney and Buchanan were, politically bad as Hayes was, this Warren Harding will go down into history, the history of the world, as still worse. Perhaps a Harriet Beecher Stowe or an Abraham Lincoln will arise to show up the whole deviltry.

Probably, James M. Cox will long outlive Warren G. Harding, who has arteriosclerosis and a blood pressure of above 200. The man who survives his enemy has an enormous advantage over him for terrestrial reputation. Cox will write the epitaphs for Harding.

They made the election of 1920 to order, it was thoroughly disgusting, it has left after effects that will last a long time. It placed in the Presidency a man without a program, ashamed of his ancestry, and afraid of exposure. We now have a president who is ignorant of history and international affairs. He will bring only contempt to America.

Within three days after the election Warren Harding left the confines of Marion, Ohio, to make a trip first to Port Isabel, Texas then to the Panama Canal. The president-elect took friends with him. He invited three Senatorial cronies to assure enough men were around to make up a foursome for a game of golf. Ed and Evalyn McLean attached their private car, the Enquire, to the two-car train and went along. The multimillionaire couple thought that being part of the President-elect group would be fun.

President Wilson offered Harding the use of the presidential yacht, the Mayflower, to use when they arrived at the Gulf. They turned down the offer.

A close friend of Harding in the senate was Albert Fall. Senator Fall of New Mexico and a native of Kentucky, led a life of a rough rider in the very wild west. He invested time in mining for gold, herding cows as a cowboy and eventually became a lawyer. Fall, bilingual, became famous among the Mexican people as he defended their land right cases in court. Senator Fall also was an expert on oil and a close friend of Doheny and Sinclair the owner of the Sinclair Oil company.

Seeing Albert Fall dressed in western style garb was a common sight. He wore a tall hat, cowboy boots with six guns included. At Brownsville, Texas Senator Fall, accompanied by E L Torres, greeted Harding dressed in his cowboys' regalia. Senior Torres represented the Mexico president, Obregon, with whom Woodrow Wilson refused to have anything to do. Senator Fall's goal was to plan with president-elect Harding a way to meet with Mexico's new president and settle their differences. Of course Fall received a handsome fee from Mexico.

Albert Fall at this time needed to make money, as his ranch was nine years in arrears on real estate taxes. His spread in New Mexico was also in disrepair.

Chancellor wrote about the trip to Texas. On November 6 Harding left Marion to go to Texas. He took with him senator friends he knew would enjoy playing golf. Daugherty and his man Friday Jesse Smith would join them in Oklahoma.

The train stopped at Oklahoma, and Jake Hamon had a fine banquet at Oklahoma City. At this affair Mrs. Warren Gamaliel Harding put her right hand upon the shoulder of the oil king and called him "our dear Jake." Florence told the people how grateful she was for the terribly hard work he did to win Oklahoma.

They took Jake, but not Clara, his mistress, to Point Isabel, Texas. Jake, supported Harding during the election, thinking they would appoint him the Sec-

Clara Smith was said to have sprung from the bed and shot Hamon in the back. Hamon would be the first casualty of at least six during Harding's short-lived term as president

retary of the Interior. Jake was to learn differently. Senators Fall, Hale, and Frelinghuyson told Jake Hamon to go back home and clean house. Warren and Florence Harding sat sadly by and watched Jake's torment. Fall, Daugherty, and others thought Jake's way of living was too flamboyant for such a respected position, especially his open affairs with his secretary Clara. They quoted Jake as saying "Where do they get that stuff? What is the matter?"

Jake Hamon went into the June Republican convention in support of Governor Lowden and switched his alliance to Harding, when they promised him the Cabinet post of Secretary of the Interior. This position he bragged was worth at least four hundred thousand, more if he could control the Naval Oil reserves. E M Reily accompanied the entourage to Port Isabel. In Oklahoma he said William Backs, an employee of Hamon talked to him on the train. Bill Backs told Reily he knew Harding was going to make Reily the ambassador to Mexico. "We are interested in that appointment because of oil interests. We want that place."

Hamon wanted Reily to step aside so he could put his own man in that position. E M. Reily goes on to say, "Harding never trusted Hamon as a friend. He was suspicious of every move of the Hamon crowd and claimed Hamon had nothing to do getting his nomination." Daugherty and Harding did not want the complications of assorting with Jake Hamon.

Harding and his entourage went to Port Isabel to discover the cottage prearranged for their visit was too small for their group. Temporary living quarters were found in an abandoned brick hotel for reporters and guests of the Hardings. The rich, pampered McLeans' had to sleep on cots and eat at a "horrible" restaurant that served mostly ham with eggs. A rare blizzard brought the vacation to a close. Harding and his group left Port Isabel. In New Orleans the group boarded an excursion steamer, offered graciously by the United Fruit company. The Navy with great fanfare escorted the steamer into port once it reached Panama.

Chancellor wrote about Hamon. Jake went back home, first to Rankin, and told the city officials to send all the "Dames and skirts sky-hooting," [he wanted them gone] which they did. Then he went down to Ardmore to see Clara. Jake told her that she would have to go. She asked for her clothes, motor car, jewelry and fifteen hundred in cash to begin again.

This made Hamon think that Clara did not love him, and he went out and took several drinks. When he came back, he was drunk. He went to Clara's room and argued with her, but she only sent him away again. Then he took some more drinks. By this time, anger and desire for her had gotten the better of his temper, and he started to whip her. She resisted. Then he hit her again, and she took up a little pearl handled revolver and pointed it at him. He seized a chair and raised it. According to reports, Clara swung off the bed, like a cat, behind him, and 'plugged' him one. The bullet entered his back behind his liver, and he ran out into the hallway and into another room.

Jake stumbled into the Hard Sanitarium reports the *Daily Ardmore* newspaper. "The oil magnate claimed he had been cleaning a gun when it went off, injuring him. He died six days later."

Chancellor wrote, Clara rushed after him, and put her arms around him, but others who had heard the shot came in. Hamon said to them, "Well, the young woman has got the old man at last." A few days later Jake died.

Ardmore Daily reported Clara disappeared from Oklahoma. A local sheriff, Buck Garret, knew where Clara went. She fled to Mexico and Buck Garret finally traveled to Mexico when the trial started in the spring. Ardmore's business community put up her bond. The Judge presiding over the case was the twin brother of Clara's defense team attorney, Joe B. Champion. One attorney came from New York and the other from Chicago. The jury deliberated just thirty-nine minutes before they found Clara not guilty. They still list Hamon's murder in Ardmore as unsolved. Investigators wondered how Clara in bed, jumped out, moved behind Jake and shot him in the back as Hamon stood poised with a chair over his head.

Chancellor wrote about the killing of Hamon. All this might have come out at the trial. Nevertheless, the Standard Oil Company said NO, but allowed the part in the record about why Clara had the revolver.

The Indictment

The jury had no desire to hang a woman or even put her away for life. Also, she might run around and tell all she knew. Therefore, they made her and her parents comfortable by acquitting her on the ground of self defense. She was at large, and she may someday tell her story.

This was the story they told us. This was no ruined young woman story. It was merely the brutal outline of the plutocracy and its tool in the raw West. Senator Fall, who did the advising of Hamon to go home, will answer to the highest court, where all men have their Great Court. He asked Hamon to do something that was virtually suicide. How will he adjust his own conscience to his part in the business?

Through this dead man's money, or that of the Standard Oil men, many of whom are very religious, Warren Harding lives in the White House. It was a sickening fact for decent men to endure. How the White House can ever be cleared of the odor of this petroleum was a serious problem for the future of our American social order. Hamon, bad as he was, was a better man than the man whom he placed in the White House, and Hamon played a finer game. The American press know this story, but they have preferred to let me now tell it.

Jake Hamon was about 45 years old at the time of his murder by Clara Smith, whom they acquitted her for reasons and from causes of the most exciting nature. As the people of Ardmore, Rankin, and Oklahoma City put it "someone had to kill Jake, perhaps it was best Clara did it."

William Nickels, a close friend of Jake Hamon, testified years later: "Jake asked me to deliver a note to Warren Harding in Panama. He told me he wanted that letter tore up after Harding read it. Jake said, 'I am going to depend on your doing it.' I did. I delivered it to the president-elect and he read it. The tears rolled down Harding's face, he handed it back to me, and I tore it up. Harding spoke at length of what a wonderful fellow Jake was. Harding said, it is too bad Hamon had to be taken out."

Chancellor was born in Dayton, Ohio, on September 25, 1867, the son of David W. Chancellor and Harriet Allen Estabrook Chancellor. In 1873 the Chancellors lived at 395 West 2nd Street west of Perry Street in Dayton. William had three sisters and one brother. His father had a store at 2nd and Jefferson streets called Chancellor, Forgy & Company, that sold staples and fancy, dry goods, carpets, oil cloths, window shades and other household items.

In his hometown of Dayton, Ohio, Chancellor sued the Burkam-Herrick Company for $100,000 on November 1, 1920. They were the publishers of the *Dayton Journal*. While this call for a judgement was very sizable in 1920, it was well below the $500,000 indemnity bond placed with the Newspaper Association in Chicago by the Republican Party, reported by Chancellor. Hugh A. Snepp, a Dayton attorney, represented the ex-professor.

Snepp sued in the Common Pleas Court, Montgomery County, Ohio. Alfred L McCray, considered a capable and impartial Judge, presided. Judge

The Indictment

McCray issued, Summons in Action, to Burkam-Herrick for judgement on November 2. They note that a mileage and service fee for the summons cost one dollar and fifty-five cents, which included 80 cents for mileage and 75 cents for the service. The Deputy H. J. Thompson handed the summons to E. G. Burkam, President of Burkam-Herrick.

Nevins and Kalbfus law firm represented Burkam-Herrick Company. On December 4, 1920, this law firm filed a demurrer or a motion to dismiss. The attorneys for Burkam-Herrick stated they did not dispute the truth of the allegation, but claimed it was not sufficient grounds to justify legal action. In other words they objected to the filing of the law suit by Chancellor and wanted it dismissed.

Kalbfus presented his strongest point first, "The plaintiff in his petition says we have libeled him. These words standing alone are perfectly harmless and are not libelous. The plaintiff has failed to state how we libeled him and what is his exact damage. No facts are set forth that we have injured him in his profession as an author and educator. We move the Court should strike the petition from the files and obliterated from the records of this court."

Burkam-Herrick's attorney continued his plea to the judge. "The sole objective of the plaintiff is to use the channels of this Court to get before the public a document he wrote. They have not filed this petition in good faith. It is a sham. They are trying to use the Court to bring public attention to the so-called Open Letter. They attached this Open Letter as 'Exhibit A.' They should not have attached this as it cannot be justified on any theory of good pleading."

"We should not permit them to use the Court in the advancement of a scheme. This scheme is one of the vilest pages in political history. The sole purpose of this Open Letter was to cast reflection upon the distinguished American citizen who is to be the next President of the United States."

Judge Mc Cary heard this argument, then Kalbfus entered his motion to dismiss. Kalbfus said, "We respectfully submit the Court should order the petition herein stricken from the files and obliterated from the records of the Court. As counsel for the defendant, we now move the Court to strike the petition from the files and from the records of this Court."

Kalbfus also filed a motion for security costs. This motion claimed that William Estabrook Chancellor was a nonresident of Montgomery County. Therefore, he should deposit sufficient security for costs of this action. Kalbfus pleas that if they do not make the deposit securing the costs by January 1, 1921, this action should then stand as dismissed.

In the docket journal of Montgomery County Common Pleas Court they show a deposit of $25 less the $1.55 for service fees. It was not clear who gave the deposit or when they made the deposit. Most likely they deposited the deposit of $25 at the time Hugh A. Snepp sued.

The docket does not show, nor do records show what the Judge Mc Cary ruled on the plea of the Kalbfus and Nevin law firm. This silence means that Judge McCary did not rule on Kalbfus's plea and they did not dismiss case. Records clearly show that Chancellor's attorney Hugh Snepp never filed an answer to Kalbfus's pleas.

They dated the last entry in the Montgomery Common Pleas court two years later, April 4, 1923 on the Chancellor case. This stated, "we dismiss this case for want of prosecution, at plaintiffs' costs with a record, for we award a judgement. They took a clerk fee of $23.45 and Sheriff fees from the remaining deposit leaving a zero balance. This entry ended the lawsuit."

On November 13, 1923, the court notified Hugh A. Snepp that they dismissed the case. A large question remains unanswered about why the Chancellor case languished two years in the courts of Montgomery County. Maybe the Republicans got to Attorney Snepp and paid him off and this was possible. It could be that Snepp could not get in touch with his client Chancellor. Professor Chancellor may have decided not to continue the lawsuit or was Hugh Snepp paid off to look the other way? Documents to prove or disprove any of these possibilities are lost. What happened were extenuating circumstances, created by Harding and Daugherty that prevented the professor from having his day in court. We can interpret these extenuating circumstances as obstruction of justice.

Despite his threat to sue others, Chancellor never did. He threatened to sue the *New York World* and the *St. Louis Post-Dispatch*. These leaned heavily to the Democratic party and its policies during the election. Professor Chancellor felt both papers were fair to him and did not sue them for libel.

The Pulitzer Estate owned these two newspapers. The newspapers helped the professor in the research of Warren Harding's background before the election. *New York World* also sent investigators in December 1920, to help Chancellor to do more research on the president-elect. Chancellor and these reporters went back to Blooming Grove, Steaming Corners and Marion. These reporters wanted to prove or disprove what Chancellor had said to date. Former professor Chancellor and reporters gathered information that only confirmed Harding's ancestry. This group explored and found many interesting items. These same reporters gave Chancellor the information on the killing of Jake Hamon. This team at first found resistance from citizens, but soon won their confidence. With new found information the ex-professor began to put a book together about Warren G. Harding at the suggestion of the reporters. Some of this information he shared with his friend at the New York Press Club.

Chancellor wrote about his investigation. Obviously, James M. Cox's first wife was a cousin of Harding and she was black. Therefore, he would not back propaganda about Harding's ancestry. I had too much common sense to do it anyway. Obviously, this was a move of the Negroes. Local Republican leaders backed them, such as D. R. Crissinger, and known to Harding himself, to get the Negro voting out and the sympathetic white votes with it.

As to saving my chair we must remember the goal of the Trustees. They did not go to Wooster that afternoon to oust me. They went to get me to sign a lie as to my beliefs. When I refused, they ousted me. The New York Press Club under their orders had me banished from their organization.

These orders came from Medill McCormick, of the *Chicago Tribune*. Others behind McCormick were Myron T. Herrick, of the *Dayton Journal*, Theodore N. Noyes, of the *Washington Star*, Edward McLean, of the *Cincinnati Enquirer* and *Washington Post*. Even Dan R. Hanna, of the *Cleveland News* supported this move.

On the ex-parte evidence of one Reverend Doctor John Timothy Stone the Wooster College Board of Trustees ousted me after a sham trial that was a lie. Another lie was to the effect that I had "retracted" that which I never did. This was an offense to Anglo American law and obstruction of justice.

They say in reply that I intended to prove that this president has a peculiar ancestry. Was this president sacred like Nero in a Golden Palace? Can they write truth of all white men, but not of men not all white? Is Negro Blood untouchable from publicity?

They object that the truth would cause public indignation or worse. It is exposure that they fear. Yet if we do not expose Harding, they will reelect him and others like him, and worse will follow. The plutocracy needs these rubber stamp men as tools.

Chapter Seven
I Will Write, I Will Write!

Florence Bernhart Kling De Wolfe Harding who Warren Harding called the 'Duchess' sits on the front stoop of her Marion ,Ohio, home.
Credit: Ohio Historical Society

In his letter to a member of the New York Press Club Chancellor wrote, "only God can stop a writer." Discharged from his teaching job, Chancellor went back to Blooming Grove, Steaming Corners and Marion with reporters from the *New York World* newspaper. The former professor and other reporters gathered information that only confirmed Harding's ancestry and Chancellor's views.

As Chancellor researched, Warren Harding would give a speech to the Congress and in it he spoke of liberty, security and rights of all citizens. He also said, "No matter what clouds may gather, no matter what storms may result, no matter what hardships may attend, or what sacrifices may be necessary, we must sustain government by law. The first allegiance of every citizen, high and low, is to his government. To hold that government will be the just and unchallenged sponsor for the liberty, security, and rights of all its citizens." This position Harding spoke of but as we will see he did not practice. The ex-professor and newspaper people would find out exactly how the Republicans felt about liberty, and the rights of all its citizens.

The Indictment

Chancellor wrote that the chairperson of the Marion County Democratic Committee was a staff member of the Marion High School. In that capacity she made favorable speeches about the League of Nations. Of course, she knew the truth about the color of Harding and she told it. They enforced an order, forbidding the chairperson to talk, after the election. This order was contrary to the Constitution of the United States.

Suppose that the Republicans could silence free speech in America, as they have gagged the press with money. Let our Republican neighbors understand this. You cannot attempt to stop free public speech. Can you stop gossip and slander? Can you stop secret pamphlets? Try it and see. What tyrants have failed to do, the plutocracy will quickly fail in trying to do.

A gang of Republicans at night entered the office of a rich old Democrat in Marion and stole all his papers. He had been corresponding with other free Americans about the Negro ancestry of Warren Harding. Cannot the Democrats retaliate? When is this crime going to end?

Nevertheless pressed by his ambitions and by his brunet, aged wife, Warren Harding has been trying to convince himself that he has too little Negro blood to count. He was too ignorant to know that the past was adamant. It takes a dull man to try to change it.

In this fierce struggle in his mind, Warren went in 1915 to Washington as a Senator. He was absent in the next five years from thirteen hundred roll-calls for votes. Harding voted for prohibition and then against prohibition of liquor when he did vote, he voted anti suffrage. Warren made very few speeches as a Senator, and none of them long. Every time they mentioned the tariff, he showed some interest. The reasons for this are several. Harding stopped what little schooling he had experienced when he was 17 years old. At this time education was under the control of high protective tariff teachers, and he has learned nothing since. The other reason was that the manufacturers of Marion are high protective tariff men and own the banks also. He has always catered to them in the *Marion Star*.

A man serving five and a half years never made a poorer record in the United States Senate than Warren Harding. He was merely a creature of his creators, and not a good one at that. We might tell much more of the records by Harding until the 1920 presidential campaign. Nothing more is worth telling beyond more support of the main point. He was in training, but severe training for the business of doing just what his masters of the plutocracy were to tell him as president to do.

The oil interests did not waste Harding's visit to Panama. They informed him that Columbia lost land from the Roosevelt administration during the building of the Panama canal. Woodrow Wilson would not even discuss the situation on a diplomatic level. Harding would remedy this situation when sworn in as President by paying Columbia for land rightfully owned by the United States. Then Rockefellers interests moved in buying and leasing oil producing sites with the sanction and blessing of the Columbian government.

The President-elect returned to the United States after a short stay in Jamaica. As his ship approached the protection of Norfolk Bay, airplanes, blimps and seaplanes encircled it. In a daring display of airmanship, pilots dropped newspaper bundles onto the ship's deck by flying low in their airplanes.

December 5, 1920, Harding appeared in the Senate and answered role call as a Senator. This appearance, when they greeted him with applause, marked the last time Harding would appear in front of that autumn body as a Senator.

At this time the professor was organizing his notes and preparing to write a book about Harding. Chancellor wrote contrary to my desire, I became involved in this race issue because I would not lie about my belief. I believed that those Negroes and neighbors of Harding that I interviewed were telling the truth, as they were. Asserting the equality of men or of races is wicked. The glory of men is in that all differ, one star different from another. Climates vary too much and the original germ plasmas differ too much. Ideas differ too much. The differences between men and the races of men concern everything that man is.

They now claim since Harding's family tree originated in New England, and he could have no black ancestry. Fully 50,000 Negroes lived in New England at the time when the Hardings supposedly moved out of Connecticut. Many other Negroes also moved out. Negroes and Indians of almost pure blood are living in Caucasian clothes and according to Caucasian manners in New England. Proving that they came from New England does not prove that the Harding blood was all white. They evidently know nothing of New England.

Do we have pure races? Very few pure Negroes are in America, as nearly all Negroes have Portugese or Spanish blood. The slave traders saw to it that every black woman who came into America was pregnant. They bore a half white child, white in the sense that the Moor or Portugese or Spaniard is white. A great Negro named W. E. Burghardt Du Bois who has Negro, French, German, Portuguese and Dutch blood, tells this in his book on the slave trade. Only 5 percent of city Negroes are pure Negro, and in the rural districts the proportion does not rise above 25 percent anywhere. To say in America that any Negro man is all black is a very risky thing regarding the truth. He probably has at least some white blood of the brunet stocks, if not of the blond stocks.

Where children in the same family differ radically, this is an evidence of hybrid origin. Many races exist and the men of each race differ from one another. In America, representatives of every race and hybrids exist. The so-called white race consists of brunets, blonds and grades between the blacks and whites, and other race grades.

George Tyron Harding the father of
Warren G. Harding.
Source Joe M Chapple

The friends of Warren Harding claim that he was also French, Dutch, and Kelt Scotch. No one imagines that Warren Harding was a black or even a brown Negro. He has china blue eyes. His flatterers call them gray. This was apparently a hateful thing to say, but the people who started the race issue were the Republicans. They set out to organize every new woman-colored voter for Harding, on the ground that he had Negro ancestry.

Soon, I discovered that colored Harding men had taken as mates the white women of their own neighborhoods. I found no concern about a formal marriage with any of them. They simply mated and usually for life. Morals were not involved, save as not having a public marriage was immoral. In their back country they were busy trying to support themselves and breed children.

Now the evidences are many that all the Hardings, are descendants from Amos, have Negro blood. The best evidence was in the father of Warren, George Tyron Harding II and the ten children born to him. Of these ten Harding children, of whom Warren was the oldest, these children are of all shades from dark brown to a very light yellow. The color of the three who are most nearly white was hard to name. Color, though the popular means of discrimination, is hardly the most useful means to the science of human traits.

No one imagines that the mother was the cause of the exceeding variety of types in this brood. She was at least nearly all white. She might have had some Indian blood, but no direct evidence was available on this point. Any who read this must get over the notion that most of the country people around Blooming Grove were white people. Mostly they were Black people like the Hardings.

After he grew up, why did not Warren Gamaliel Harding resent his nickname 'Nig.?' For the sufficient reason, as he has told United States senators, that he has Negro blood. Every man is secretly proud of his race elements, as he ought to be. They have quoted Warren's father to saying that he was smarter then most, because his ancestors come from three races.

It was true that Warren had the blue eyes of the white man, but his sister, Mary, had the dark brown eye of the black race. One child who died was very dark.

In early January 1921 a reporter from the *Post* in an excited tone told ex-professor William Estabrook Chancellor that he found the William Chancellor named by the Republicans on the flyers. "This William Chancellor lives near Mt Gilead and he was black," said the reporter. The reporter said "D R Crissinger came upon the black man with your first and last name and it amused him to no end. I interviewed this black Chancellor and he said it was his pleasure putting one over the white men." The reporter told Bill, "It was their desire to do no harm but only good with the flyers."

This news excited Bill Chancellor and he left Wooster, with the reporter to meet the black man with his family's name. Former professor Chancellor, sought a notary so they could take and use an affidavit in his court case. What they found was an elder black man that could barely write his name. Out of pity Chancellor took no affidavit or deposition from this black man. Instead he continued to work on his notes.

Chancellor wrote, the American people would like to know now, at the beginning of his administration what Harding's dominant trait is, and what is his other influential trait. His dominant trait is a love of ease. He likes to be well provided for. To have plenty to eat, plenty to wear, warm housing, tobacco to smoke, chew, and take as snuff. Harding revels in tobacco and in times past plenty to drink. For which habit in its final stages he was, occasionally, treated in the private sanitarium of Dr. C. E. Sawyer.

They have just made Doctor Sawyer a Brigadier General, where at public expense he will continue as Warren's private physician. This appointment also conveniently limits unwelcome scientific observation.

Give Harding ease and he is at peace with the world. He does not care how the ease, was secured. Because he loves ease, he was the perfection of laziness. He hates to come to the time when he must do something. "Do Nothing" would be a far better name for him than Harding.

His next diminutive trait is caution. He has no prudence, no prevision. Warren never bothered learning geography on the notion that some day he might be a member of the Senate Foreign Affairs Committee. Harding knows nothing of international law or of ordinary law, in the prospect that some day he might become the head of our foreign affairs as president. Still, he has caution, but he looks about circumspectly. The man does nothing. He looks about with his eyes half open and his ears wide open to adjust to the turn of affairs. Warren was a commonplace man to whom things happen, but who was ready for them when they happen.

Warren Harding loves to appear more than what he is. He likes to be well thought of and a born imposter, poser, mimic, and a masquerader. His wife has tamed down his original love of loud clothes and loud colors.

His need to keep out of trouble was another trait. Warren can sidestep all blows and he makes no decisions that he can avoid. Harding will move rather than take a blow and fight. In which respect he was no Kelt like Andrew Jackson and no fighting Dutchman like

Nan Britton bore a child of Warren Harding that she named Elizabeth. Harding refused to see the child.

Theodore Roosevelt. These men loved fighting for its own sake. Harding hates it. He was a born pacifist.

Evalyn McLean, the wife of Ned McLean, often saw the self-doubting traits of Harding. While in Panama, she noticed a change. She records, "The constant adulation of people was beginning to affect Senator Harding. He was more, inclined to believe in himself." Harding had told her that "that when they elevated a man to the presidency his wits by some automatic mental chemistry increased to fit the stature of his office." The heir and owner of the Hope diamond, said Harding began to realize what power the president had. He used this power to place his friends in office and he called to them in the tone, "as an olden times, a King called to his jesters." Evalyn would see other changes in Harding as the responsibilities of his office loomed over him. The selection of close friends would contribute to the change over Harding.

Warren Harding told the press he planned to have a cabinet consisting of the "best minds" available. While at Port Isabel, Warren contradicted this statement. He gave Ed Scobey, a close friend of his, the job as Director of the Mint. Ed Scobey's qualification for that job was his experience as a Sheriff of Pickaway County, Ohio.

D R Crissinger organized in Marion, Ohio, the Harding for President Club and worked to get Harding elected. They give him the plum of Comptroller of the Currency. Crissinger's financial qualifications consisted of a few months on the board of directors for a Marion bank.

The Indictment

Warren then appointed Doctor Sawyer at the insistence of Florence Harding to be the White House physician. Harding gave the rank of Brigadier General to this homeopathic doctor. Dr. Sawyer purchased a uniform and wore it constantly.

Reverend Heber Votaw's qualification to be the Superintendent of Federal Prisons was his marriage to Harding's sister Carolyn. A major consideration of Mr. Votaw's selection was the fact he was unemployed at the time and Harding's brother-in-law. Carolyn "Carrie" Harding Votaw, Harding's sister, took a departmental job in the Veterans Bureau. Appointments to other important posts, Harding procrastinated.

In Wooster the unemployed professor of political science wrote. The Phillips case illustrates his sex instincts. Several times, even after the nomination, Harding and Mrs. Phillips visited together at Upper Sandusky. Phillips went to Japan early in October, but not until Mrs. Phillips, who was a very talkative woman, had told all her friends just what she was to receive. Warren shrugged his shoulders and said he could get another woman.

In sex morals Warren advocates no reservations. Some of Warren's affairs with the ladies were almost disastrous. For instance, they called the police to the house of his regular lady friend, in Washington, to sober him up and stitch the cuts in his back. This resulted, according to her, from a dispute over finances. This woman, who was about 35 years old, they never prosecuted for this almost fatal attack upon a member of the senate. The Department of Justice and the Washington police gave this matter to the Democratic National Committee, but the Democrats were too decent to use it.

Warren Harding waited to resign as Senator until the time was right to have the newly elected, Republican Governor of Ohio, Harry L Davis in office. Governor James Cox offered to nominate the recently elected Willis, but the Republicans did not want any favors from the Democratic Governor. Harding formerly resigned as Senator when Harry Davis was sworn in.

Harding returned to his home base, Marion, Ohio. The Hardings then rented their Mt. Vernon Street house to a local contractor, Millard Hunt. Hardings had their furniture put in storage and left for Florida on another vacation before announcing any more Cabinet appointments. Before leaving Marion, the president-elect gave a speech at the newly named high school that still bears his name. They record his speech at Harding High School of Marion, Ohio, as inspirational.

In Florida Warren became sullen. In a short time he lost all the confidence he exuded in Texas and Panama. Harry Daugherty discovered the reason for the sudden turn of personality. Someone was blackmailing him. A young lady of ill repute wanted a thousand dollars for letters he sent her while a senator. Daugherty typically made discreet phone calls to get information about the woman and where the letters were.

The Indictment

Chancellor continued to write, the question whether or not Warren was a Negro and that a black man is now the President-elect, Americans take one of many different positions. Let me list these reasons.

Some do not care. A president might be a Hottentot or a German from Berlin and they would not care. It was not a matter important or even of interest to them. They have other business to which to attend. The government is a thing apart. It does not concern most people who are in the White House. Presidents may come and go. The presidency is a kaleidoscope to them. University graduate or a Negro school attendant, it was all one to them. Why worry? We cannot change him, and the case might be worse than it was.

Some feel it was a good thing to try the experiment and let us all wait and see what the Negro will do! With fifteen million black people in the country, every race has a right to try. He may be a very desirable man. All races are equal, and we are all Americans. Back him up!

Some are interested and hesitant about having a Black president. They are disappointed they have made such a choice, but it might be worse. These people would say, after all, a good Negro was better than a bad white man.

Several regard the charge that Harding was black as pure invention of malicious politicians. They believe it was not worth even noticing, because government politics was bad and rotten. These people believe every wicked move by politicians was only an impulse toward the end.

Few admit that Warren was considered colored but he has lived it down. He was not any longer a Negro roustabout but our foremost man. Race means nothing when a fine specimen comes along. Some think that even a little Negro blood was acceptable. Since he has so much white blood, what was the harm in the choice, Octoroon was really, after all, a white man.

The thought of the president being of Negro blood horrifies other people. The thing was too awful even to think about. They believe his election was an insult to the white women. These people want to impeach him to absolve this outrage to the white race.

The North and South hopelessly divide the Negro question. It was a wonder that America has remained one nation. Some people in the Southern states regard the Blackman as an evil presence. Most southerners believe the white man must keep him under and that they should never allow him to mate with a white woman. They think Negroes should live in a segregated part of every city or of the countryside. He may individually work as a servant or field hand, but they should frown upon all endeavor on his part to rise even to industrial equality and when possible, defeated. These people do not hesitate to lynch an accused black or black man on the same premise that causes them to kill a wild beast.

While the Blacks remain in the land, we must treat them decently. No one should kill an unoffending Black or Black man or rob him of his goods or wages. Some leaders of Southern opinion think that every person with Negro blood should be placed in a part of the South where they will exclude the whites. They want to set aside certain counties for Blacks alone.

We will have hangings, and we will have them until the whole population is all white or all black, for race instinct is behind the sins and the lynching. This was the antique fear of many Southerners.

In the United States, among the several hundred thousand Negroes, are those of pure Negro ancestry. They also class these among the groups of Malays, Barbers, Arabs and Moors. This was a false assumption. These Negroes, fourteen races in all, are Senegambians, Hottentots, Mozambicans, Pygmies, Sudanese, Kaffirs, Zulus, Gold Coast, Plateau, Ethiopians, Abyssinians, Congoese, and Senegalians. The differences between these various races of Negroes are as great as those between the white races, in culture and even in external appearance.

Northern people do not know many Negroes and have a distorted notion of the Negro. According to this idea, he was kinkily haired, pot-bellied, black as coal, with big brown eyes, a projecting jaw, flat feet, and long arms and legs and the knees not standing straight. A few such Negroes in the United States may exist, but they are very few. To say that Warren Harding has Negro blood was not to assert that his ancestry was from the Senegambian Negroes, or from plantation field hands enslaved to white masters.

What are the questions about Harding? Did his family rear him with the notion that he was a black boy to be a Negro man? The light and truth are the opinions of the neighbors, a thousand of them in the three counties, Crawford, Morrow and Marion. Here the thousands of Hardings live and have just one answer, Yes!

From St. Augustine, Florida, Harding made public his announcement of his choice for Secretary of State. The announcement of Charles Evans Hughes as Secretary of State surprised many Republicans. He was not popular with the bosses, especially Boise Penrose. Harry Daugherty said, "Considering his age, experience, training and general qualifications I believe that he was today the ablest man in the United States."

Charles Hughes managed the estate of Joseph Pulitzer that owned the *New York World* and the *St. Louis Post-Dispatch*. With Hughes appointment as Secretary of State, these newspapers ordered their reporters working with Chancellor off the story.

Chancellor wrote about Hughes, it so happens the Pulitzer estate owns two great Democratic newspapers, the *New York World* and the St. Louis *Post-Dispatch.* These two papers and others were the only ones that were fair with me to get all the facts out about Warren Harding. The *World* was an organ of public opinion that values the truth and they had special reporters out after the election to look into the facts. Charles Evans Hughes was drawing the salary set at thirty six-thousand dollars per year as a trustee and legal estate advisor. The appointment of Hughes would not control the editorial opinion of the newspapers. Yet the edge of hostility to Hughes and to the administration of Harding was off after his selection. Also, the search into the records by their reporters of the Harding ancestry ceased. These newspapers remain Democratic in view but should Hughes error in office a very awkward situation will develop.

Reporters from the *World* and *Post-Dispatch* gave William Chancellor their collective notes before leaving Ohio. One suggested that Chancellor should write a separate book of Harding instead of just updating his "Our Presidents" publication. With these notes and his own Chancellor continued to work on the book he would entitle The *Illustrated Life of President Warren G Harding.*

Chancellor wrote, Doctor George Tyrone Harding, Warren's father, would never have considered himself anything but a black man until Amos Kling's death. If Warren had not married the rich banker's daughter, they would regard Warren with his brothers and sisters as black. They would have gone back and forth to Blooming Grove and have shared the views of their colored relatives, who are half the population. Still, fate had something else in the store. It had in stock the effort of George T. Harding and of his children to defeat the truth of social opinion.

Again the question about Harding was whether he was reared as a Negro boy with the training and notions of black people. He has escaped that social classification. He did this, but he left some bitter enemies in Marion, where the better element has had him in their homes. Senator or president, though he was, he will never again live in Marion. When he becomes an ex-president, he will go to some city where they will ignore his past.

The actual question was, in the physical sense, has Warren any Negro blood? If so, what was the line of proof? Socially, a man is what his neighbors report. He has to take their classification or get out from among them. When they call him a Negro, it does no good to sue them for slander. They still think so.

In September and October, when I, newspaper correspondents and others by the score went to Blooming Grove, New Caledonia, Iberia, and Steam Corners, not one reporter found one man or woman who denied that the Hardings was anything but Negro people. The

Hardings themselves agreed that everyone so called them.

Of course, after the tremendous furor over the matter, the neighbors became naturally silent. Many ignorant persons now believe that President Harding could put them in jail for telling the truth about him. This they felt could happen with Daugherty and the secret service at his call.

Mrs J. C, a descendant of
Elizabeth Madison Harding
Library Of Congress.

Yet, once Harding ceases to be president, what will then happen? Give the neighborhood time to recover itself. Especially bitter are the darker Negroes whom the Republicans have failed to reward as promised. They will settle scores that will make the old feud, as Harding calls it, mild.

The Republicans promised they would appoint many Negroes into responsible positions if they helped to get Harding elected. Harding would renege on this promise.

"Harding's treatment of Charles A. Cottrell of Toledo, Ohio, who had stuck by him so valiantly at the convention has caused much gossip," wrote A. N. Fields in the black owned Abbot Magazine. Field says, "We thought it to be a matter of course Harding would take care of Cottrell."

Charles Cottrell had worked diligently with Harry Daugherty to make the Colored Voters Day in Marion a large success. President Taft had made Cottrell a collector of internal revenue of Hawaii. Cottrell got nothing from Warren. Harding did reappoint the Negro Judge Robert Terrill to the Municipal Court of the District of Columbia. "We expected this. It was not considered as indicative of friendship for the Negro," stated Fields in his magazine series.

Harding did select Walter L Cohen, a prominent Negro, as the collector of customs in Louisiana. Fields in his writings reflected the feeling of most Negro politicians. "Apart from this Cohen's appointment Harding selected white men of lower intelligence and less standing in their communities than any president since the time of Grant in 1869."

Chancellor continued to work on his manuscript. He wrote, Warren Harding said that "the people have been calling his family and kin Negroes for eighty years." He has given this out twice in long interviews. It was curious how Harding does not dare to pronounce it a lie. He says that people have a right to their opinions and that he was sorry about their opinion. Many people sent telegrams to him from all parts of the country asking Harding to deny the truth about his ancestry. Harding never has yet said that he has no Negro blood and deplores the discussion of the subject.

Was he afraid of the ghosts of his Negro ancestors? No man should ever deny his ancestors. That was like denying God Himself. No man should be ashamed of whom his ancestor was.

All of Blooming Grove cannot be wrong about Warren. They cannot be wrong about his father, George T. Harding II, and his grandfather, Charles A. Harding, and his great-grandfather, George Harding I, and the second wife, Elizabeth Madison, who were black. Elizabeth was Warrens' Great-grandmother. No Harding descended from this Elizabeth has ever had the courage to tell who their parents were. They acknowledge that no picture exists. Yet this was the fact.

Any person with ears questions the truth for one moment what Elizabeth was. She was well remembered by eight old persons still living as late as October 1920 in Blooming Grove and nearby. They all say that Elizabeth was Negro. One woman, past 90, said she was so dark skinned, that she frightened the white children of her neighbors. Her son, the grandfather of Warren, lived until past 1880. He also was well remembered with pictures enough of him. He had curly, kinky hair, and a dark complexion, and a wide, big body, and great nostrils. Also, he left many children.

Five of these descendants of Elizabeth live in Blooming Grove and nearby. One of them was Mrs. J. C. She was a fine old dark Negro woman who has never offended anyone, and she was a good woman. She allowed me to take six pictures of herself. Mrs. J. C. has a large heavy body, big brown eyes, very dark skin, and was a typical mulatto. She had her pictures taken with her Bible under her arm, and that she said warded off evil spirits. Elizabeth was not a Moor, or an Arab, she was a dear old colored "mammy" and very dark.

Four others in the Harding family are all black. We might give their names. They live in Blooming Grove and Galion where anyone can see them anytime. One of them, smaller in stature, was equally dark. All of them are plainly Negro. Such are the nearest living relatives of Warren Harding in that generation.

Let us go on to the court records. In 1849 David Butler killed Amos Smith. David Butler and Amos Smith were blacksmith partners in Blooming Grove. The wife of David Butler was a Harding descendant. She owed 50 cents to Smith's Wife. One afternoon, as they were closing the shop, Smith asked Butler to have his wife to pay the money to Mrs. Smith. David replied that his wife denied that she owed any money. Then Smith told Butler that he had a Nigger for a wife. David Butler replied by throwing a piece of iron at Smith, about an inch square and ten inches long. This iron hit Smith on the side of his head, and down he went. Mr. Butler immediately ran to him and carried him into a house nearby.

He sent for a doctor, who treated the skull fracture. A few days later, fever developed and the doctor bled him, the same doctor who afterward taught George Tryon Harding II all the medicine he ever knew. A fortnight later Smith died.

In 1850 the grand jury of Morrow County, which they had just created out of Crawford County in the wilderness, tried and indicted Butler for manslaughter. The attorney for the defense said he was justified in killing Smith because his wife was a Negro woman. Defense also contended Smith died of malpractice. The jury said Butler had no malice because he immediately tried to revive Smith. They thought it was a hot instant of wrath between friends and Butler was a man of good character.

The prosecuting attorney was a famous lawyer named Columbus Delano. We sent men to a dozen states to find the copious notes that Delano kept of this trial.

We saw at Mt. Gilead the original brief records of the indictment and steps of the trial that lingered in court seven years. In the midst of the search of this record a low brow man confronted an investigator. This square-jawed hecklers' only business apparently was to maintain the curtain of darkness over the skeletons of family history. An investigator found another busy guardian had extracted the pardon papers from the files at the state house at Columbus. This was after we took photographic copies of the papers.

Intense neighborhood feeling became aroused, mostly against David Butler. Hardings countered as best they could. The jury found, that it was does not slander to call Mrs. Butler a Negro, since they always so called her and the Hardings. This jury found that Smith died of the fracture, not of the bleeding by the doctor. Yet, since David was of good character, they recommended mercy. The court sentenced David Butler to the penitentiary for five years. After two years, the Governor pardoned him on a petition presented by his Harding relatives.

They have charged two other killings to the same feud. Country people decline to take the Hardings as all white. When they try to escape from this social classification, quarrels result. The presumption in Blooming Grove was that every child was not white until they prove the opposite. Blooming Grove was a fugitive slave district. More than half the people have colored blood. The presumption was that colored blood was somewhere in the ancestry. They do not charge this as a crime, but as a fact. Nothing was 'bar sinister' about it. Warren Harding was not an illegitimate son of a white man nor was his father before him. I was not engaged in slander and libel in finding these facts, but in investigation.

In Florida with his friends Warren Harding tried to relax. Many felt the awesome duties of being the next president began to overwhelm him. Daugherty wrote, "Harding wanted all political debts paid and this embarrassed him. I gave personal aid to the President-elect in a task that all but overwhelmed him."

Daugherty wrote about this time. "I was tired of politics. The longer I was in the current of politics the more difficult it became to retreat, until I found myself helpless. Mortally tired of political fierce feuds, savage battles, bitterness, lies, slanders, foolish myths, and devastating demands upon a man deep in the game." Friends and enemies of Daugherty thought the attorney general elect enjoyed being in the limelight.

James M. Cox the defeated Democratic candidate went to Florida to relax from the strains of his failed election bid. He wrote, "I saw Daugherty and Harding's social groups. This included Ned McLean, Senator Frelinghuyson, Senator Fall and Jess Smith. I had a long talk with Daugherty. He was in unusually high spirits due, I felt at the time, to his own consciousness of power he was exerting. I remember remarking to a discreet friend of mine that I thought I saw considerable mental instability in Daugherty then."

Chancellor wrote, reports spread that Warren Harding had Negro blood. During the campaign, the city editor of the Republican *Post Intellingencer,* of Seattle WA, turned to his most experienced of reporters.

The Post's editor said to a reporter, "A Niece of Warren Harding lives here in Seattle. I do not know who she was or where she lives. Take the photographer and find her. We will print her picture and show up the bughouse professor out there in Ohio."

It took the reporter two days to find the woman. He brought back the photographer and had the pictures developed. He refused to write any story, and the city editor was wrath with rage. In an hour or so, the developed plates came down from the sky room. The city editor looked at them and he told the veteran reporter this, "That college professor out in Ohio is not so bughouse after all." The veteran reporter told this to the people of Seattle after the election! Still, the people have not yet seen the pictures of the niece of Warren.

Daugherty left Florida to return to Columbus, Ohio. One of his goals was to see what could be done about a woman blackmailing Harding. After learning more background about the woman he found the letters she had, contained nothing really damaging to Harding. He also found out the woman had a damaging character. Through trusted friends he began negotiations to get the letters back. Bid price for the letters went immediately from one thousand dollars to five thousand dollars. Daugherty found out, the woman was political vulnerable through a member of her family. Samuel Adams who recorded this event, said, "They brought counter pressure into play and they surrendered the documents without price."

Harding had learned Chancellor was writing a book that would reveal his background. After solving the blackmail problem, Daugherty turned his attention to Wooster, Ohio, and William Estabrook Chancellor. Harding returned to Ohio.

January 7, 1921 Warren Harding became a member of Columbus's Aladdin Temple, Ancient Arabic Order of Nobles of the Mystic Shrine. He spoke to his fellow Shriners, "I wonder if you know the feeling of a man whom they have called to the greatest office in the world. There is an aloofness of one's friends, and that is one sad thing. In me is a deepening sense of responsibility. I have found already that there is intrigue and untruth against which I must guard. One must ever be on his guard. This everlasting being on guard, spoils a man."

Ex-professor Chancellor wrote, In his early days Harding applied for admission to a certain secret society. He failed in three lodges. They blocked him from all others until after he was elected president. What was the personality of such a man?

Warren Harding has no program. He has no depth and reflects what was near that appeals to a very few primitive instincts. He was genial enough and, in a light way, affable. How can a man who has never studied American history or government beyond the elementary school books converse on politics and jurisprudence and economics? Warren can seem to listen. As his pastor, the Reverend Doctor McAfee, says in an interview in the *New York World*, he was an eloquent listener.

Before proceeding, we have a word to say about this Reverend C. P. McAfee. He was a Baptist and preacher where Harding goes to church occasionally. Being a preacher, he looks professionally for the good in men, and for nothing else. This preacher knows nothing of the past of this man. McAfee has no familiarity with Harding's Washington life. Because Warren pays his church dues, or Mrs. Warren does, McAfee regards him as a useful church member. The minister admitted that Harding was never at prayer meetings, has no Bible class, and makes no personal contribution to the Christian world. This was not cause and effect, but it shows the mental and physical instability of the man they cite as authority for the fine Christianity of Warren Harding. Of course, being a Baptist, he wished that Warren won. Even preachers are human.

The Marion Lodge, Loyal Order of Moose, presented Harding with a life membership card before he left Marion. When he spoke, he spoke with tears in his eyes. He mentioned he may be unequal to the ordeal ahead of him. A member told Samuel Adams, "It appeared he was reluctant to take up the responsibilities of the Presidency."

While Daugherty investigated Chancellor, Harding took up the responsibility of taking care of Nan Britton. After going to New York Nan returned to Chicago because of ill health and her inability to find a suitable job. Warren wrote Nan a letter and asked to have her sister meet him in Cleveland, so they could work out a suitable plan for the adoption of their baby, Elizabeth Ann.

Secret Service agent M.C. McCahill called the Cleveland office and informed agent John Washer that president-elect Harding would arrive in that city at 4:55. McCahill requested two automobiles, one open and one closed. A local Pierce-Arrow dealer supplied the two automobiles and the secret service escorted Harding to Doctor John Stephens office, for minor dental work. Later, special agent James Sloan made sure Harding had privacy so he could talk to Elizabeth, Nan's sister.

Elizabeth spoke with Harding and returned to Chicago. She told Nan about the arrangements that they made for the baby and her conversation with Harding. Elizabeth told Nan that Warren said, "My God, Elizabeth, you've got to help me. Nan is just a child in so many ways." Warren then discussed the few options available. He suggested, "I would not hesitate a minute to give you and your husband Scott three to four hundred dollars a month to care for Elizabeth Ann if you will adopt her."

Nan talked to Elizabeth about this adoption. She said, "I wanted so much to have the baby with me. To give her up completely through a legal adoption meant the greatest sacrifice of my life. It was presented to me that I had to do this to help and protect Warren Harding. The most difficult problem was telling Scott Willet, Elizabeth's husband to agree and keep the affair very secret." Scott Willet finally agreed to the adoption of Warren's child, Elizabeth. Harding sent three hundred dollars in cash to pay for an attorney.

Completely unaware of Nan Britton until later years, Chancellor continued to work on his book. Like the rest of the people in the United States, few knew about this love sex affair Harding had with Nan Britton. They would learn more about her and her affair when she published her book, *The President's Daughter.*

Chancellor wrote, it was "incredible" that a man who has so little mental life should have been lieutenant governor and United States senator and now the President of the United States. Yet this has happened. Warren Harding was very ignorant about many things. They have asked him often, what is an association of nations? He failed to answer this simple question. He knows no geography outside the United States, and he knows little of the world.

Harding knows no Latin and no foreign language. Warren knows only English words, and not even English grammar and rhetoric. Warren Hardin did nothing in business as an accountant.

A man may be both ignorant and confused but very shrewd according to his own lights. When they nominated him so suddenly, he turned to his advisers and asked, 'Is not this too premature?' Harding knew that they had brought up the convention with money, and he was afraid that Hiram Johnson, Wood, and Lowden would 'blow up' and tell the press. However, they did not.

Hunger, lust, vanity, these are his dominant instincts with a gaming passion, and a love of playing for good stakes. Warren was no open fighter and prefers to get at the backs of men, as the Republican Convention proved.

Victory Way in Marion, Ohio.
Ohio Historical Society

We are plain and direct here. Great parties in American history have created several great political crimes. One was the Mexican War. Another was the Fugitive Slave Act, with the infamous Dred Scott Decision, which made Abraham Lincoln President. Any of these crimes will seem minor, compared with the crime of making Warren G. Harding president of the United States.

Harding was selecting his cabinet. A member of the cabinet selected by Harding who was not a millionaire and was Harry M. Daugherty. This was the most criticized and censured of all the appointments. It was purely personal.

Here it is enough to say that Daugherty was good as a business getting lawyer. He knew how to get out and get suits and clients while his partners furnish the law service. During the World War, he and others built an envelope factory and got a contract to make envelopes for the Post Office Department. This contract, with the factory, he sold to Dayton envelope makers for just twice what the factory cost him, giving him a profit of $300,000. How much of that he could keep for himself was unknown. No one ever accused him of being a book-learned lawyer. Daugherty has been a very shrewd party politician all these years. He made Harding first a Senator and now President. Daugherty was an Irishman and vindictive against his political opponents.

Harry Daugherty may prove the ruin of the man he has used

so skillfully. He remembers his friends and his enemies, which was bad for a man who has so much power as the Attorney General possesses. Daugherty was the wettest of wets. If he develops a sense of honesty, it will be a miracle of regeneration. Believing what he does and cherishing his natural instincts to reward and punish by using the government to advance his own cause. This man was a danger to the freedom of many individual Americans. With him America becomes a land of men, not laws.

Thinking of a man like Daugherty who can exercise selfish use of power was unpleasant. The attorney general can set free tremendous forces. Nothing in the record of this man inspires confidence. He will conform only to help the rich and to help himself.

Suppose that a college professor exposes or gets in the way of a man like Daugherty? What will happen to him and to his mail and to his personal freedom?

Chapter Eight
Let Freedom Ring!

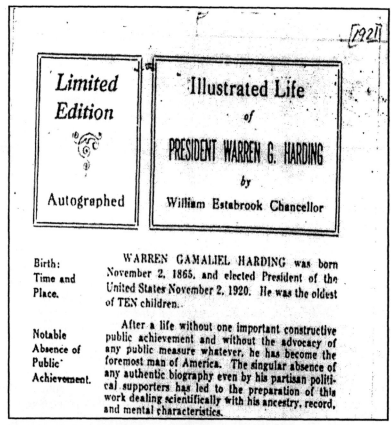

Limited Edition

Autographed

Illustrated Life

of

PRESIDENT WARREN G. HARDING

by

William Estabrook Chancellor

Birth: Time and Place.	WARREN GAMALIEL HARDING was born November 2, 1865, and elected President of the United States November 2, 1920. He was the oldest of TEN children.
Notable Absence of Public Achievement.	After a life without one important constructive public achievement and without the advocacy of any public measure whatever, he has become the foremost man of America. The singular absence of any authentic biography even by his partisan political supporters has led to the preparation of this work dealing scientifically with his ancestry, record, and mental characteristics.

Top part of a front page of a flyer sent by Chancellor to solicit prepublication sales for his book. A Toledo, Ohio, businessman had sent this to Harding, who set into action Secret Service agents to destroy the manuscript.

Bill Chancellor continued to write his book titled *Illustrated Life of President Warren G. Harding*. Chancellor planned publication sometime after inauguration day because he wanted to include his observations about Harding's inauguration speech and Harding's cabinet selection. Inauguration day was March 4, 1921.

The professor had a unique way of writing a book. First he would write chapter numbers and titles in sequence on a sheet of paper. If he needed another sheet, he would continue the list, then tape them together. This became his outline for his proposed book. When finished he rolled the pages scroll-like together. Using this as a guide he would type his book and neatly place the sheets into the box in which the typing paper came. On the box, in block letters, he put the title.

Chancellor typed his manuscripts on a manual typewriter and he marveled about how easy writing was using this machine. His first few books he wrote with a pencil and then rewrote them using pen and ink. He rewrote his first book seven times before feeling confident enough to send it to the publisher. The professor commented that most people do not realize the amount of hard work and how much time it takes to write a book.

Chancellor formed a company called the Sentinel Publishing Company with a Wooster, Ohio, address. The Sentinel Publishing company was never officially incorporated and the professor planned to print a limited edition numbering only eight-hundred.

MacMillen publishing company continued to print the professor's education series. The book Graded City Speller went into its ninth printing in 1921. This book and others from that collection sold between six cents and eighteen cents. Sentinel Publishing had an asking price of five dollars for the unpublished book and promised delivery by mail or express if a subscriber prepaid. Those who prepaid would receive a numbered issue autographed by the professor. A brochure suggested to the subscriber that large orders would cost less and political organizations would get special treatment.

Twenty different publishers had published at least one the professor's thirty nine books. Any one of these publishing companies should have accepted this well-known author's latest effort but none did. The pamphlet stated that the author was "bearing the entire expense as he bore alone all the expenses of his long and careful investigation in the interest of truth."

Word got around of Chancellor's new book and Walter A. Jones from Columbus, Ohio, became interested in this project. Jones agreed to bear the expense and be responsible for the printing.

Sentinel Publishing printed and mailed flyers to potential buyers in January of 1921. The front-page of the pre-publication flyer outlined the contents of the book. A lead paragraph stated, "After a life without one important constructive achievement and without the advocacy of any public achievement he has become the foremost man of America, its President. The singular absence of any authentic biography even by his partisan political supporters had led to the preparation of this work dealing scientifically with his ancestry, record, and mental characteristics." Of course Chancellor was referring to his main subject of the book, Warren G. Harding.

This flyer said, "Immediately after March 4, 1921, the book will go to press containing a review of the inaugural address." A back page of the flyer had a reservation coupon with the return address of William Estabrook Chancellor, a member of City Council in Wooster, Ohio.

This advertisement familiarized the reader of Chancellor's six-month investigation into the ancestry of the president, including a report about whether

Harding's parents were ever married and if not why? The pamphlet stated, "Read the record of his wandering life and his incomplete education that was not equal to an ordinary rural high school. A story of his marriage to a divorced woman and of her father's opposition to him, which was not for the reason, falsely alleged, that he was a poor painter. We explain his political office seeking before the campaign of 1920."

RESERVATION COUPON

William Estabrook Chancellor.
Member of City Council,
Wooster. Ohio.

Dear Sir—Please reserve 1, 2, 3, 4, ... copies (as indicated by underscored number) of your illustrated life of Warren G. Harding, President of the United States, at Six ($6.00) Dollars a copy, to be delivered by mail or express, prepaid in advance. To insure reservation and autographic verification, I enclose herewith.................Dollars, being Thirty per cent of price

Six copies only be reserved in advance for $30.00

Terms for cash full paid in advance are offered as follows: 1 copy, $5.00; 2 copies, $9.50; 6 copies, $25.00.

The coupon on the back page of the advertisement
sent out by Sentinel Publishing Company

The circular confirms he was an author of thirty-eight different books, including *Our Presidents and Their Office*, and five other historical works. It also states that the author was formerly the City School Superintendent in Washington, D.C., and connected him with the College of Wooster.

Then the flyer quotes Mr. Scott T. Bone, Publicity Agent of the Republican National Committee when he was an editor of the *Washington Daily Herald*. It was Scott Bone who said, "The whispering campaign so insidiously and wickedly carried by the conscienceless Democratic party is now out in the light and condemned by the press of the country. Originating in Ohio with no other foundation for it than the vapors of a miserable person of unbalanced mind, it spread from state to state. They designed it at the cost of many thousands of dollars. The author of the calumny, professor Chancellor, has now borne this expense." They printed this quotation in newspapers right after they ousted the professor from the College of Wooster.

Chancellor used another quotation from Scot Bone in his brochure. How the Republican reacted to this bit of burlesque is unknown. Chancellor quoted Bone, "Everyone knows that Doctor William Estabrook Chancellor is a genius of the first water. He had a uniform and brilliantly successful record in New Jersey and is making a notable administrative record in Connecticut." This quotation came for an editorial that appeared in the *Herald* on December 16, 1909.

The flyer asked the questions, "Who bought the nomination for Harding? Whom did they pay off and at what cost? Why was it alleged Clara Smith killed Hamon?"

A feature of the book, claimed the handbill was, "The inside story of President Harding's financial relations with Colonel Jake Hamon, multimillionaire oil operator. Hamon was killed November 21, 1920, by Clara Smith, as reported at Ardmore, Oklahoma. This book explains the defeat of Georgia Harding Hamon as candidate to succeed Jake as member of the National Republican Committee from Oklahoma. We give a true account of the nomination and election of 1920 by which Harding was elected president. Read the disclosures of his friendships and enmities involving Congressman Theodore Burton, former Governor and Ambassador Myron T Herrick, the late Senators Mark Hanna and Joseph B. Foraker and President William McKinley. Know the explanation why the Senate of the United States was so especially concerned in his election. Learn the motives behind the cabinet choices under the new president."

The brochure states, "The *Illustrated Life* contains an account of a race experiment at Blooming Grove, a main Ohio station in the underground railroad, formerly called Harding Corners." This and the following statement are the only references to the race issue that they continually accused the professor of conceiving. The second reference reads, "First, professional interest and duty inspired the careful investigation now public. Interest commands publication of facts that the American people, men and women, white, red, black and colored have a right to know what manner of man lives in the White House." These statements gave no cause or reason to threaten Harding. However, this would be the reason used of what happened next.

The unexpected result of this exercise of free enterprise astounded not only Chancellor but his contemporaries. Somehow Warren Harding got a copy of this flyer. He became livid with anger and wanted Chancellor smashed. He told Harry M Daugherty he must find a way to suppress the book and quiet the professor in Wooster!

All biographers of Harding said the President refused to acknowledge the race issue. This was not true. Writing to his cousin in Chicago he affirmed and denied this stand on the race issue. He wrote, "I have always been averse to dignifying this talk with attention or denial. If finally deemed necessary, we will stamp it as the unmitigated lie it is." Harding became upset when he heard Chancellor was writing a biography about him and he told Daugherty he wanted the book quashed.

Daugherty asked the presiding attorney general to help in suppressing Chancellor and his book. Attorney General A. Mitchell Palmer officially held office and would until replaced by the incoming administration. This attorney general had predicted that on May Day, 1920 there would be a major uprising of communist reds in the United States. When this did not happen, Palmer suffered a credibility crisis with the public and especially the press. Daugherty would in a similar vain blame many of his future problems on Reds or Communists. Using information supplied to him by Daugherty, Palmer had the postal department and secret service alerted on the pretense that Chancellor had threatened the life of president-elect Harding. President Wishart of the College of Wooster, stated that was beyond Chancellor's demeanor and character.

Secret Service operative Joe E. Murphy's temporary job was to insure the safety of the president elect. Murphy took it on his own to insure Harding's accommodations. On January 16, 1920, he wrote to the Director of the Secret Service M. H. Moran about a special letter forwarded to him from Warren Harding. The content of the letter was about Professor Chancellor of Wooster, Ohio.

This letter prompted the special investigation of Chancellor in Wooster. President elect Harding had postal inspector agents sent to investigate. These agents walked around Wooster asking questions about William Estabrook Chancellor. They wanted to know if anyone could give them any information about the book the former professor was writing about Harding. Their investigative report included a copy of the pre-publication flyer.

Secret Service agent John Washer remembered the bitter cold morning of January 30, 1921, and recorded in his daily log, "Severe Cold." On this day secret service agent James Sloan visited the Cleveland secret service office. Sloan, Warren G. Harding's special body guard, went to Cleveland to oversee the Chancellor matter.

Secret Service operative, John Washer, wrote in his daily report. "Mr. Sloan was familiar with the fact that Chancellor was about to publish a book dealing with the ancestry of Mr. Harding. He advised me that he would return in the morning to take the view toward suppressing the publication and circulation of the book in question. Sloan said that they incensed Mr. Harding about the Chancellor matter. It seems that they had detailed a Post Office inspector for some weeks to the Chancellor-Affair at Wooster. Sloan told me he had previously talked to US Attorney Edward S. Wertz, who referred him to me."

The investigation was not discreet and word got around Wooster that they were watching the former professor. The Wooster *Daily Record* in its February 8, 1920-edition headlined on the front page, "WILL NOT DISCUSS CONTENTS OF BOOK, A SERVICE MAN WAS HERE." This *Record* reporter wrote, "They created last week considerable discussion about the visit of a secret service representative who asked questions about William E. Chancellor. This agent wanted to know about another edition of *'Lives of Our Presidents'* that he will publish in the future."

The article stated that those interviewed by the secret service agent, said he wanted to know if the material of Chancellor's book was to be about the recent political campaign. This agent seemed concerned that Chancellor would write about the Negro background of Harding or the publicity used during the last election. Other people thought the agent was in the city about the defense of a suit Dr. Chancellor started against the *Journal*, a Dayton newspaper. Word of the secret service's alleged investigation spread around the college city.

We must address this article about the alleged investigation of Chancellor by the secret service as erroneously reported by the Wooster Daily Record. Secret service did not send any agents to Wooster at this time. It was the postal department that conducted the investigation as revealed by agent John Washer.

A Wooster *Daily Record* reporter went to Chancellor who told him that he had a new book ready to publish. "I will issue just eight-hundred copies. We will sell these to those who subscribe for it in advance." He explained to the reporter, "Under the circumstances, I will not discuss the proposed contents of the book and will not do so until we publish the book." The reporter also found out the secret service agent while in town did not visit or interrogate the former professor.

Chancellor addressed a letter to the Attorney General of the United States, dated February 9, 1921. He enclosed two clippings from the *Daily Record*. One clipping was about his suit against the Dayton *Journal* and his discovery of an important witness. That article said the witness admitted sending the circulars during the election and he lives in Morrow County. The witness said, "The intent was to send the circulars where they thought it would not harm anyone." The second clipping was the *Record*'s most recent article about the secret service agent being in Wooster.

> In his letter the professor refers to the articles in the *Record*. He states, "I am unaware that the defense of a libel suit offers any occasion for this splendid service to investigate me." He continues, "I am glad anytime to see any officer of the U.S. Government. If you will examine the war records, you will find that my sister, Florence M. Chancellor, was one of the last discharged from censoring foreign mails during the war period. I come of the oldest colonial Massachusetts and Virginia white stocks. Also, I am anxious to obey the laws in every least particular." Chancellor closed the letter by saying, "I have no objection to being shadowed by the Secret Service if you advise me of this." Below the signature line Chancellor wrote, "I never retracted, for I had nothing to retract."

Three days later assistant Attorney General R. P. Sterart answered Chancellor's letter. Sterart replied, "We advise you that the records of this Department do not show that we have assigned any member of the Bureau of

Investigation to the work referred to. It must by an error on your part, unless it is some operative from another branch of the Government."

Attorney Sterart was correct in making this observation. The secret service came under the authority of the U. S. Treasury department not the Attorney General's office. However, the attorney general and the President often used the Secret Service at their desecration. Here a president-elect was using the Postal Department and the Secret Service to satisfy his own needs.

As the postal agents investigated Chancellor in Wooster, Ohio, Elizabeth Ann Britton, Harding's illegitimate daughter, became the legal ward of her aunt and uncle. Nan wrote that Harding paid for this adoption. The president made this move in hopes the knowledge this affair would remain secret. Harry Daugherty later claimed he knew nothing about Nan Britton or her child.

Edward S. Wertz was very well known in the city of Wooster, Ohio. Being a good Democrat, Woodrow Wilson had appointed him to be the Cleveland U. S. District Attorney position. He had attended the College of Wooster for two years then continued his education at Ohio State University in Columbus, Ohio. At OSU he received his doctorate degree in Law by the year 1900. Not only was he a neighbor of Chancellor but he attended the same church and belonged to the same Masonic Lodge as well.

Edward more affectionately known as Edwin had prosecuted the socialist presidential candidate, Eugene V. Debs for obstructing recruitments of soldiers during the World War. With pride he said that he put Debs away for thirty years. Debs claimed in court that the constitution guaranteed his freedom of speech. The Wooster attorney convinced the jury, that the constitution did not warrant freedom of speech against the U.S. Government and the jury convicted the Socialist leader. Wertz would not be of any help to his neighbor, fellow church member, fellow Democrat and Mason, William Estabrook Chancellor.

They transferred Michael Bolan Jr. , a special operative, to Cleveland from a New York office to become the temporary operative of that office when John Washer had quit his job. At a February 11, 1921, meeting, a Michael Bolan Jr greeted agent James Sloan and US District Attorney Ed Wertz. Bolan Jr. wrote, "Attorney E. Wertz went over the prospectus of the book proposed by Dr. Chancellor. This book deals with the genealogy of Mr. Harding and claims to prove he was descended from ancestors of mixed blood."

The only prospectus available on Chancellor's book at this time was the four-page flyer the Sentinel Publishing Company had mailed. No such reference like this was in this flyer.

Ed Wertz stated, "The book may incite a deranged person to do damage to the President, but it is not a violation of public act 319. Based on this law, we have no legal grounds to prosecute Chancellor." Secret Service agent Sloan did not like what he heard from the District Attorney and wanted the postal department involved.

Bolan Jr. reported to his superiors, "Sloan suggested that Wertz had to call postal inspector Zimmerman into the case. We all concluded that would be the best and safest manner to employ in this matter." Zimmerman's office was in the same building and they asked him to attend the Secret Service meeting.

Zimmerman told the men when he arrived that they allowed the postal department to confiscate material that may incite, or is inflammatory in character or intends to incite. Zimmerman said, "The code is Section 480 of the postal regulations and 211 of the criminal codes. This law defines the deposit, publication or circulation of any printed form having used the United States Mail, that may cause a person or organization to do physical damage, murder, arson or assassination."

Ed Wertz read the law and told those present, "I think that section of the law is broad enough in its meaning to handle the Chancellor matter. I think Mr. Zimmerman should take up the matter immediately with a view of finding the publishers, the book and secure all the information he can on Dr. Chancellor."

James Sloan, Harding's body guard said, "I must advise you to go to the limit in the suppression of this man. They have aroused Mr. Harding's temper and he will give full cooperation to see Dr. Chancellor prosecuted. If Attorney Wertz thinks, he has a case strong enough to present to a court this will be acceptable to the Harding organization."

Agent Bolan Jr. finished his report to the secret service director. He wrote, "they have throughly aroused Mr. Harding. Attorney Mr. Wertz assured us that he would give us full cooperation of whatever evidence he could secure against Chancellor. I told those present, that I would keep in touch and assist in any manner."

Attorney Ed Wertz

The meeting lasted most of the day and Bolan Jr. left his office about 6:00 in the evening. Zimmerman said he would take up the matter with the view toward finding the publisher or the book and securing all the evidence he could find against Chancellor.

Zimmerman visited Michael Bolan Jr. on the fifteenth of February. The postal inspector told him he wanted to bring him up to date on the Chancellor matter. In Wooster he had instructed the postmaster, Frank C. Gerlach, to list letters sent to William Chancellor. They also instructed the Wooster postmaster to keep a list of names to whom Chancellor was sending mail.

Frank Gerlach, the postmaster of Wooster, lived just two blocks from Chancellor on the same street. He was a fellow Mason, a staunch Democrat and appointed by President Woodrow Wilson as the postmaster of Wooster. Gerlach never informed the former professor he was under investigation.

Zimmerman also told Bolan, Jr. that he met with Harry Daugherty and

The Indictment

agent James Sloan in Columbus. "Daugherty is to leave this evening by train to Florida and we talked this matter of putting a stop to this man Chancellor. Before leaving he asked me to look into the sanity of Chancellor."

Chancellor in his research discovered Warren Harding went to the Kellogg Sanitarium in Michigan for nerve treatment. Dr. Sawyer treated Harding and his wife for the same reason in a sanitarium just outside Marion. This treatment by Sawyer was kept from the public's knowledge. Now Daugherty will accuse Chancellor of being a patient of such a mental institution. In 1922, they would treat Daugherty for a nervous breakdown.

Agent Bolan Jr. wrote to his superior about what Daugherty had told Zimmerman. Daugherty had stated, "that he had heard a rumor that they had confined this man (Chancellor) in a sanitarium some years ago, but he could not secure any information about it. He did not say when this confinement took place, the time, reason or where they had confined Chancellor. I am requesting you to find out if any evidence exists that Dr. Chancellor was in an asylum for the insane." Daugherty suggested to Zimmerman, they should put this crazy man away.

Chief Inspector, Moran never found any supportive evidence to Daugherty's allegation that Chancellor was ever in an asylum for the insane. The postal inspector, Zimmerman would later use this threat to intimidate the former professor.

Mr. Daugherty wanted the secret service to look for and collect any mail that was threatening to Warren Harding should they have to go to court. The attorney general-elect also wanted the postal inspector to see what could be done to have Chancellor drop his law suit against the *Dayton Journal*.

Harry Daugherty went to Florida about the middle of February, to join Warren Harding and his partying colleagues. While in Columbus, he checked his finances. His taxable property amounted to only eight thousand dollars and he owed about twenty-seven thousand dollars. Daugherty after many years as an attorney and a Republican boss had a negative net worth of nineteen thousand dollars. His effort to get Warren Harding elected was an expensive ordeal. When congress in 1924 investigated him, his cash position astonished the investigators. More than two hundred dollars in cash and bonds were found in a safe-deposit box belonging to the Attorney General.

When Daugherty arrived in Florida Harding announced to the press that Harry M Daugherty would join his cabinet as Attorney General of the United States. This news did not take many by surprise. Attorney General-elect, Daugherty, talked to Harding about his two immediate problems. The first was the settlement of the blackmail threat and the other was about William Estabrook Chancellor. He told Harding there was a report that Chancellor was just about ready to publish his biography in Wooster. Warren Harding and Daugherty discussed their options of handling the stubborn and persistent former professor. The pressure to select members to Harding's cabinet temporarily preempted any move against Chancellor.

Warren Harding in his last speech of the campaign had said, "I am

The Indictment

unpledged! I am unowned! I am unbossed!" He went on to say, "I am the most unbound, unpledged, untrammeled candidate ever offered by the Republicans for president!"

Senator Penrose thought differently. He insisted it was his right to select at least three men to the cabinet because that was part of the deal made at the Chicago convention. Daugherty went to talk with the Pennsylvania boss. Senators Knox, Lodge and Penrose opposed the idea of having Herbert Hoover in the cabinet. Their reason was that Hoover vacillated from the Democrat party to the Republican party. The powerful senate cabal stood poised against Hoover.

Daugherty told Penrose and Senator Knox, "We should allow the president-elect to assemble his own cabinet and you should be the last men in the United States to abort this prerogative." Senator Philander Knox agreed with Daugherty but Penrose kept pushing. The senator became visibly irritated and cussed when Harry Daugherty told him Hoover was going to be in the cabinet. Penrose wanted Andrew Mellon in the cabinet, because he had recently underwritten the Republican Party's huge debt accumulated during the election campaign. It was Penrose's duty to get "Uncle Andy" in the cabinet. Harry Daugherty used cuss words liberally in his everyday conversation, but as he said, when Boise Penrose got mad at him, "I listened to my master."

Senators Knox, Penrose, Lodge and Daugherty finally came to a meeting of the minds. Andrew Mellon would be secretary of Treasury and Davis from Pennsylvania would be Secretary of Labor. With this compromise the leaders of the senate cabal agreed to stop all opposition to the nomination of Herbert Hoover to a special cabinet post. Hoover became Secretary of Commerce with an annual pay equaling the President's seventy-five thousand dollars per year. Harding immediately announced "his" additions to the "best minds' only cabinet" to the public that he "selected" and not the bosses.

Chancellor wrote, Harding's Cabinet, has already shown to be a clutter of unrelated and discordant minds that will not work together in any system of leadership. Habitually all things to all men, his cabinet mirrors himself. Not one man in the Cabinet has shown the leadership necessary to help our domestic situation. As Daugherty deals with Penrose and Smoot, the Cabinet will have no influence whatever upon the processes of the Senate or of the House. The President carries no weight, and never did carry weight.

Consider the case of Secretary Andrew Mellon of the Treasury. He was forced upon the President by Senator Boise Penrose, of Pennsylvania. Mr. Mellon was the richest man whoever drew a salary from the United States Government. He was richer than any other Senator has ever been, even Senator Clark of Montana, the copper magnate. No one knows what Mellon was worth. Like every active plutocrat in business, Mr. Mellon was richer some years than others. Born rich, for his father made a great fortune, he increased this fortune. He may be worth two-hundred million dollars. [Andrew Mellon may have been close to being a billionaire in the early twenties.]

The Indictment

Mr. Mellon will preserve the present money system by which banks get twice as much paper as they hold in gold. If a bank has five million in gold, it may lend out ten million of paper money. Instead of making three-hundred thousand dollars in interest on five million dollars they can now double that amount with paper money. This was very attractive for the stockholders of big banks authorized to issue the wild currency known as Federal Reserve notes.

Andrew Mellon was a philanthropist, giving away vast sums of money every year. He has been, of course, a lifelong friend of J. Pierpont Morgan of New York and London. Andrew Mellon was shy, reticent, quiet, self effacing, diligent, gloomy, patient, wise, and far sighted beyond most men. He played a gentleman's game of poker. It was his only sport.

The selection of only the "great mind's cabinet" continued in Florida. Senator Fall dubbed Harding into making him the Secretary of the Interior. Senator Albert Fall sent a telegram to Warren Harding signing Harry Daugherty's name to it. Daugherty found out later that Fall paid the fee for the telegram. This telegram urged Harding to appoint Fall as the Secretary of the Interior before the fourth, with Daugherty's name as the sender. Harding made the announcement official after spending two days fishing with the New Mexico senator. Albert B. Fall got his appointment to the post promised to Jake Hamon at the June convention. Fall, ruthless at times, caused some to speculate he had something to do with the murder of Jake Hamon. They never proved this.

Chancellor wrote, next to Daugherty among the objectionable was Albert B. Fall, who was in oil. No one knows how rich he was. By some they style him a millionaire, which was doubtful.

A. B. Fall was committed to the policy of armed intervention in Mexico. Oil, and copper and silver are the prizes in Mexico. He has publically stated we must have a war with Mexico. He thinks that Mexico will never be safe until an American army teaches the Mexicans respect for American rights. If we have a war with Mexico, we may charge it to Secretary Fall. Temperamentally, he was unsound. He had no guiding and controlling doctrines of action and was a natural imperialist.

Like Harry M. Daugherty, Albert Fall was almost broke at the time of his nomination. The senator needed cash to pay back real estate taxes on his land holdings in New Mexico. His ranch needed repair work and his herd had diminished in size and value every year.

Chancellor wrote, Herbert C. Hoover, who might have been President, and was playing for the Presidency. Mr. Hoover had some false notions, such as the desirability of exporting capital from America to help the rest of the world. Mr. Hoover had shown in many fields superb executive abilities, a warm heart for all men, a tremendous talent for getting people together and, in short, a genius. Herbert Hoover should have been either Secretary of State, the Interior or Secretary of the Treasury.

Harding's selection for Secretary of State was Charles Evans Hughes. Hughes carries no weight because they dislike him and because he lost the Republican Presidential campaign of 1916 through blundering. This involved perma nent alienation from Senator Johnson and most Republican party bosses.

Most Senators are indifferent to Cabinet Secretaries. To the Senate, even Hoover was unimportant. A Cabinet Secretary lives in the sunshine or dies in the shadow of the President. For an elective office there was no recall and in that respect is better than any appointive office.

Robert R. Woods, a banker, a member of the Masons, a democrat and a member of the College of Wooster board of Trustees.

Chancellor's lawsuit against the *Dayton Journal* laid dormant in Montgomery County common-pleas court. Harding and Daugherty thought it was the time to get information about Chancellor's attorney Hugh Snepp. In Cincinnati, Ohio, Secret Service agent Bolan Sr. received a letter and call from Washington. His instructions were to get all the information he could on Hugh A. Snepp. Bolan Sr. wrote in his daily report, "Went to Dayton, Ohio, to investigate H.A. Snepp an attorney who sued the Dayton Journal for William E. Chancellor. I will investigate his business and personal standing."

Bill Chancellor in the quiet of his home promoted his new book the *Illustrated Life of President Warren G Harding*. The cost of publishing should have been no problem to the successful author. Some of his educational books, purchased by school boards numbered in the thousands. His royalties since 1904 exceeded his combined salaries as a teacher and professor.

To promote the book, Chancellor used a mailing list he compiled over the past year of those who wrote him about Harding and the election. Most of his mail requested a copy of his new book about Harding. This promotion had the impression of being a success as every day the former professor went to the Wooster post office to drop off mail and pick his up. Unknown to him, Wooster postmaster Gerlach listed Chancellor's mail coming and going. Then he turned over this list to the postal inspector Zimmerman, who gave a copy to the secret service agent Michael Bolan Jr. in Cleveland. Bolan Jr. then sent the list to W. H. Moran the head of that bureau in Washington, D.C. The chief inspector then made the list available to Daugherty who then passed this information onto President elect Harding.

Faithfully Zimmerman kept agent Bolan Jr. informed about the people mailing letters to Chancellor. Most of the mail requested a copy of his new book about Harding. Suddenly, the postal inspector was not present in Cleveland. On February 24, 1921, the secret service agent wrote in his daily report. "Tried to get hold of Zimmerman during the afternoon, but they advised me he was not available." Four days later he wrote, "Zimmerman was out of town. His stenographer advised me that nothing new developed in the Chancellor matter. She gave me a list of names who were corresponding with Chancellor at Wooster."

Zimmerman was in Columbus, Ohio, at the special invitation of Harry Daugherty, getting special instructions. The postal inspector told Bolan Jr. later, "Daugherty told me that Harding had thought it best to suppress William E. Chancellor. The president did not favor prosecution but thought it best to approach Chancellor and see what could be done about this matter. Harding wanted the professor to desist from any more attacks against him."

U.S. District attorney Ed Wertz had instructed Zimmerman and the secret service to work together on the Chancellor matter. However, the postal inspector decided to make a move on his own. Monday, February 28, 1921, the postal inspector took a train from Columbus and went directly to Wooster, without telling the secret service of his movements. In Wooster, Zimmerman talked to the postmaster Frank Gerlach about his instructions from Harding. Colonel Gerlach thought that involving Robert Woods would be best. Robert Woods was owner and teller at the Wayne County National Bank. Mr. Woods knew Chancellor very well and thought he would know how to handle this problem.

Woods knew almost everyone in Wooster and he counted Chancellor as a friend. They attended the same church in Wooster and were fellow Masons. Robert Woods was a trustee of the College of Wooster and was present when the board dismissed the professor. Robert Woods voted not to dismiss Chancellor. It was Woods who had a "hot" argument with Reverend Timothy Stone that night at the College of Wooster trustee meeting.

Zimmerman explained to Gerlach and Woods that he had orders to arrest Chancellor for using the mails to incite people. His book could encourage "nuts" to do physical harm to President Harding and this violated a postal department rule. He told the men that all Harding wanted was for Chancellor to stop his attacks on him and to drop his plans to publish his book. The inspector asked these men what they thought should be done concerning the suppression of Chancellor and the publication he intended to circulate. The three men discussed their options and Robert Woods thought it best to have Chancellor come to the post office and see what his attitude might be.

Former professor Chancellor arrived at the post office. Zimmerman explained to Chancellor what U.S. District Attorney Ed Wertz cited about the criminal code and postal law. The postal inspector told the former professor that he was violating this code. He told Chancellor he had the power to place him under arrest and continue with prosecution in court. Zimmerman advised Chancellor that Mr. Harding wanted him to desist his attacks against him. He told the professor the secret service and the postal department had Harding's orders to suppress his book. This postal inspector also told Chancellor that Daugherty wanted to place him in an asylum for the insane.

Chancellor had fainted when he received the telegram informing him his wife had died. When on the stand in Washington, D.C. he also passed out. At the College of Wooster inquisition the professor felt faint but had successfully fought it off. Chancellor fought the urge to pass out as he heard what the postal inspector was telling him. This urge to faint was strong, but he was successful in fighting the pressure that day.

Zimmerman noted that Chancellor acted very scared and "after talking to him a few moments he agreed to stop all work on his book. He also said he would refund the money secured from persons who subscribed and he would not molest Mr. Harding in any manner." Gerlach, Woods, Zimmerman and Chancellor went to his home and Chancellor handed over to Zimmerman a box that contained a typed manuscript. The two men went into the basement and opened his coal-fired furnace. Page after page they tossed into the furnace. The flames consumed the author's manuscript. The postal inspector kept some pages of the manuscript to use as future evidence against the author.

In the presence of Wood and Gerlach, Chancellor wrote a statement "in which he expressed contrition for the worry and trouble his actions had caused Mr. Harding. He promised to cause no more trouble." Gerlach and Zimmerman witnessed the signature of Chancellor on the document.

Zimmerman asked Chancellor where he had planned to print the book. Chancellor answered, "I do not know. An attorney in Columbus has encouraged me and that obligation of printing and paying for it was his." Chancellor did not give the inspector a name and address of the attorney in Columbus, Ohio. The postal inspector took a train to Cleveland that night. If it bothered him that he just violated the first amendment of the constitution by burning Chancellor's manuscript, he did not record it.

Tuesday, March 1, 1921, Zimmerman called at the secret service office in Cleveland. Agent Bolan Jr. learned for the first time from the postal inspector that Harry Daugherty had returned from Florida and had asked the postal inspector to meet him in Columbus, Ohio, at his law office. Zimmerman told the agent, "Mr. Harding wants Chancellor's book suppressed but will not prosecute him for criminal activity at this time, if he cooperates."

Zimmerman than told the secret service agent about his successful trip to Wooster and that the Chancellor matter could be considered closed. Bolan expressed his concern that Zimmerman went to Wooster, without having someone from the secret service with him. Almost in a tone of innocence the postal inspector said, "everything broke so fast in Wooster he just had to take advantage of it."

Zimmerman said he was going to Columbus to find the person who was supposed to be responsible for printing the book. This person was "part of this conspiracy," explained Zimmerman. Bolan Jr. told the postal inspector he would go to Columbus with him.

Agent Bolan wired Washington that they had burned Chancellor's book and that he had agreed not to harass Mr. Harding. The agent sent in a new list of people corresponding with the former professor. They passed on the news of the Chancellor's suppression to Daugherty and Warren G. Harding.

Assistant Chief Joe Murphy wrote the same day in his daily report, "Sloan says they settled the Wooster matter. I will wire tomorrow before leaving Jacksonville, Florida."

Wednesday, agent Michael Bolan Jr. went to the postal inspector's office early, but never got in touch with him till mid morning. Zimmerman in an excited tone, said he had received a telegram from his postmaster in Wooster saying that Chancellor had left town. Postmaster Gerlach had called Cleveland and told the postal inspector, "I have tried to find Chancellor without success. I checked the railroad station, his home and other places but I have been unable to find him."

Without revealing any sources, Bolan Jr. wrote to his father, Bolan Sr. in Cincinnati. "We believe that Hugh A. Snepp, Chancellor's attorney, was supposed to be responsible for the publication of the book. The postal inspector would like to arrange to meet you at Dayton to check out this lead." Agent Bolan Jr. also told his father about the burning of the manuscript in Wooster. He wrote, "I should have been at Wooster when Chancellor agreed to give up his attack against the President. I am very much disappointed that everything broke the way it did."

An urgent call came from Washington. Chief Inspector told Bolan Jr. that Harding wanted Chancellor found. The chief instructed the secret service agent to drop everything and go to Wooster. After closing the Cleveland office late in the day, agent Bolan Jr. boarded a train to Wooster. The local train took three hours to travel the ninety-miles distance. When he arrived, the secret service agent called postmaster Gerlach who confirmed the information that Chancellor could not be found. Bolan Jr. learned that Zimmerman went to Dayton because one of Chancellor's daughters said that was where she thought he had gone. Bolan Jr. was growing to dislike Zimmerman's off handed methods. Then Frank Gerlach told the operative that the statement that Chancellor had signed was not acceptable because it would not hold up in court.

In Cincinnati, agent Bolan Sr. also received an urgent message from director Moran requesting all the information, he had on H.A. Snepp. He reported his findings. "Special agent, M.F. Mitchell, went to Dayton to investigate the character and business of this subject. Mitchell talked to the postmaster, Forest May. He has known Snepp since boyhood. May said he had never heard anything derogatory to his character. Hugh Snepp was a graduate of Ohio State University, had been a principal of school once and was born in Miamisburg, Ohio. Some people said that at times he may be lazy. His law practice was very small and he was in charge of the law suit against the *Dayton Journal*. He once had an office on Lindsay Street but recently moved to 501 American Building on the corner of Third and Main Streets, Dayton, Ohio. Mitchell made other inquiries and found Snepp was a man of respected morals and a good church man. Snepp has three brothers in Dayton who are Arthur, Reverend Samuel and L.H. Snepp who was a druggist." The secret service agent's investigation did not say that Hugh Snepp had anything to do with the publishing of Chancellor's book.

Susan Chancellor came home for lunch on March 3, 1921, and postmaster Gerlach was there waiting for her. The platinum fair-haired Susan told Gerlach, "You can reach my father through his attorney Mr. Snepp in Dayton." She also told the Wooster postmaster that he had left town to seek employment and would not return until he was successful.

Agent Bolan wired his superior in Washington, D.C. "We must reach Mr. 'C' through his attorney 'S' in Dayton. Daughter states he has gone seeking employment and will be gone until successful. Await your instructions."

Susan did not tell the agent that a friend had come to the house and advised the former professor it would be best if he got out of the country. This friend advised Chancellor that it was not beneath Harding or Daugherty to have him put away. This meant they would kill or place him in an asylum for the insane. If they incarcerated him, Chancellor may never experience freedom again. The family arranged a secret method to transmit messages with each other without using the mails before the professor left.

After sending his telegram to Moran, agent Bolan Jr. telephoned the Chancellor home. A woman answered who told Bolan Jr. to call Mr. Chancellor's attorney in Dayton. The woman told the agent she did not know where Chancellor was. Bolan went back to the post office and instructed Gerlach to "cover" Chancellor's incoming and outgoing mail. This meant Gerlach had to open each letter and make notes of its content.

Bolan Jr. continued his search for information about where Chancellor may have gone. He visited the office of President Wishart at the College of Wooster. Dr. Wishart told the agent he thought that Chancellor had gone to Columbus, Ohio.

March 4, 1921, the day of Harding's inauguration, agent Bolan Jr. went to the Wooster telegram office. In his report he wrote, "Mr. T. O. Wertz received a wire from a man signing himself as 'Sneff' and they addressed it to Miss Susan Chancellor. 'Sneff,' was advising her that he would arrive in Wooster that day."

Agent Bolan Jr. interpretation of this telegram was that Hugh Snepp was planning to see Susan that day. The secret service agent checked the schedule of trains that were to arrive in Wooster. One was due at noon and the other at 3:20 that afternoon. At the post office he wrote a special delivery letter addressed to William E. Chancellor then stationed himself near the Chancellor home. He watched as a delivery boy attempted without success to deliver the letter.

That same day, as the secret service agent continued his surveillance of the Chancellor home, President Woodrow Wilson prepared to turn over his office to Warren G. Harding. The crippled Woodrow Wilson depended upon others to help him move about. The simple task of getting in and out chairs required help. Walking was out of the question. His eight years of service as President cost the professor from Princeton University dearly. Harding with his permanent "Bermuda" tan, high in spirits, contrasted sharply with the pale Wilson as they rode in an open car to the swearing in ceremonies. Anxious to take on his new duties, Warren ran up the steps to the podium leaving the crippled Wilson behind. Observers thought he should have waited and gone with Woodrow to the inauguration stands. Democrats would never forgive him for this affront.

The world focused on the news of the current leader of the United States taking office. This man from Blooming Grove, from a family of ten, raised his right hand and placed it on the Bible used by George Washington. Chief Justice Edward White administered the oath. Warren Gamaliel Bancroft Harding swore to uphold the constitution of the United States.

Later, Nan Britton would read and reread the oath as her lover and the father of her child became the twenty-ninth president of the United States. Not invited to the ceremonies, Dr. George Tyrone Harding, Harding's father languished in Marion, Ohio. Harding did not invite any of his brothers or sisters to his inauguration although his sister Carrie Votaw did attend. Carrie Phillips, banished to Japan, sought newspapers to read about her lover's political triumph. The prostitute who attempted to blackmail Harding knew what kind of man was taking office. Harry M. Daugherty, Attorney General of the United States, looked with pride as Harding said, "So help me, God!"

By this time William Estabrook Chancellor was in St. Louis, Quebec, Canada, fleeing prosecution for speaking his mind. In Wooster, Ohio, agent Bolan Jr. watched for the arrival of attorney Snepp in Wooster, but he never saw him. In desperation he went to the Wayne County National Bank to seek the help of Robert Woods. Woods told the agent he did not even know the "old fella" had left town. The banker called the Chancellor home and told young Susan he needed to get in touch with her father on a very important matter. Robert Woods suggested to Susan there was no danger in telling him the whereabouts of Chancellor.

In tears Susan told the family friend her father had left home Tuesday morning and said he was going to Cleveland to seek work. "I believe he might have gone to Ardmore, Oklahoma, to attend the Hamon hearing. He talked about going there for some time, and I believe he was going to stay at the Statler Hotel in Cleveland. My dad told me he had gotten into trouble over the attempted publication of his book. He ran away, fearing repercussions from the government." She told Robert Woods that Mr. Snepp came today and he was looking for her father as well.

Woods listened to Susan until her sobbing and crying made it difficult to understand her. He hung up the phone and told agent Bolan Jr. everything that Susan had told him on the phone. It disturbed Bolan Jr. to learn that Snepp had come and gone driving a motor car rather than taking a train. The secret service agent telegraphed Washington telling what he knew about Chancellor.

The Indictment

At the telegraph office waited a message from the secret service agent's father who worked out of the Cincinnati office. The message from Bolan Sr. was an update about Hugh Snepp of Dayton, Ohio.

Warren Harding loved automobiles and relished the thought he became the first President to ride in a car to the swearing in ceremonies. The use of a loudspeaker and microphone heralded another milestone at this inauguration. Unfamiliar with a microphone and loudspeaker he at times during his inauguration speech tried to speak over it. Another first, was the broadcast of his speech over a radio. Those who had receivers and were within range of Pittsburgh marveled at this innovation.

Harding in his fine speaking voice in the opening of his speech said, "We have seen a world passion spend its fury, but we contemplate our Republic unshaken, and hold our civilization secure. Liberty, liberty within the law, and civilization are inseparable."

Democrats who had taken guidance from Woodrow Wilson focused their campaign upon the United States entering a world order through the League of Nations. They listened as Harding alluded to normalcy and "America first" in his speech. Harding said, "We recognize the order in the world, with closer contacts which progress has wrought. Yet America, our America . . . can be a party to no permanent military alliance." The men who wanted the United States to be part of the League of Nations knew it was a dead issue.

Harding spoke about the maimed and wounded soldier who fought in the war. "A generous country will never forget the services you rendered." Within less than a year he would veto a bonus to them.

"Our supreme task is reconstruction, readjustment and restoration . . ." This meant low taxes for those with high incomes. Harding stated, "Prices must reflect the receding fever of war activities. Perhaps we will never know the old levels of wages again." This alerted the leaders of labor unions the stand Harding and his administration would be taking on labor. The writer of Harding's speech then wrote the following, "Our most dangerous tendency is expecting too much of the government, and at the same time, do for it too little." Years later, John F. Kennedy would paraphrase the same sentiments in his inauguration speech. Harding ended his speech with a quotation from the bible. "What doth the Lord require of thee but to do justly and to love mercy and to walk humbly with thy God?" Obviously meaning to say *pledges* he ends the speech with a typical Harding error, "This I *plights* to God and country."

Chancellor wrote, the order to seize and destroy my manuscript was a violation of the Constitution. Let the Republicans fill up the cup of their iniquity, but they will drink it themselves. They have built a gallows upon which they will hang them themselves until they are dead. I wrote before leaving to escape the lawlessness of certain persons nominally in the pay of the Government. The tools of the plutocracy were trying to defeat my law suit.

The most humiliating and fearful fact confronting Harding, was the attempt to suppress the publication of the facts. By intimidating me with use of an alleged warrant that I was assured they would quash it if I would destroy my manuscript on the Harding biography.

I have many reliable reasons for believing that the Republican leaders know that my statements concerning the ancestry of the President are true. The activity at suppression was due to the fear that they will rebuke them at last for its imposition upon the American people.

All the Republicans lied about the situation and me. They bribed many and terrorized the women by telling them that the League meant war. Then they predicted that our factories would close down because the Republican capitalists would not use their funds if Cox should be elected. They appealed to every mother and wife whose men they had drafted and farmers who wanted a better price for their wheat and wool. Republicans organized the Negroes by saying that if the Democrats had their way, they would disfranchise them.

Republicans told the big capitalists that they would reduce the income tax and told the railroaders that they would raise their wages. They tore out of the Democratic party every man and women whom fear, self interest, greed, patriotism, pride of country, and every class interest could reach. Then they told ministers that all the leading Democrats were on the straight road to hell.

We have left a period when Woodrow Wilson held high ideals of a world of peace, righteousness, humanity and world fellowship. Before us are periods that remind me of Jerusalem and the Dead Sea. No living creature can cross that Sea. Its waters are pestilent. Its heat is terrific, and its odors cut the lungs. I for one rejoice that I belong to the Democrats, whom they could not bribe, terrorize, seduce, or mislead. Nevertheless, as I stand with you upon the high hills of Mount Zion, I watch with interest, the flight across the Dead Sea of one Black Crow.

Chapter Nine
Run Man Run!

Tearful Susan Chancellor told Robert Woods that her father had run away from home because he feared prosecution by the government. Susan told the banker she thought her father went to Cleveland. Her father told her he may go onto Ardmore, Oklahoma to witness the court trial of Clara Smith whom they accused of murdering Jake Hamon.

The understaffed Secret Service tried to find Chancellor. Secret service agent Bolan Jr. received a wire from Director Moran that Chancellor was not in Dayton, Ohio, as suspected. Bolan Jr. checked some hotel registers in

Most biographers said Harding knew nothing about Chancellor's book. This was not true.

the city of Cleveland to see if Chancellor had been there. He reported that Chancellor did not register at any of the better hotels. He called the Cleveland Hotel Association and asked them to tell him immediately if Chancellor showed up in one of their members' hotel. Every day the postal department and the secret service checked the mail sent to Susan Chancellor.

Most researchers had a difficult time finding out where the ex-professor went after leaving so abruptly for Wooster, Ohio. Walter Boroson wrote an article in 1955 for the now defunct magazine called the *Fact*. Boroson reported that a letter he received from Ralph W. Bentley of Medomak, Maine conclusively gave the whereabouts of Chancellor. Bentley wrote, "The Chancellor Story, is a weird one. My father was a college chum of Bill's. Bill Chancellor lived with us here in Maine when things got too hot for him in Ohio because of his attempted publication and distribution of the book. When Daugherty started opening Chancellor's mail, Dad brought him here to hide and protect him. Both feared with good reason that Chancellor was to be committed as insane to discount any evidence he might submit to the public."

The former professor had left Wooster as fast as he could. The fear of being admitted into an asylum for the insane prompted his fast exit from the town of Wooster. His family thought he also had a fear of his life being taken.

Many thought he went to Maine and stayed with a friend, but Chancellor fled to St. Louis, Quebec, Canada. Here he found a French-speaking peasant family who offered him room and board at a reasonable rate. Chancellor later wrote he stayed with this family for over a year. Speaking and understanding the French language was not a barrier to the author who could speak and write the language fluently.

In Quebec he carefully mailed any letters he sent to the states from different post offices because he suspected the Secret Service was monitoring his mail. Sometimes he drove to Montreal and other places to post his correspondence. The former professor felt confident using the telephone and found out from his daughter Susan, she was receiving mail that looked like they had tampered with the envelopes. William advised his daughter to move out of Wooster to Columbus.

Just eighteen years old, Susan tried to keep her composure when confronted with questions about the whereabouts of her father. Susan did not know who to trust. March 9, 1921, she went to the Wayne County Bank and spoke with Robert Woods, a person whom she trusted. Susan told Woods that her father had gone to Canada but she did not know where. She also told the banker that she and David were leaving Wooster and moving to Columbus, Ohio.

Her next stop was the Wooster post office where she told Frank Gerlach all future mail to her and father should be forwarded to General Delivery, Columbus, Ohio. Woods called Gerlach and told him that Chancellor was some place in Canada. Gerlach then notified the agent Bolan Jr. in Cleveland, who in turn wired Chief Director Moran in Washington. President elect Harding and Attorney General Daugherty knew the suspected whereabouts of Chancellor before the day was over. In a few days these same people knew that Susan had moved to live with her sister Catherine at 209 West 11 Street in Columbus, Ohio.

The Chancellor matter bothered Harding and Daugherty. They did not want this loose cannon out of their control because of his ability to ferret out facts. President Harding was obsessed with crushing the ex-professor. Attorney general elect, Daugherty had invited Postal Inspector Zimmerman to Washington. This invitation was more of an order then a personal request. Daugherty was very pleased to speak to the man who burned that "pack of lies" that the former professor had written. He instructed the postal inspector it was his duty to find Chancellor.

Agent Bolan Jr. wrote to Washington, "C. M. Zimmerman called at the office and advised me that he returned from Washington yesterday. He said Attorney General Harry Daugherty told him he must interview Chancellor, with the view of having him stop his suit against the Dayton Ohio newspaper for libel. I told the postal inspector that Chancellor was somewhere in Canada and we had the family mail covered in Columbus."

As Chancellor became a fugitive in Canada, the Hardings took over the White House in Washington. Mrs. Florence Harding immediately opened the

White House and surrounding grounds to the public. This was a dramatic change from the Woodrow Wilson era when that president, cherishing his privacy, kept the White House unavailable to the public. Mrs. Harding would scold the housekeepers if they attempted to draw the curtains at night. She said, "Let the people look in if they want to, it's their White House." This policy of openness brought an end to any private life Warren Harding enjoyed. It was not long before he called the White House his personal prison.

It would not take long for Daugherty to set his Ohio Gang into high gear. Agents found ways to extract money for government favors, according to special agent Gaston Means. He said in his self published book, *The Strange Death of President Harding*, that at times his wife had $60,000 in cash strapped to her body. They created a special cache in the rear of his Washington home. Agent Means claimed they once had more than $500,000 cash in this cache. Gaston said, Jesse Smith, the special White House entree and friend of Daugherty, counted the money and distributed it around. To whom this illicit money went, Means never fully revealed. The investigator admitted he kept some of this illicit money. Gaston Means lived the good life. He maintained an expensive house, two butlers, a chauffeured Cadillac on his $49-a-week salary from the Bureau of Investigation. This bureau was the predecessor to the FBI.

President Harding soon began his routine of playing golf, poker twice a week, following baseball and boxing, and sneaking off to burlesque shows. Also, he found ways to get the mother of his illegitimate child in the White House to make love with her in a five-by-five closet.

With the intent of prosecuting Chancellor Daugherty had one of his staff write to Edward Wertz the U.S. District Attorney in Cleveland. The letter noted that Wertz had forwarded a letter to the Attorney General's office in February, about his investigation of William Estabrook Chancellor. They informed Wertz this letter was lost and they wanted the District Attorney to forward a copy to Washington at his earliest convenience. It is unknown if Ed Wertz ever sent a copy of that letter.

During his investigation of Chancellor district attorney Ed Wertz wanted the Secret Service to collect threatening letters to Harding. Wertz needed these threats if he had to prosecute Chancellor under the postal criminal code. They sent all threatening mail to Washington and then they sent copies to district agents to investigate. Agent Bolan Jr. wrote to Washington on March 13, 1921, "Neglected to acknowledge the receipt of three post cards sent by Chief Murphy. They addressed the post cards to President Harding. A Mr. Rause who called Harding a nut signed the first. A second came from Mr. F. Sandi of Cleveland. He wrote that Harding is a big cheese, a nut and a stiff. The third mailer notified Harding that he had saved the world from destruction and the next president would be George Washington." The agent filed these so-called threatening letters and would interview the senders later. Along with the post cards he filed copies of mail sent to Chancellor and his family in Columbus, Ohio.

Although they were enforcing prohibition, liquor flowed freely in the

The Indictment

White House and in the Washington home of Daugherty. Newspaper reporters were quick to pick up on this disregard of the law and Harding thought this criticism was a serious menace to popular government.

Within days of taking office Harding lifted the protection of postmasters from Civil Service regulations. It was his desire to have revenge and remove any postmaster who had sent out flyers about his ancestry, during the recent campaign. Most of the Republicans frowned on the use of this presidential power for personal revenge.

Harding had selected Will Hays as the General Postmaster for the United States Postal Department, the former chair of the Republican National Party. The new postmaster-general let the president know it was not a good move to dismiss postmasters for revenge. They called a meeting.

Washington correspondent, Charles E. Morris, former private secretary of Governor James M. Cox, in a message to the *Dayton News* wrote March 9, 1921. "Since conferences here between Governor Myron T Herrick, Howard Mannington, President Harding, former President William Howard Taft, Walter F. Brown, and others, a noted abandonment of a policy has occurred. They agreed not to make vicarious sacrifices of Democratic office holders. They give some postmasters and internal revenue collectors the opportunity for immediate resignation. This instead of the more embarrassing experience of being summarily fired for having engaged in scurrilous propaganda during the campaign."

Soon other newspaper articles appeared and publically President Harding declared an amenity. He said the election was over and he forgave all. Postmaster General Hays took this literally and selected postmasters based upon ability instead of politics. The post office service almost immediately improved efficiency under Mr. Hays guidance. The Republican party grumbled about the postmaster-general's underhand methods of not exclusively putting Republicans into these positions. This leave-alone-forgive and forget attitude declared by the President included most everyone, except former professor William Estabrook Chancellor.

They temporarily assigned Secret Service agent Bolan Jr. to be the head of the Cleveland office until Robert J. Hynes replaced him. The last entry Bolan Jr. made in his daily report log was on April 16, 1921. Bolan Jr. wrote, "I met post office inspector Zimmerman in the building and he told me he just came back from Columbus, Ohio. He told me that a Mr. Jones was making statements that Chancellor had put one over on the inspector. Jones said he was responsible for the publication of the professor's book about President Harding. This man said Chancellor only surrendered to Zimmerman what he wanted to and kept the original manuscript. Jones promised he will still publish that book." Agent Bolan Jr. reported this to Washington along with the report that Chancellor's latest letters bore postmarks from Montreal, Canada. Daugherty belligerently demanded that the Secret Service find Chancellor in Canada. Walter Jones of Columbus was placed under surveillance by the postal department.

President Harding heard from Nan Britton who mailed her letters directly to secret service agent James Sloan. Sloan would then deliver the letters to Harding. She told the President that a Dr. Barbour had thought she needed to have an operation. Nan never mentioned what type of operation the doctor was recommending. Harding sent four hundred dollars in cash by agent James Sloan to cover her costs. Nan would then learn Barbour, for some reason, refused to operate and he guessed correctly who the father of the baby was. Nan kept the money intended for her operation.

Robert J. Hynes took over the Cleveland secret service office toward the middle of April 1921 and at the end of the month meet with postal inspector Zimmerman. The postal inspector informed Hynes about the Chancellors' affair. Hynes wrote, "During our conversation Mr. Zimmerman informed me that the mail of Susan Chancellor of Columbus was under cover. He was covering Hugh Snepp's mail in Dayton and Walter Jones of Columbus. The postal inspector told me they were tracing all the addresses of mail sent from Chancellor whose letters they postmark from Toronto and Montreal, Canada. His daughter Susan moved and now lives at 1560 Worthington Street, in Columbus, Ohio."

Hynes continued his report to Washington, "Attorney general Daugherty has berated the postal inspector for his inability to find the whereabouts of Dr. Chancellor. The attorney general has the intent of making immediate contact with Chancellor when he was found. Zimmerman asked for my full cooperation and I told him I would help him. I arranged to meet him in Columbus where he thinks his head postmaster was not doing a satisfactory job. I plan to be in Columbus about the second of May."

At the insistence of friends in the United States, Chancellor added "The Constitution and the President" to his manuscript. Chancellor wrote, the latest apologist for the President was one William Crawford who has known Harding for twenty years. This writer has an article in *The World's Work* for the month of May 1921. In its editorial the author deals forcefully with the inability of the president to formulate a policy in foreign affairs.

Mr. Crawford describes the president as, "A man under whom the power of the executive will voluntarily fall lower than it has for the last twenty-five years. Incidentally, many believe with Mr. Harding that the reduction of presidential authority was urgently necessary for the preservation of our democratic form of government."

If the presidency under Harding falls lower, any lower than it fell under McKinley and Taft, have God save the American people! Mr. Harding has no desire or intention to dominate the entire government. We will have for the first time in many years three separate, distinct, and independent branches of the government. Now this statement was nothing less than subversive of the Constitution itself.

In respect to Mrs. Harding, the writer of this apology said, "Evidence was everywhere that she has been a helpmate and advisor to the president in his upward climb." Then he adds, as an admirer of Wilson I was more than exasperated at what I consider the unjust calumny heaped upon him during the campaign for partisan political purposes. Consequently, I came to my task with no prejudice favorable to the new president.

Operative Hynes went to Columbus, Ohio, and found Susan's new home south of the Ohio State University's campus but did not harass her. The secret service was unhappy with the postmaster in Columbus. He was not being helpful in the covering of mail to and from the Chancellors. Hynes visited the postmaster at the Columbus post office. To Hynes he expressed cooperation by making his assistant responsible for covering Susan and Walter Jones' mail.

Zimmerman and Hynes then went to Dayton, Ohio, to plan on the investigation and cover of Chancellor's attorney Hugh Snepp. Before returning to Cleveland, Hynes stopped in Akron, Ohio and discussed with postmaster E. K. Alrich the need of a cover on a Mrs. Chancellor. "We arranged to cover all mail addressed to Mrs. D. Warwick Chancellor, care, YMCA, Akron, Ohio. She is a sister-in-law of Chancellor," wrote the agent. Hynes was wrong in this assumption as Mrs. D. Warwick Chancellor was the elderly mother of the former professor.

Chancellor wrote in Canada. The administration of President Warren Harding has now continued several months. We can see, and according to our lights what the policy was to be, scruples do not exist.

Already Harding has done several things that ultimate history will regret. He has broken the heart of the world by setting aside the League of Nations. In doing this, he has broken his promises to millions of persons who in good faith believed in him. It was a melancholy decision, based entirely on immediate expediency.

President Harding had broken the hearts of the Black people of America. The Republicans told them that Harding had Negro blood and he would remember the Negroes in his appointments. Warren Harding failed to place many Negroes in office. This man was ashamed of this element in his blood, ashamed of his own great-grandmother, Elizabeth Madison. He was ashamed of the Negroes that contributed their blood to his great-grandfather, George Tyrone Harding II.

More then fifteen million Negroes are in this country and it was a safe guess that, from now on, some of them will be Democrats. The Republicans have appointed only one important person to any office who has any discoverable Negro blood. This was no better than other Republicans have done before him.

Harding has shown by his messages and his letters to societies and to individuals that the Presidency has fallen into ignorant hands. He could not write English that was understandable. The American political system was rotten to permit the election of a person who was unable to speak authoritatively upon public questions.

Chancellor's point in case, during the war, farmers of America supplied a European market that was unable to feed its populace. With great optimism American farmers expanded their operations and production increased. As Europe recovered, its farmers began to deliver produce to their own market at a lower cost than the America farmer. Excess European production began to find its way to America. The farmers heavily in debt were unable to compete and they passed an emergency tariff in Congress to keep farm prices high in America.

A *New York Times* reporter interviewed Harding in June. This reporter asked the President about the recently passed tariff and what effect it would have on international trade. Harding answered, "The United States should adopt a protective tariff of such a character as will help the struggling industries of Europe get on their feet." The stunned reporter read his notes back to Harding to see if he understood what he just said. Harding told the reporter to print it.

Susan Chancellor sought a secretarial job at the Pure Oil company in Columbus. She asked Agent Robert Hynes to give her a letter of reference that she could use to secure her job. Robert Hynes wrote her and said he would be happy to give her such a letter in exchange for her father's address in Canada. Susan would not have to give Hynes the address.

William Chancellor had moved to Bloomfield, New Jersey in 1899 when he took the job as their school superintendent. Louise, his wife, talked Bill into buying property, which they did. When she died, Chancellor never cleared the title of this property. Before leaving Wooster they informed him that certain parties wanted to buy it. A bank in Bloomfield sent papers that needed his and his children's signatures. Chancellor informed Susan he needed her to sign some documents. He wrote that he would tell her by telegram where to meet him. A classified ad would give her the proper instructions where and when to meet him.

Through the postal department the secret service found out that Chancellor had to return to the United States to have these papers signed. Immediately agent Hynes boarded the train in Cleveland when he received a telegram from Zimmerman about Chancellor. The train left Cleveland about five o'clock in the afternoon and arrived three hours later in Columbus. He went to the Neil House Hotel where he met with Charles Zimmerman. The postal inspector showed Hynes a copy of a letter addressed to Susan from her father in Canada and opened by the postmaster. Chancellor had informed his daughter he would be sending her instructions by a telegram within a few days where to meet him. In the letter he explained the first National Bank of Bloomfield wanted her to sign some papers so he could transfer the property. The former professor stated he had already sent other papers required by the bank using certified mail.

Postal Inspector Zimmerman wired the postmaster in Bloomfield, New Jersey, and asked for the return address on Chancellor's certified letter. About fifteen minutes to midnight Hynes and Zimmerman knew Chancellor's address in Canada. It was 38 Rue Street, St. Louis, Quebec, Canada. Hynes informed Washington within the hour. Moran passed this information onto Daugherty and

The Indictment

President Harding.

The next day agent Hynes covered the telegram office in Columbus, waiting for the wire from Chancellor to his daughter. The day finished late for the agent who never saw the telegram arrive. Chancellor would meet with his daughter at some unknown place, sign the papers and forward them to New Jersey. Chancellor then returned to Canada.

This prompted agent Hynes to go to Washington and discuss the Chancellor case with Chief Director Moran. After this meeting the secret service lost all interest in the Chancellor matter. Hynes returned to Cleveland, Ohio, and the investigation of Chancellor by the secret service all but stopped. The chase was over for the secret service but Chancellor did not know this. He continued to take evasive moves in case someone was on his trail.

Chancellor wrote in Canada. President Harding has continued to pose as a common man, anxious to please the common people by a variety of poses. These appointments show he was a dealer in offices, a political debt payer. He was not thinking of America first and last, as he promised during the campaign. This president does not understand the morality of a man like President Hayes, who upon becoming President said, "Now I have no friends. I will appoint only the best men available." Instead of taking this, the only patriotic and honorable position, Warren Harding was paying his political debts at the expense of America, which was corruption at its worst. Open bribery, the direct sale of offices, was less dangerous than the course being pursued.

Daugherty has made him what he was, and he names this low-grade man Attorney General of the United States, to occupy a place of very great personal power. They should protect the Department of Justice from the presence of any such man who was not fit to be even a clerk or janitor in it. Harding's appointment of Harry Daugherty as his attorney general was a disgrace. This low grade man occupies a place of very great personal power.

Other appointments by Harding are just as bad. Mr. Harvey went to England as an ambassador, in payment for his services and for his betrayal of Wilson. Harvey was the man who printed in his *Harvey's Weekly* a sacrilegious cartoon against the League of Nations. He was a man of low-grade mind and obviously low-grade character. Harvey in his speech before the Pilgrim Club has offended the patriotic sense of his own party associates by insulting the British.

Herrick, who was mentally a better man, was morally lower than Harvey. This man was in politics to make money and to get power. Herrick goes to France as ambassador whether the French really like him or not.

They made D. R. Crissinger, who sold out to the Republicans the Controller of the Currency. A high-grade financial and economic expert should fill this position. He has recently relieved the National

Banks from serious responsibilities. They now can report general figures to fool the people.

George W. Aldridge, one of the lowest New York State politicians and some shameless corruptionists was now the collector of the Port of New York. At the convention he used Jake Hamon's money to buy forty-six votes from delegates to nominate Harding.

The former professor kept in contact with Walter Jones in Columbus. To prevent interception of mail he had to send mail to other people who forwarded it to Jones. Years later, Chancellor stated that he traveled and sojourned in Canada, in business affairs and hunting and fishing. He said he became acquainted with a foreign country on this side of the Atlantic.

In a paper titled, *We Journey to Fashion the Soul*, Chancellor wrote about his sojourn in Canada. I've heard the call of the mountain and worked down canyon walls to drink the crystal fountains. I have fished by rainbow falls. Through mist I have climbed to many a summit to its snow white peak. Down a sheer precipice I plummeted and have ridden the raging ocean by Aleut Isles. Icy seas swept over the decks in commotion and made my blood stream freeze. With friends I roamed unbroken prairies and held off wolves with fire. From Cougar Caves to where the ice-floes grind and roll to reefs of coral and lava, I traveled to fashion the soul.

The last entry in the year 1921 made by the secret service about Chancellor was that he was in Winnipeg, Canada and mentioned he was living at a cheap hotel. The agent sent this report to Washington in September of the year. From Winnipeg the former professor went to Edmonton, Alberta, Canada. In this city they hired him to sell bonds and he began to specialize in selling Provincial bonds. It did not take long for the author and former professor to find a way to sell Canadian provincial bonds on the New York and Chicago market exchanges. He later noted that he sold millions.

Walter Jones of Columbus, Ohio continued to encourage the former professor to finish his book on Warren Harding. As time permitted, Chancellor would read about political events taking place in the United States. As he hunted and fished and expanded his travels across Canada he lost touch with his friends and the political scene in the United States.

Chancellor did find out the Harding administration started with the cooperation of the Senate cabal and Congress but in less than a year this would end. Congress voted to pay Colombia twenty-five million dollars to pay for land and rights allegedly taken in the building of the panama canal. Shortly after that Standard Oil announced it had purchased a large island in the harbor of Barranquilla, Columbia. They expected these oil fields to yield 25,000 barrels of oil per day.

The *New York Tribune* printed, "Evidence accumulates that the Standard

Oil interests consider the Colombian oil fields among the best for future operation. Several months ago the Standard Oil Company got control of the International Petroleum Company."

With little effort Congress approved a sweeping change in spending by creating a budget system. It was the goal of new Secretary of Treasurer Andrew Mellon to create restrictions on Congressional spending based upon income taken through taxation. This plan worked for a short time and with excess income Mellon reduced the national debt. The national debt amounted to about twenty-five billion in 1921. Mellon reduced the debt by seventeen billion, after recommending the reduction of the high taxes created by Woodrow Wilson to pay for the war debt. The reduction of taxes encouraged capital investment that created more jobs and the economy began to prosper under Mellon's expert directions.

Mellon, a quiet, but persuasive man, immediately had Harding remove Harding's hometown friend Crissinger as Controller of the Currency Controller. Harding proved his lack of judgement even more by making his boyhood friend a governor of the Federal Reserve Board. He had no qualifications for this new position. Many believe some policies recommended by Crissinger set the stage for the great crash of 1929.

Harding selected Elmer Dover of Ohio as Assistant Secretary of Treasury. Mellon rebuffed the president by getting rid of him after Dover fired employees of the Treasury Department for political reasons.

"Charlie" Forbes, liked by Harding, became the Director of the Veteran's Bureau. They would catch Forbes selling government goods for personal gain and rigging construction bids for pay backs. Forbes would serve time in prison. The coordinator of the budget, Colonel Smithers had to approve any inventory sold by the Veterans Bureau. Forbes would add pages of items to the list after Smithers gave his approval. Forbes hired an attorney by the name of Charles N. Cramer to help him. Afraid of being convicted with Forbes Cramer wrote a letter to Harding then shot himself.

Daugherty selected W. J. Burns of Columbus, Ohio, to head the Bureau of Investigation. Under Burns the bureau became a weapon for use against enemies of Harding and Daugherty. Harding placed under investigation anyone whom he considered offensive. The Bureau worked up a flimsy case against Senator Wheeler and harassed him. Senator LaFollette had his office looted. Congressmen Johnson and Woodruff were subjected to espionage. Gaston Means, an agent of the Bureau, said the information sought by Harding was to blackmail them. Colonel Jim Darden threatened to interfere with Fall and they ordered the Bureau to snoop for compromising information about the legislator. They investigated Senator Walsh who would expose the Teapot Dome scandal. If an agent investigated a friend, they transferred or relieved him of duty. The Bureau of Investigation became a corrupt political tool under Harding and Daugherty.

Harding appointed Edwin N. Denby Secretary of Navy. Secretary of the

The Indictment

Interior W.B. Fall and others informed Denby that Rockefeller oil companies had encircled the Navy oil reserves. They were attempting to drain the oil fields' dry. Denby learned that top Navy officials would not allow private companies in the reserve. He learned the Navy refusal was because all the revenue from extracted oil would go to the U.S. Treasury and not to them.

Doheny a Democrat, a contributor to Harding's election observed that the Navy should benefit and not the Treasury. Doheny had donated twenty-five thousand dollars to pay for articles to lessen the alleged effect of the roorbacks during the election. Harding and the Republicans did not forget this. Through A.B. Fall, Doheny learned about oil magnate Doheny's suggestion.

Secretary of the Navy Denby, suggested to Harding that instead of giving the Navy money for the oil, they would issue certificates. The Navy then could convert the certificates to oil when the need arose. Harding sought the advice of Fall who he knew was an expert on oil. Fall recommended letting one private party drill for the oil in the reserve instead of many. Fall suggested the leaser should provide storage facilities in Hawaii. He felt it was a matter of time before the Empire of Japan would strike the Philippines and Hawaii. The threat of war with Japan loomed heavy over the Harding administration. Should Japan strike, the Navy would need the oil in the Pacific to keep naval forces afloat. They gave this information to Harding and he approved it.

The order from Harding, giving Fall authority to lease the western land was marked top secret. Later at a special investigation of Fall this order remained a top secret, never shown at the investigation. The investigation committee ruled Fall leased the land on his own for selfish gain. Fall would serve time in jail.

William Chancellor predicted in his writings that the Empire of Japan was ready for war. Only a natural catastrophe prevented the expected attack on the Phillippines and Hawaii islands. In 1923 an earthquake destroyed Japan's only munition factory and storage facility. The heavy seas generated by the earthquake, wiped out two thirds of their naval fleet. It would take Japan more than a decade to regain their losses. Oil from the western reserves would find its way to Japan to help them rebuild their military might.

Secretary of Interior Albert Fall tried to defend his case on patriotism. For this he received from the oil magnate Doheny, liberty bonds totaling $223,000, two loans amounting to $71,000 in cash. D. L. Doheny also "lent" Fall another $100,000 in cash, and he advanced extra cash for expenses of $5,000. Doheny and his oil company were on the road to make $100 million off the oil deal. Jake Hamon had said the position as the Secretary of the Interior would be worth more than four hundred thousand dollars plus revenue from the oil fields. Doheny paid that to get the lease of the oil rich government land.

Within the first six months after becoming president Harding selected William Taft to Chief Justice of the Supreme Court. Taft had aspirations of running for President again but he coveted a position on the Supreme Court. Harding and Daugherty fulfilled Taft's dream and eliminated him as a future candidate for president.

The Indictment

The congress, at Harding's suggestion, signed a treaty of peace directly with Germany and that country opened diplomatic offices in New York City for the first time in six years. The League of Nations took this as an insult from Harding and the United States. Within days of signing the peace treaty Warren Harding refused to make law a Soldiers Bonus bill. Month by month Hardings popularity ratings became lower and fulfilled Chancellor's prediction about Harding's ability as a president.

John L Lewis called a strike of coal miners. Effects of the coal strike were immediate. Harry Daugherty told Harding the Reds were behind the coal and railroad strike. The attorney general created a war map, showing train wrecks, where a riot had broken out, where they had kidnaped a worker or a murder was committed. Daugherty claimed, "they have maimed and killed and were covering up these crimes." Harding appealed to the Governors of the states where the coal strikes were occurring and did nothing to stop the strikes.

The threat of force against the coal miners had no effect after the Railroad Labor Board ordered a 13 percent wage cut for railroad workers. To complicate matters, this board ordered to cut the wages of all railroad shop men along with clerks and signalmen. Railroad shop men walked out and went on strike encouraging the coal miners to be in defiant of the President's orders. Now two major strikes threaten the country's welfare.

Harding faced with this major problem wanted to conciliate and Daugherty wanted to bring this alleged Communist inspired conspiracy under control. The mentor of Harding said he looked like a President but watched with disgust as he shrank under this decision. Daugherty told Harding, "either we have a government or we do not!"

Attorney General Daugherty thought the railroad and coal strikes were a conspiracy of the communists and treated it as such. When the army failed to bring the expected peace, Daugherty resorted to the courts. A Federal Judge filed an injunction against the Unions. This Federal Judge was an appointee of Daugherty. The threat of violating an injunction issued by the Federal government hung over the heads of the Union leaders and workers. They quickly realized that fighting the government in court would be futile and the strikes were broken. Daugherty did this with approval of Warren Harding.

Mitsui, a Japan manufacture of airplanes, had a contract with the U. S. Defense department during the last war and failed to deliver. A law suit by the Justice Department threatened them. A Japanese representative of Mitsui paid one hundred thousand dollars in cash to Jess Smith, Daugherty's personal aide. The Mitsui investigation came to a halt. Harry Mingle whom Mitsui had hired to handle their claim was found shot to death in New York City.

Charles Forbes saw a stack of money on Jess Smith's desk one day and asked whose it was. Jess told him it belonged to the General (Daugherty). Jess said he was going to deposit $175,000 of eastern money in his hometown bank in Washington Court House, Ohio. Jesse Smith was on the take and said, "the money keeps rolling in."

The Indictment

Swiss bankers filed a claim for seven million dollars for confiscated patents thought to belong to a German owned company during the War. These Swiss bankers claimed they owned the patents and wanted their money. The Swiss applied to the Department of Justice knowing it might take a long time. The process should have taken months, at the very least, but Daugherty approved it in two days. Jess Smith received cash of one hundred thousand dollars and forty thousand in bonds. They deposited this into Daugherty's account at the Midland Bank found in Washington Court House, Ohio. Daugherty's brother Mally owned Midland Bank. The government paid seven million dollars to the Swiss.

In the middle of the 1921 summer George Christian, Secretary to President Harding received a letter from a John O'Dwyer of Toledo, Ohio. This Republican for some reason received a flyer about Chancellor's book, "The Illustrated Life of Warren G. Harding." This was the exact flyer Chancellor or the Sentinel Publishing company had sent out in January. O'Dwyer wrote, "I was against this kind of stuff in the campaign, last year and I'm against it this year and forever. I don't approve of these methods."

The author of this letter made a suggestion. "If you think it worthwhile, and you know best, send out a Secret Service man to see where they are publishing it and who was financing it. You can probably bust it up."

George Christian made a polite reply to O'Dwyer that he would pass this information onto the "General" under the instructions of President Harding. Christian made no statement that Harding had already sent the Secret Service and the Postal Inspector to confiscate this manuscript. Nor was anything said that the former professor Chancellor was in Canada running from false persecution.

Late in the summer Nan Britton visited the White House and Harding had sex with her in the small closet just off the oval office. With the limited time allocated to her Nan showed Warren the photographs of their child and discussed her need to find a job. Harding on White House stationery wrote a letter of recommendation to George Aldridge. Aldridge headed the New York Port Authority, a position given to him by Harding. The president gave her a few hundred dollars before she left. Nan went to New York, but failed to get a job with Aldridge.

In December 1921, the Washington Conference for the Limitation of Armament convened with England, France, Japan and Italy. This was the culmination of a plan introduced by Senator Borah but he was left out of the meeting. Secretary of State Hughes and others represented the United States. Hughes stated, "the way to reduce was to reduce." All the nations at this meeting agreed to reduce the size of their fleets. They said Hughes sank more ships in thirty-five minutes than all the admirals of the world have sunk in the cycle of centuries. In reality it gave all the nations a chance to get rid of outdated ships. Also, the treaty canceled the Anglo-Japanese Alliance. They did not accept this plan until July of 1923.

President Woodrow Wilson had more than fourteen thousand people put in jail for political reasons. They arrested most for disagreeing with Wilson or those who had objected to the draft during the war. Eugene Debs the Socialist Party leader was still incarcerated in jail for political reasons. It was through the efforts of District Attorney Ed Wertz of Wooster, Ohio that they sentenced Debs for thirty years. Daugherty thought it would be a good political move to free him.

Daugherty interviewed Debs for more than half a day and recommended his release. To the surprise of Debs they allowed him to go to Washington without a guard or escort. At the White House, Warren Harding interviewed him and signed the order to make him a free man on Christmas eve. Ed Wertz would resign from his position as U.S. District Attorney.

Warren Harding loved to play poker and he was famous for all the side bets he would make during a game. At one game he lost an entire set of White House china, including the silverware. Charles Forbes and others attended these card games at the White House. Liquor flowed freely despite the ban on it. One evening Forbes and Harding strolled on the White House lawn after a long drawn out card game. Harding talked about his job as President and how unhappy he was. To Forbes amazement Harding broke down and cried.

Daugherty never liked Charlie Forbes and avoided him as much as possible. When he heard that Forbes was selling hospital supplies for personal gain he had agents investigate. Daugherty knew Warren and Florence Harding really liked Forbes and he presented the problem very delicately. He told the President that it was his duty to investigate the Forbes matter. Warren knew Daugherty did not like Forbes but promised to look in the matter. Soon they announced the reorganization of the Veterans Bureau. The deceit was too much for Harding. He confronted Forbes in the Oval Office and lost his temper. Coming around the desk he lifted the smug Forbes and pushed him against the wall. Gripping his neck, choking him, he called Forbes, "You yellow rat! You double-crossing bastard!" An aide, hearing the noise, came into the office and put a stop to Harding's attack. They sent Forbes over seas on a special assignment to get rid of him for the time being.

Cries from the strikers that Daugherty had violated their right to freedom of expression guaranteed under the constitution and a threat to sue got the attention of Congress. Senator Wheeler and others passed a resolution to have the attorney general impeached from office. In his book Harry Daugherty spoke of this impeachment effort under his chapter titled, "Impeached for High Crimes and Misdemeanors." The outline of the charges read, "Harry M. Daugherty, Attorney-General of the United States has used his office to violate the Constitution. They charge him with abridging freedom of speech, abridging freedom of press and abridging the right of the people peaceably to assemble. Other charges were that he conducted himself in an arbitrary, oppressive, unjust and illegal manners. This indictment charged him with using the funds of his office to prosecute individuals and organization of certain lawful acts."

The senate investigation failed to impeach Daugherty who burned, destroyed or hid papers needed to convict him. He claimed he did this to protect secrets of the United States that its enemies could use. This investigation, however, would reveal many inside dealings of Harding, Daugherty and the administration. The senate committee found that Harry Daugherty listed his taxable property as eight thousand dollars and his liabilities were twenty-seven thousand dollars, before going to Washington. He lived the good life as the attorney general. He paid seventy-eight hundred dollars a year to Wardman Park Hotel for a housekeeping suite. Jess Smith's book keeping said their annual expense was about fifty thousand per year. Daugherty's annual income as attorney general was twelve thousand dollars a year. Daugherty never explained where the extra money came from to maintain his high style of living.

South of Columbus, Ohio, is the town of Washington Court, the attorney general's hometown. His brother Mally owned the Midland Bank in that town. The senate committee sent investigators to check the books before Daugherty had them destroyed.

The committee found a certificate of deposit amounting to seventy-four thousand dollars in Harry Daugherty's name. Jesse Smith had liberty bonds equaling a cash value of sixty-three thousand and another fifty thousand in bonds were in Mally's name. They credited Liberty Bonds from the American Metal Company to Daugherty. The book showed five deposits of ten thousand each from the American Metal Company. Mally closed the books to the investigators and his brother, Harry had them destroyed. He claimed he did this to protect national security. Mally will be found guilty of violating banking laws, sentenced to ten years in jail, but on appeal they dropped the sentence.

Senator Boise Penrose died after a long battle with sickness. Senator Penrose had dedicated his delegate votes to Harding during the Convention in Chicago earned just a Senator's salary over the years. The Hamon people said Jake had paid $250,000 to Penrose to get votes for Harding. They knew him as boss whom they could buy with money. In a strong box they found $700,000 in cash. Many bills were in one thousand dollar denominations and a ten thousand-dollar bill was found in the cache. This news raised some eyebrows of the Republicans and got the attention of all the Democrats.

The turmoil in Washington encouraged Chancellor's friends to have the ex-professor fulfill his dream of publishing a book about Harding. Chancellor had started Sentinel Publishing Company in Wooster, Ohio. Walter Jones of Columbus, Ohio, agreed to see to the printing and selling of the book. A Mr. E. Furthman appeared as Secretary of the Sentinel Press company on correspondence sent to the White House. This is all that we know of this publishing company but they would print a book about Harding. The exact location of the printing press is speculation and guessed at by biographers of the Warren G. Harding.

Howard Lowry claimed in a paper he wrote for Samuel Hopkins Adams that two strangers negotiated with Hugh A. Snepp for Chancellor's data. Their goal was to form Sentinel Press and publish a book about Warren G. Harding with Chancellor as the author. Lowry thought the men were from Cincinnati and he did not know of any Sentinel Press in that town. Lowry speculated the printing press was in Dayton but well hidden. Howard Lowry claimed he got this information from Hugh Snepp's brother, the Reverend Samuel Snepp.

Author Samuel Adams in his well written book *The Incredible Era* repeats the information that Lowry suggested to him in the special letter. Adams claims Hugh Snepp was dead in 1922 but, it was a brother of Snepp, who was a druggist that had passed away. Then this author said the publisher may have been the Sentinel Press, "an enterprise, similar in name, that operated in southern Ohio and printed Ku Klux Klan literature." In an otherwise very well researched book, Adams states that a Mr. Sharts claimed the press was undercover in Dayton, Ohio.

At the beginning of 1922, Jones and Furthman still wanted more information from William Estabrook Chancellor to put in the anticipated book. William corresponded with Jones from British Columbia, Vancouver, Canada, just across the bay, from Seattle, Washington. Chancellor's oldest daughter, Louise Marie, lived in Seattle. While in Vancouver he stayed at the YMCA and visited his daughter in Seattle.

Chancellor wrote that Harry Daugherty encouraged the press to promote a set of Republican politicians as the greatest lawyers in the country. They hired these attorneys for swift prosecution of war grafters, which the attorney general claimed amounted to $192 million in defaulted contracts. The attorney general seemed to have ignored he was sowing seeds of public distrust of all government agencies including his own. Making wild charges of Wilson's administration boomeranged and did Harding great harm. The pro-Harding *Ohio State Journal* in the home city of Daugherty printed in their editorial the following paragraph.

The Journal printed, *Our own unparalleled offer for the day:* "We will give $2,500 in gold for every grafting war contractor Harry Daugherty puts in jail. An extra prize of a genuine Packard Single-Six every time where the grafting war contractor is placed in jail, is a Republican." They ever made no claim to the Journal.

Whatever a man sows he will also reap and justice pursues wickedness and the wicked. To those who have won by force or by fraud what was not theirs by right, they have sown the wind and will reap the whirlwind. They have the notion that the wages of violence, fraud and deception are often success. Harding has on his hands a resistant Congress and openly antagonistic people. Southern slave lords are gone and the plutocracy operating though the Republican machinery may go as suddenly. Let us hope that it will be by the lawful means of free speech, free press and the ballot.

In America elections ordain powers. Those who deny the right of free speech regarding a President are Un-American who belong in the parts of the world not yet freed from monarchy. They say we cannot speak freely about a President until he was out of office. What they really intend is to secure him for reelections. Tyrannies perpetuate themselves by silencing free speech. Former postmaster general Hays talked much about ordered freedom. Now in the movie industry he said, "The principle of liberty is incompatible with any censorship." Mr. Hays was out of the sphere of authority and he just began to perceive the ideas of liberty.

A President should be master of all those immediately about him and the servant of the public and its posterity. Our valuable Presidents did not surround themselves with self styled "best-minds" and wait for the pull of wires before they began to act. We did not afflict these Presidents with the notion that Presidency was a four-year throne for the servant of individuals and groups. They never worried about the private mail of ordinary citizens. They did not employ agencies, public or private to prevent the publication of the story of their life. These Presidents did not have their own private physicians who were mangers of sanitariums for delirium tremens.

The occupant of the white house was nursing his health, playing golf, going fishing and whiling away the days and nights in pastimes. Millions now believe that he occupies his time this way, because he is incompetent to do otherwise.

The dismal earlier work of the Republican Convention at Chicago gave us this man as President and his results do their own talking. Disclaimers of understanding are useless. Republicans whipped the nation, wheeled it, persuaded it into line and they decided not to place intelligence in the white house. Some politicians care little about ideals or parties. They only want the control of the organizations. They have for sale offices, legislation and court decisions and are habitually engaged in the commercialization of government. These men would rather see their party defeated since they are left in control. It is logical these men deplore primaries and look upon removing control of politicians as undesirable.

With Presidential primaries the nomination of such a man as Warren G. Harding would be impossible. The pre arranged appointment of officers would be impossible. Even primaries will not entirely solve the problem of how to get a competent President every time, though it will be a step forward. Free men will tell the truth and malicious operating politicians will not, by intrigue, control the government. A well-informed citizen is the requisite to justice and freedom. Those who are merciful to the agents of tyranny are cruel to the victims of weakness and ignorance.

Chancellor while in Vancouver, Canada, sent a letter to the Editor of the *New York Times* and he wrote this letter March 19, 1922 but they published it on the twenty-fifth. It was the first letter the author had sent to the *Times* since discharged from the New York Press Club. This letter had nothing to do with politics, it was about comparing real life in Alaska with the way it was presented in movies.

The writer, the author, former-professor of political science depicted a wild untamed Alaska being conquered by men just as wild. He told of gold miners spending two to three thousand in gold at taverns having a joyous time. Chancellor wrote that the men adapted tamed wolfs to pull their sleds over the snow. Indians interbred with Scots, and French would break the snow trail for the dog sleds in the great trails in Newfoundland. Chancellor wrote about the greatest enemy to man and beasts were giant swarms of insects that often killed herds of Moose.

The professor found some peace of mind in Canada. Just before Harding and Daugherty stormed him again.

Chapter Ten
Burn Baby Burn!

Warren G. Harding wrote a reply letter to Colonel Creager of Texas. He told Creager that he would serve at the head of the Postal Department in a "masterly way." The president then told Creager, "It is more than possible that you will be visiting Washington before they finally settle the matter."

Colonel Creager had written to Harding on January 24, 1922 and informed the President that Chancellor was about ready to publish a book. President Harding replied, "I noted, of course, your letter concerning the Chancellor's publication. They have pointed it

Gaston Means agent of the Bureau of Investigation seemed to enjoy this moment during senatorial hearings. Gaston collected a fortune selling under the table liquor permits. He would serve time in a jail and later co-author a book.

out from several sources. I am grateful to you for your consideration in this matter. Also, I will remind General Daugherty to promptly return the documents forwarded to him."

Within weeks after Harding replied to Colonel Creager, Secret Service agent Robert Hynes in Cleveland, Ohio, received a telephone call from Postal Inspector Charles Zimmerman who requested a conference. Hynes wrote in his daily report, "Upon my arrival at Inspector Zimmerman's office, he took up with me the matter of the Dr. William E Chancellor case. I will submit the result of this interview as a special letter." This conference took place February 14, 1922.

Hynes wrote in his daily report, "Feb. 23, 1922. At 10:00 A.M. they called me into a conference with Zimmerman in the latter's office. He told me the latest developments in the Dr. Wm E. Chancellor case."

Records of what happened at this meeting do not exist. However, neither

The Indictment

Hynes nor any other secret service agent became involved with Zimmerman who was trying to find the publishers of a new book allegedly written and published by Chancellor. Soon the postal department lost interest in looking for and suppressing the former professor.

Only sketchy details remain about when, where and how the book, the printing press and people involved were found. Fire destroyed the postal department archives and that valuable source is gone. Mrs. Harding burned documents and so did Attorney General Daugherty to hide their involvement. Without supporting documents we must speculate on time and places, although we know some people who were involved. Authors have speculated and confused this episode in the past. We will try to reconstruct this event with information available.

A biographer of Harding placed Chancellor in Dayton, Ohio in early 1922 under an assumed name. This author wrote that Chancellor was "registered in the Beckel Hotel where he got in touch with two local shysters, Hugh Snepp and Cedric C. Brown." This is not true, because at this time Chancellor was in exile in Canada.

The author of the *Shadow of Blooming Grove*, Francis Russell claimed that Chancellor worked "from the corner of their office." That "he sent an endless chain of flyers' advertising the forthcoming book. Chancellor supposedly offered shares in the publishing enterprise at one hundred dollars each that he claimed would be worth eighteen hundred dollars within six months." The flyers and prospectus of the publishing enterprise are extant, nonexistent and he was not in Dayton at this time because he was a refugee in Canada.

We know that on February 19, 1922, William Estabrook Chancellor was in a YMCA room in Vancouver, British Columbia, Canada, writing a letter to the *New York Times*. He also visited his oldest daughter and his grandchildren who lived across the bay in Seattle, Washington. He wrote his poem *We Journey to Fashion the Soul*, in Vancouver and signed his name as Estabrook Chancellor rather than William Estabrook Chancellor. This was in February of that year.

Secret Service agent Robert Haynes and Charles Zimmerman would discuss the Chancellor matter often. March 11, 1922, Hynes stated he would forward a special report to Washington covering the Chancellor matter. This March entry would be the last entry ever made by the Secret Service concerning Chancellor. Despite the pressure that came from President Harding the secret service took no action. The agency wanted to have nothing to do with the "Chancellor matter."

Within the preface of the published book an unnamed editor wrote about the confiscation of the original manuscript in Wooster. This has been confused with the confiscation of the published book.

Friends of Chancellor wrote. The most humiliating and fearful fact confronting the reader are the attempts to suppress the publication of the facts. The suppression was through the agents of the Post office Department and the personal representative of Harry M. Daugherty. They intimidated Professor

The Indictment

Chancellor by use of an alleged warrant, which they assured him they would extinguish if he would destroy his manuscripts on the Harding Biography.

Thus a man who has written the recognized work dealing exclusively with the lives of the Presidents is now forbidden, on principle of lese majeste, from revising his work on the lives of the Presidents. His work includes an account of all the Presidents except Woodrow Wilson.

This publisher has reliable reasons for believing that the Republican leaders know that the statements of Professor Chancellor and others concerning the ancestry of the President are true. This activity of suppression is due to the fear that they will rebuke the party at last, for its imposition upon the American people.

Postal inspector Zimmerman learned that Walter Jones of Columbus, Ohio, was planning to publish the book and that another manuscript of the *Illustrated Life of Warren G. Harding* existed. With encouragement of Jones and other friends, Chancellor sent additions to his original manuscript back to the states as he traveled in Canada. These additions were about the first year of Warren Harding's presidency. From these additions one can date the time that Chancellor wrote the new material. Comparing recorded events and his writings it was about April 1922 when he wrote the last edition for the new book. It would take months to prepare the plates, bind the book and get it ready to market. Although some biographers claimed the FBI closed in on Snepp, Chancellor and others in early 1922, the dated material in the book belies this fact.

May 2, 1922, George Christian, the secretary to the president, wrote a letter to representative Walter F. Lineberger of California. Christian wrote, "I have your letter of May 1, with enclosure and I want to thank you very cordially for your interest in this matter. I will take it up with the Attorney General." The enclosure referred to by Christian was a letter Lineberger received from Mr. William E. Baum of Saugus, California. Mr. Baum said that they sent him a brochure soliciting a subscription to a book published by Professor William E. Chancellor. Mr. Baum told representative Lineberger he would aid in suppressing this scurrilous publication and offered his services. The brochure came from Dayton, Ohio, the publishing company was the Sentinel Publishing Company, sent by E. Furthman, its Secretary-Treasurer.

Sentinel Publishing Company was the same name Chancellor had used on his pre publication flier that he sent from Wooster, Ohio. None of the new flyers have been found, and the dated letter also proves they had not found the publishers by May 1922.

Title of this new book was *WARREN GAMALIEL HARDING, President of the United States*. It was bound in a red cloth cover. This book consists of two hundred sixty-seven pages without an index, but it has a table of contents and a foreword. The table of contents lists twenty chapters.

An obvious error on the title plate was that the typesetter spelled

Sentinel Press as Sentinal Press. The miss spelling was most likely an error by the typesetter. This would be one of many typesetting mistakes in the book. The title page said, "by William Estabrook Chancellor, formerly Professor of Economics, Politics and Social Science of Wooster College, Wooster, Ohio." As in the flyers or roorback, sent out in October 1921 the College of Wooster, they list the College's name incorrectly.

Prefacing Chancellor's name the publisher printed, "A review of facts collected from, Anthropological, Historical and Political Researches." In small print on the title page was the notation, "This book is sold and distributed by agents only."

Confusion created by the title page caused the Library of Congress to use both spellings of Sentinal and Sentinel Press when it listed the book. They credit the copyright to Chancellor although neither the publisher nor Chancellor filled out or payed for any application. This title page fails to note the publication date. The library of Congress states the date as 1922. Chancellor never acknowledged the authorship of this book.

An unnamed editor titled the book's foreword as the Publisher's Preface. His first sentence sets the racial slant of this book and would mark Professor Chancellor as a racist. This sentence reads, "The whole destiny of the world falls on President Harding's leadership, the fate of the white civilization hangs in the crisis."

Another paragraph states, "Undoubtedly the times are out of joint and blind, and selfish false leadership will be calamitous." This paragraph sets the political tone to the book.

The New York Times book review section wrote decently about previous publications by Chancellor. Other newspapers followed suit. *Warren Gamaliel Harding, President of the United States*, did not get any book reviews by the newspapers. In later years, authors and historians wrote about this book.

Russell Francis the author of the *Shadow of Blooming Grove, Warren G. Harding and his Times* wrote the following. "Cheaply bound, wretchedly printed, with uncorrected typographical errors strewn across the pages and scattered blurred photographs. The book held the possibilities of a major scandal that might overthrow Harding in the next election. They described the president as big, lazy, slouching, confused, ignorant, affable, yellow and cringing like a Negro butler to the great." Mr. Russell also wrote, "Chancellor accused Harding of resorting to cosmetics to make himself look-more-white, than he really was. The author also accused Harding of being an Army deserter and having had several attacks of delirium tremens."

"The book," continues Russell, "was a mishmash of obsessive fantasies, lies, occasional shrewd political observations, and several unrecorded facts. With the author's obvious paranoia and the scurrility of his approach, it is a wonder that no historian has tried to sift the facts from fantasies. Yet facts are there. While in Marion Chancellor picked up the story of Harding's liaison with Carrie Phillips and mentioned her name until the discovery of her long-hidden love letters in 1963."

Author Reverend James R. Blackwood has among his literary credits is the book *Howard Lowry, a Life of Education*. Reverend Blackwood wrote how Dr. Lowry, who as a college student, defended Chancellor that night in Wooster, Ohio, when drunk citizens wanted to tar and feather the Professor. Reverend Blackwood had the pleasure of talking to Russell Francis. When asked about his sources about the professor, Russell replied, "My interest in Chancellor was peripheral."

Russell Francis experienced a very traumatic time when writing his book because of the love letters of Carrie Phillips. An attorney in Marion, Ohio, gave these letters to him to read. He quoted the letters in his manuscript but had to delete the words at the insistence of Dr. Harding of Worthington, Ohio, who obtained the letters after a prolonged law suit. This relative of Harding thought that suppressing the truth would be best. At least he kept up the Florence Harding tradition to destroy and suppress. The Ohio Historical Society was involved in this suit because they had microfilmed these letters as a safety measure in case the Harding family planned to destroy them. The microfilms lie in the Library of Congress and the originals in a bank vault. They will make these historical documents public after the millennium. Whenever they release these letters to the public domain, they will confirm the known morals and scruples of the twenty-ninth president of the United States.

In defense of Russell Francis's statement to Reverend Blackwood that he researched Chancellor peripherally, Russell seemed preoccupied with the Carrie Phillip letters. This was reason enough to discourage any historian or author to be weak on some of his research.

Reverend Blackwood mentions the book *Warren Gamaliel Harding, President of the United States*. Mr. Blackwood wrote, "A casual reading would suggest that Dr. William E. Chancellor had written and published the volume. One thing, however, lay beyond argument, Professor William E. Chancellor did not look on Warren G. Harding as a man of genius, wherever he came from and whatever his racial background might have been. This was the man the college trustees hastily summoned, who, denying that he had anything to do with the broadside on Harding, with equal intensity refused to say that he thought Harding all white. He had made inquiries at Blooming Grove, Ohio, Harding's hometown, and firmly believed that the reports concerning his Negro blood were true."

Samuel Hopkins Adams in 1930 had published his book titled *The Incredible Era*. This author wrote a remarkable book about President Harding and his times with a great asset and a hindrance. His asset was the fact he lived the times as a political newspaper reporter. He had met many individuals, who appear, disappear and reappear around a President. His hindrance was secrecy created by and encouraged by those who knew Harding and not having access to secret service daily reports. At the time Adams researched his book, Chancellor was alive. No documentation exists that the author tried to talk to the professor. If he had, his book could have been a sensation.

The Indictment

Adams wrote, "Around no other President of the United States has there been cast such a smoke screen of obscuration as that which beclouds the personality of Warren G. Harding. This is largely defensive. What little remains, outside a scattered specimen, was in the archives of the Harding Memorial Association, which denied access to them. The rule held fast to the general reading public and individual researcher."

We should note, most of the Harding papers are in the Ohio Historical Society archives, some are in the Library of Congress and others are in the National Archives. The richest source of information lies in the archives of newspapers that number into the thousands. These newspaper articles proved refreshing.

Samuel Hopkins traveled to Wooster, Ohio, and interviewed Dr. Wishart of the College of Wooster and corresponded with Howard Lowry. This author contributed more space to the epic of Chancellor than any author to date.

Adams wrote, "Whatever Professor Chancellor's qualifications in the highly specialized field of genealogical research, it is undeniable he studied the Hardings. Before the appearance of the leaflets, he spent a fortnight in Blooming Grove and the vicinity, interviewing the oldest inhabitants of the region and tracing down family lines. Though he advances a sometimes contradictory claim that there was a Negro strain in several branches of the clan. His main contention was that the second wife of George Tyron Harding, born in 1799 was a Negress." Adams felt, "a strong bias on the Negro question impairs Professor Chancellor's judgement and impugns his testimony."

Adams erroneously stated that Hugh A. Snepp was dead in the year 1922. A brother of Snepp died, not the attorney, this happened in the year of 1923. Samuel Adam's book was well written and exhibits a tremendous amount of research. An excellent book to learn more about the Harding Era, it was a not good source for understanding anything about William Estabrook Chancellor.

Samuel Hopkins Adams' book relied on the research of a college student who was collecting information to write his thesis for his doctorate degree. This student was Harold F. Alderfer of Syracuse University who titled his work, *The Personality of and Politics of Warren G. Harding.* Alderfer went to Blooming Grove, Marion and followed the same trails that Chancellor had. When Alderfer researched for his thesis he had additional information not available to the Wooster Professor. Both Adams and Alderfer used the congressional records of the investigation of Daugherty for sources. Dr. Alderfer cites the book *Warren Gamaliel Harding, President of the United States* in his bibliography.

Dr. Alderfer commented about this book. "This is a difficult volume to evaluate. They ousted the author as Professor of Social Sciences at Wooster College because he allegedly spread the rumor about Harding's tainted-blood during the campaign of 1920. This he denied and after he was subjected to various humiliations, which is a story by itself, he gathered material and wrote this book. The book has the appearance of hasty editorship, and it abounds with typographical errors, repetitions and dogmatic assertions without adequate proof.

These deficiencies cannot hide the knowledge of intimate and personal politics the author had at his fingertips. Nor can it obscure some profound observations on Harding and his cabinet, which although prophecies when he wrote them, became fact. For example, he pointed to Fall and Daugherty predicting failure. The volume is partial, it has a point to prove and it deserves more attention than one would give it after receiving a first impression. Due to the lack of substantiation, many of its alleged facts and its material can only be of use as leads. The author and his activities since 1920 deserve attention."

The Sentinel Press has acquired unreserved legal title to my original papers relating to my investigations into the ancestry and life of President Warren G. Harding. Such references as may be made to me as the source of information concerning facts therein should be credited as authentic.

An Afro-American author J. A. Rogers, wrote a booklet titled *The Five Negro Presidents*. On the cover of this book is a photograph of President Harding and his paternal granduncle, Oliver Harding. Oliver Harding's photograph depicts him as having Negro blood. Rogers used the research done by Chancellor in the assertion that Warren G. Harding was of black ancestry. Roger's booklet is still in print.

Dr. Auset BaKhufu, author of *The Six Black Presidents, Black Blood, White Masks U.S.A.* also uses William Estabrook Chancellor's book as her main source of research. Dr. BaKhufu explains her fierce pride of being Black and discusses Harding's ancestry at great length. This book is still in print under the label of A & A Distributors, Temple Hills, Maryland.

Now comes Warren Boroson who wrote an article titled *America's First Negro President*. Mr. Boroson in a letter to an author, researching Chancellor, stated the author should leave his home and spend more time in the libraries. In the same biting sarcastic fashion Boroson claimed, "William Estabrook

Chancellor was a crank, but a formidable one." Warren Boroson's article printed in the January-February 1964 edition of Fact Magazine was about Chancellor, and his trails and tribulations. Many of Boroson's statements are not true.

We say this in defense of Boroson because they have scattered Chancellor's papers all over this country. After traveling more than four thousand miles in all directions I had managed to get letters and articles about this private man, Chancellor. New found information would have changed much of what Boroson wrote, had he traveled the roads and not stayed at home as he admonished another author.

Boroson reviewed the book *Warren G. Harding, President of the United States*. "The book itself is a melange of shrewd political observations and violent denunciations of Warren G. Harding and Negroes overall. Chancellor very ably exposes the corruption of the Harding Administration and castigates Daugherty, Will Hays and Albert B. Fall as inferior members of the Cabinet. As for, *Our first Negro President* (Warren Harding), no slur is too petty or too extravagant."

A collector of President Harding paraphernalia is Judge K. William Baily of Wooster, Ohio. He owns a copy of the banned book that Chancellor allegedly wrote. In response to me Judge Baily wrote, "I have suspected the book is an unholy composite of some of Chancellor's writings. For example the criticism of economic polices and the ranting of someone else, with a vast difference in grammar, style, etc. from one chapter to another."

Let us now go to the author William Estabrook Chancellor the man credited with writing this book. First the reader must understand that disproving anything that Chancellor researched is very difficult. As Scott Bone said of Chancellor, "he is a genius of the first water." The professor researched throughly any subject he wrote about and did not commit to print a falsehood. William Estabrook Chancellor wrote a letter in response to an inquiry from Samuel Hopkins Adams.

Chancellor wrote to Adams. "I did not write this book. I did not authorize its publication and do not have a copy of it. No one ever paid me a dollar for it, nor did I ever contribute a dollar to its issuance."

This letter from Professor Chancellor must have stunned Samuel Adams as it did this author when I read it. As I have already cautioned the reader, not believing anything that Chancellor wrote is very difficult. After the title page of the printed book, the publisher put in the following statement written by Chancellor.

The unknown editor, publisher and compiler of this book used the Professor's notes and manuscript to write this book. After careful study the title page does not say that Chancellor was the author. Chancellor stated he gave Sentinel Press the legal use of his original papers. He always denied that he wrote this book.

As a writer I have written many, many pages of research that will most likely never see the light of day in the publishing world. Should anyone ever use these notes, although I wrote them, I would not be the author. They would only credit me as the source of the information and not as the writer. Those who used my notes would be the authors. This is the case of Chancellor and publisher of the book. The unknown publisher and other unnamed people wrote the book, *Warren G. Harding, President of the United States*, not Chancellor. He was in flight in Canada when they wrote, compiled and printed this book. President Harding learned to set type when he was very young. He set most of the type for the newspaper, the *Marion Star*. Looking at old copies of the Star one realizes that Harding was good at setting type. The person who set the type for the book was not good at his job. After type is set, a good proofreader should check for errors and one has to believe that nobody proofread the book. On one

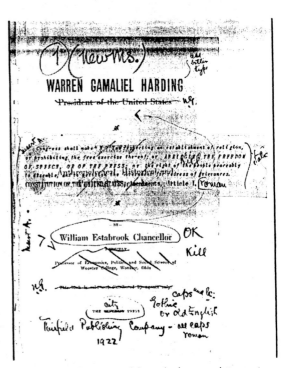

The front page of the revised manuscript.

page alone I counted twenty typographic and type setting errors. The publisher clearly shows he was not familiar with the printing of a book. Flow of the book is erratic, repetitive at times and lacking continuity. Chancellor would have attempted to correct some of these mistakes.

From Vancouver, British Columbia, Canada, Chancellor wrote a letter to the editor of the *New York Times*. The next letter the *New York Times* printed written by Chancellor dated August 16, 1922 and the subject matter was the Professor's view of a Northcliffe matter. This is not so important as the fact that he wrote from Columbus, Ohio and most likely from his daughter's house, who lived at 1560 Worthington Street. At this time the book about Warren Harding was in print. Chancellor took enough copies to give one to all of his children. These are still in the family except one. A grand daughter of Chancellor told me she tossed her copy away, because she did not like the book or anything about the whole affair. Chancellor left Columbus and returned to Winnipeg, Manitoba,

Canada.

In some unknown place near Winnipeg, Canada Chancellor went to work on the book. He tore the book apart, page by page. He sorted the pages and put order into the presentation. The professor overhauled the title page dramatically. The title changed to *Warren Gamaliel Harding*, and he deleted the rest of the original title *President of the United States*. On onion skin paper he made additions and inserted them in the text. He glued the tissue paper on a page and marked it as an insert.

On the title page an insertion read, "Congress will make it a law respecting an establishment of religion or prohibiting the free exercise thereof, of abridging the freedom of speech, or of the press or the right of the people peaceably to assemble and to petition the Government for redress of grievances. Constitution of the United States, amendments, Article I."

A page of Chancellors last manuscript about the life of Warren G. Harding.

This new title page clearly states Chancellor is the author. They deleted reference to the College of Wooster. Also deleted was the statement "This book is sold and distributed by agents only." Sentinal press was crossed out and in its place City Press was handwritten in. They inserted a new line on the bottom of the page, reading Fairfield Publishing Company. Notations state the publisher's signature is to be in Gothic of Old English, all caps, with its publishing date as 1922.

The second page also had a dramatic change. Chancellor added below a printed speech of Andrew Jackson. Also he included the following, "I know not what course others may take, but as for me give me liberty or death." This was from Patrick Henry's speech that he gave in Richmond, Virginia just before the

Revolutionary War. Chancellor also quotes from the Declaration of Independence, "We hold these truths to be self-evident."

Frustration created by the suppression of his manuscript. Chasing across Canada, unable to live in the United States with safety, ousted from his coveted position as a professor, manifested itself in his full edit of the book erroneously credited to him. Like a warm knife going through butter, he had torn out the pages from the printed book, tossing most, correcting others to create his version of Warren G. Harding's biography.

The newly composed book had just twelve chapters with the last entitled, "Nemesis Marching on the Trail." Included in the new version is an appendix about Florence Kling DeWolfe Harding.

While editing, the professor deleted the word "Nigger" out of the book and in its place came the words, Negro, Afro-American, colored or Black. Chancellor deleted scurrilous comments of race, although the author included many more pages giving facts about the ancestry of Harding. He made corrections in pen, or with type written inserts pasted to the page. More than fifty new pages were added and more than that amount deleted. The over all change showed his writing ability, coordination of subject matter and the presentation of historical facts that proved he was a Professor and not some hack writer. He replaced the long, grammatically incorrect sentences as he worked diligently on this final version.

Even in the banned book most of the subject matter, taken from his notes, was not on racial issues. Most of that book and his manuscript and his Winnipeg version dealt with political matters. Most authors in the past appeared to have followed his leads and included what he wrote in their books. To say the banned book was just about race would be wrong and unjustified.

Using a pencil, Chancellor wrote on the last page "Wincks-Oct 20," "Fess-Oct 25," and under these notations he wrote, "both, to *Jones.*" These notations date the manuscript but we are clueless who Wincks and Fess were. Another contribution to this manuscript truly dates it. On page twenty eight of the new manuscript Chancellor added his last insertion. This insert reads, "November 1922, the city of Marion elected as Mayor George W. Neeley, Democrat, by a vote of four thousand to three thousand. Mayor Neeley was the grandfather of the two grandchildren of Florence Kling Harding."

The "Jones" Chancellor referred to was Walter A. Jones who lived on East Broad Street, Columbus, Ohio. Jones' house was close to the center of downtown Columbus. In fact it was not that far from Harry M. Daugherty's house in Columbus on East Town Street. Michael owned a wholesale distribution company that specialized in glass windows sold in large lots. Walter Jones would have known nothing about printing a book and the result proves this statement.

Chancellor wrote the preface to his new book last. At the bottom of the page he wrote in ink, "November 1922, Winnipeg, Manitoba, Canada." So I call his last biography of Warren G. Harding the Winnipeg manuscript.

Harding and Daugherty knew about the new book being printed in the early months of 1922, but they had yet to confiscate it by early November of that year. They occupied them with the railroad strike and the aftermath of fury caused by the Federal injunction filed against the strikers. It is possible that is why they did not confiscate the book by this time.

Daugherty in his exuberance attacked labor unions with vengeance. Congress began to talk about impeaching Daugherty and Harding was not spared any unkind words. This caused the Labor Defense Council in Chicago to publish a booklet titled, *The Burns and Daugherty Attack upon Labor and Liberty*. They sold this booklet for ten cents. This labor organization was a Socialist Party front and its vice chair was Eugene V. Debs, the man Daugherty and Harding freed just the year before. The raids on their union by Daugherty and the Bureau of Investigation prompted this publication. We show this to prove the tactics and the mind set of Daugherty at this time.

This booklet verbally attacks William J. Burns head of the Bureau of Investigation and attorney general Daugherty. Its author called Burns and Daugherty the "awful scourge" of trade unionism, masters of mercenaries who accuse organized labor of importing un-American ideas from abroad. They say, "It is sheer effrontery for them to make such a charge against anyone other than themselves. Violent searches and seizures, raids, confiscations and arrests, without the due process of the law and violation of the American constitution" they charged against Harding. "These angels of vengeance beat helpless prisoners before they have tried or even accused them of crimes or misdemeanors. These lawless, slugs, killing crews, reaching back into the past for inquisition methods have the sullen and defiant audacity to brand radicals and labor men as persons who import ideas and conduct. This charge comes from lawless devotees of the doctrine of force and violence. They themselves had already, largely, destroyed the American form of Government. They have raped it." Others have accused Harding, Daugherty and Burns of these tactics, but not as eloquently as the unnamed author of the pamphlet.

William J. Burns lived in Columbus, Ohio. Harry M Daugherty appointed him head of the newly formed Bureau of Investigation that would later become the Federal Bureau of Investigation or more commonly known as the FBI. Many in Congress did not welcome William J. Burns because of his underhanded methods of obtaining information, but they had no control over this appointment. William J. Burns they knew as the Front Page Detective, fame he earned by solving cases that got national press coverage.

Gene Caesar, author of the *Incredible Detective, the Biography of William J. Burns* gives some insights into the times. Caesar wrote, "the Bureau of Investigation that Burns headed was hardly a political-free organization. Daugherty commonly made appointments of agents as favors, and they informed the Director after the fact. Moreover, the President, Warren G Harding and even his wife, Florence, felt perfectly free to borrow Bureau men for confidential missions about which they told Burns nothing. Harry Daugherty, unabashedly played politics with every move he made."

Edwin Wertz, U.S. District Attorney, had examined Professor Chancellor's original flyer and he thought it violated a criminal code of the United States Postal Service. By the spring of 1922 Ed Wertz was no longer interested in Chancellor and neither was Zimmerman, the Postal Inspector. The Secret Service refused to follow up on the Chancellor matter and concentrated its efforts on looking for counterfeiters of United States currency. This frustrated President Harding and Harry Daugherty.

The Secret Service failed to give Harding and Daugherty any information of the whereabouts of Chancellor or where they were printing the book. Mail sent to the White House increased by the day that told about the book "published" by Chancellor. Sales men began to approach prospects to sell the printed book for the Sentinel Publishing Company. Some books found their way to Washington.

Any effort to obtain records from the FBI, the Secret Service or the Postal Office by the author about this event was stopped cold in its tracks. These agencies cited different parts of the Freedom of Information Act that "prevented" them to reveal any information, pro or con. The reluctance of these agencies to allow a search of records and the fact Mrs. Harding destroyed documents impedes proper research. Therefore, we must rely on what other authors have said. We must take some of these revelations with a large dose of salt and skepticism but they tell the story.

Samuel Adams spoke or wrote to people who were living at the time they gave him testimony. One man was Secretary Greer of the Democratic State Committee who had a law office in Dayton Ohio. Greer said two of the promoters came to his office and were "tough-looking guys." The sales agents said they were from Cincinnati, and offered a special deal to the attorney. He could act as a state agent for the book, appoint subagents and rake off a fat commission. The attorney invited the sales men to leave his office.

Russell Francis claimed the book was a fast mover and that attorney Hugh A. Snepp had a printing press in the loft of the Crystal Restaurant in Dayton, Ohio. Investigation shows that next door to the restaurant was a printing company by the name of Quality Press that had the equipment to print such a book. Research belies the fact they printed the book above the restaurant or at Quality Press. Russell speculates, "Snepp felt he had a gold mine and he planned to market four million volumes at five dollars each."

A George Durgan of Lafayette wrote a letter dated October 28, 1930 addressed to no one in particular. The letter tells us something about the book. Durgan writes, "I purchased for five dollars this copy direct from the author, William Estabrook Chancellor. The book came to the Mayor's office in Lafayette, Indiana, by express several weeks before the election of 1922." Chancellor was in Winnipeg, Canada writing the revisions to the book about which Durgan writes. This letter dates the delivery of the book to Durgan late October 1922.

The last entries in Chancellor's revision date the information to the beginning of November 1922. Not long after that Harding and Daugherty, for whatever motives ordered the confiscation of the book, its plates and manuscripts. They wanted Chancellor smashed, the book suppressed and Chancellor prosecuted.

Gaston Means was the only author who writes about this suppression. He was a special agent, often working directly with Florence Harding and Harry M. Daugherty. This agent of the Bureau of Investigation led a very colorful life and accused of murdering a widow for her money but acquitted. Later they would catch him conning one hundred thousand dollars from Mrs. Evalyn McLean. He told her the money was to pay the ransom for the Lindbergh's baby. Gaston kept the money and he knew nothing about the kidnaping. For this crime they put him in jail, where years later he would die of a heart attack.

How many copies of this book supposedly written and printed by Chancellor, remains hidden in the "fog of time" as they destroyed these records. The agents came to Ohio, found the books, the printing plates, the original manuscript and notes Chancellor had written and his latest Winnipeg version. They took to Washington what they did not destroy in Ohio. This act had to take place in mid November in the year 1922.

Gaston Means using a ghost writer self-published a book titled, *The Strange Death of Warren G. Harding.* In this book he intimated that Florence Harding poisoned Warren, because she feared all the scandal would do him great harm. Author Means also reveals the suppression of the new book.

Gaston Means wrote, "A Professor of an Ohio University wrote a book proving in a scientific dissertation, as he claimed, that Harding had a taint of Negro blood in his veins. I myself had helped to light a bonfire that burnt up the entire edition of this book, copyright and all, bought at a price. They destroyed the printing plates for this book also. They made the bonfire in the rear grounds around the palatial home of a Mr. [Douglas] Boyd, a wealthy friend of Hardings. These books and plates came to Washington in a guarded express car. The express car was packed full of the confiscated books."

Flames consumed the books. Flames consumed freedom of speech and the hard work of the former Professor. The bonfire larger than the one ignited in the coal-fired furnace in Chancellors home in Wooster, Ohio, turned free thought into ashes. The fire added some warmth to Warren G. Harding that at last he silenced William Estabrook Chancellor. Within the pages of the book Florence burned, Chancellor accurately predicted that Harding had a high blood pressure that would lead to a heart failure. In less than a year after they ignited this fire, President Warren G. Harding died of a heart attack.

Florence Kling Harding made it her duty to go through all of Harding's papers and burn anything she deemed harmful to her dead husband, Warren. They estimate she burned more than 60 percent of his letters and papers. Gaston Means notes that one day he saw Mrs. Harding demolishes two more boxes of Chancellor's book.

Evalyn McLean, owner of the Hope diamond, helped Harding's wife, Florence remove papers from the White House to her Washington home. At first

Florence would read every paper she thought would be harmful to his reputation before they went up in flames. Evalyn then watched as Florence grew tired of the task and would toss in an entire box of papers without reading them.

The box containing Chancellor's Winnipeg manuscript Evalyn kept. This manuscript survived the burning. When Evalyn died, her attorney gave the manuscript to the Library of Congress where it rests today. They filed the Winnipeg manuscript in the Mc Clean papers under the heading of Warren G. Harding and not Chancellor's name. In fact the Library of Congress archivist did not realize that they held any of Chancellor's papers. The Library does hold copies of some of Chancellor's other books. They have a copy of *Warren G., President of the United States* that Chancellor did not write. We list all of Chancellor's published books in the appendices of this book.

The suppression was not complete. Copies of the confiscated book are in The New York Public library, Princeton University's library and the library of the Ohio Historical Society. Russell Francis wrote, "A Marion Lawyer is the only private individual I know of who owns the book." This is not true.

The College of Wooster recently put a bid in for a copy being sold by a Baltimore firm. A local bookstore, in Columbus, claims to have a copy of the banned book and wants $750 for it. West Virginia University and Maryland University have a copy. University of Michigan has a hard covered copy and a microfilm of the book. As mentioned a collector in Layette, Indiana, purchased two copies. Some professor's heirs have copies of this book. In all more than eighteen copies can be found in existence today. It is the author's feeling that as interest in this book increases, so will "found" copies increase. The author has a xeroxed copy of this banned book.

You have been reading excerpts from this banned book. We prefaced his writings with *Chancellor wrote*. Harding did not succeed in getting all of the published books. Nor did he suppress the writings of an author, as Chancellor said, "Only God can stop a writer."

Chancellor did not write the banned book that clearly shows a hatred of the Negro race. The Editor or other contributors of the Sentinel Press may have used this platform to express their views and not Chancellors. His Winnipeg manuscript clearly shows what he wrote and what he did not in the banned book. The professor had extensive opinions on more than just the Negro issue.

Regardless, motivated by self interest, a President of the United States violated his oath of upholding the constitution by destroying free thought expressed in print for others to judge. President Harding and Harry Daugherty were the causes of this melancholy day in the history of this country. Daugherty and the Harding gang cannot justify the violation of Chancellor's constitutional rights as an author and citizen of the United States. No justification can explain this act either in the 1920's or now. A fear of exposure by the Harding gang motivated them to suppress the writings of the former professor from the College of Wooster.

Any biographer of Warren G. Harding must investigate the writings of Chancellor because of the printed accusation that he had Negro ancestors. The book allegedly written by the Professor was the prime source of information by biographers in the past. In fact recent publications dealing with Harding still call this Chancellor's biography of the twenty-ninth President. Now the researcher must see the third manuscript that Evalyn McLean's attorney gave to the Library of Congress. No one has recorded what motivated Evalyn McLean to keep the manuscript. She later wrote a book about her family and it was possible she empathized with Chancellor. This book, *Father Struck it Rich,* gives no clues about her intentions.

The modern researcher is limited to the carefully culled papers of Harding now at the Ohio Historical Society's archives in Columbus, Ohio, as the primary source on Harding's life and tenure as President. Secondary sources are richer and more descriptive. Mrs. Harding could not destroy the records held by the Secret Service nor letters held by private individuals. Nor could she burn and destroy the printed newspaper articles that when studied become a good source of information. Chancellor's Winnipeg manuscript one would think is a rich resource for the researcher.

The burning of confiscated books, letters and pamphlets by Mrs. Harding was appalling and violates constitutional rights of Chancellors and other authors. Almost as restrictive to freedom of speech are the new laws concerning copyrights. When Chancellor wrote, copyrights lasted for twenty-seven years. This gave him and his legal heirs exclusive intellectual rights to this book written in 1922 up to and including the year 1949. After this date his writings became a public domain. An amendment of this copyright allowed an extension of the copyright for additional twenty seven years if the author or his heirs filed the correct forms with the Library of Congress. So this would extend all rights from 1922 to the year 1976. The latest copyright law automatically extends this copyright for seventy-five years and is retroactive. Right now any book written on or after 1923 gives exclusive rights to the author and his heirs till the year 2020. Unpublished manuscripts have even greater protection. Chancellor died in the year 1963 and his unpublished manuscripts remain the property of his heirs until the year 2033. Authors may quote small parts of his works, but not in substance, unless they have the written permission of his heirs. The confiscated book and its contents are in the public domain, but his Winnipeg manuscript is not.

Because of the nature of the manuscript and its contents, the Winnipeg manuscript is really a historical document. Letters written by public officials are historical documents. Historians need these documents to understand how and why certain events unfolded and their impact on future history.

As an author I believe anything I write, deserve credit financially and intellectually. I question the wisdom of protecting my intellectual rights for seventy years after my death. For large companies like Walt Disney and others the protections of their creations become another question. The point is the copyright law is no different then the bond fire that consumed confiscated notes, letters, affidavits and books, when it comes to historical documents. The law suffocates, hinders and prevents good research of politicians and office holders.

It gives them a protective barrier against probing minds who are trying to seek the truth.

Therefore, we cannot quote from the Winnipeg manuscript written by William Estabrook Chancellor. He wrote this to replace a really poorly done book to tell the public his thoughts about the inadequacies of Warren G. Harding. Tyrannically, the very subject of the book ordered the book confiscated and destroyed. This was done to silence a critic by a man holding the highest office the United States offers. Ironically, the Congress of the United States protects those in office by preventing publication of letters, notes and manuscripts written by them and their colleagues. All this in the name of protecting authors' intellectual rights. As an author I will say this, if you need to hold a public office what you write deserves no protection at all. Democracy thrives on knowledge, timely information, truth of the moment, not old information decades or a century later. Office holders, employees of governmental offices deserve no protection under the copyright law. No argument by a politician, a public employee, a public office holder should have validity because they have this position as the trustees of our rights.

I have read the Winnipeg manuscript and it is in the Library of Congress for anyone to read. I cannot quote the entire manuscript but I can tell you about its contents. The new manuscript has two hundred seventy two pages plus nineteen pages that are missing. Most of the pages missing are about the ancestry of Harding. No surprise. Chancellor had three chapters on ancestry, the kin of Harding and race. These are extensive and personally he spends too much time on these subjects. Still, since this was the reason they expelled him from the College of Wooster it is understandable.

This manuscript has four chapters about Ohio politics, business and politics, the election and Hamon are pretty much the same as in the original book. The biggest differences are the corrections of typos, misspelling and grammar. New chapters cover government of laws and not men, the first year of Harding's administration, policies of the administration and one titled "Nemesis Marching on the trail." The new chapters reveal the truth of Harding and his Ohio gang.

The former professor shows that from Canada he kept abreast of what was happening in the United States. However, they lack the personal touch that his earlier writings had, because his source had to be just newspapers. Occasionally he writes with great authority with some inside information he must have gotten through the mails.

Chancellor in his new manuscript writes about current events that we now accept as part and parcel of the Harding "legacy," but in 1922 it would have been news. His writings clearly show he was looking toward November elections and a possible rerun for the presidency by Harding. His views were timely, revealing and pointedly negative of Republicans and Harding. Agents who confiscated the book and manuscript reaped a larger harvest then expected. All research notes, affidavits and notes had to taken on the search and seizure. Two affidavits survived the burning by Florence Harding, and they took both in 1921. The professor had taken over a dozen affidavits while researching the background of Harding. In all the archives only four have survived the ravaging destructive mode of the Hardings.

Chancellor had taken many photographs of Harding's ancestors to enhance his claims of the Negro ancestry of Harding. These are gone and only one was in the McLean papers, a duplication of Mrs. J. C. The rest are extant. The reaper like confiscation of important information is now lost forever. Suppression, is the hallmark of President Harding's era.

In his new manuscript Chancellor clarifies his position on the Negro issue. He was not for violence, hangings, or repression. He predicted that in time the leaders of civil rights would leave the Republican party and join with the Democrats to get their deserved civil rights.

Last Chapter
Chancellors Retreat and Chase

The worst blow to Chancellor was the loss of his wife, Louise in 1908, when she became ill and died of typhoid fever. Louise's father Edward Beecher accompanied the professor to Rhode Island where they interred her remains in the Beecher's family plot.

Chancellor, the widower returned to his family in Washington, D.C., and he gathered all his children in one bedroom and noticed the baby David was not there. He had his oldest daughter bring the infant into that room because he wanted the family together. Then he knelt and had his children do the same and together they prayed for their mother. William told them to cherish their mother and remember only fine things about her. William would never remarry and he raised four daughters and one son on his own. He educated all of his children and they all received degrees from a college.

Dr. William Estabrook Chancellor

source Index College of Wooster

A man whom they tossed around in the political ring so severely, he never wrote a bitter word about it, although he had every right. Years later, three different publishers approached him and wanted to do a book about his experiences and he refused them. The professor told them he was tired of the publicity.

Chancellor may have carried a hatred for Daugherty and Harding but it never manifested itself in any of his public writings. In a scrapbook of his, some bitterness showed with one clipped newspaper article accompanied by a note on a cartoon. The cartoon depicted a man with an axe in his hand ready to strike a bear had the notation, "sunlight glittered as he sought revenge." Next to it was a clipping of the obituary of Ruth Hanna McCormick who was behind his dismissal at the College of Wooster. The implication is clear.

In 1922 Isabel, Catherine and David moved from their Worthington Street address to a frame duplex at 2261 Neil Avenue, Columbus, Ohio. This two-family house is found just north of the Ohio State University campus. In 1922 it was close to a trolley car line that passed in front of their new home. Catherine, could take the trolley car downtown to work at the offices of her employer, Hain & Miller at 240 North High Street. Isabelle was within walking distance to her classes at the University. Susan continued her education at Ohio State University, but she also had to work. David, the youngest, attended school at North High School until he graduated. He would later attend Ohio State University and graduate with a BA in Engineering in 1931. The daughters very seldom heard from their father who remained in exile in Canada, while the young women's wages went to maintain their home.

Chancellor stayed in Canada after the confiscation of his manuscript, the book, and all his notes, papers and letters held by Jones and others. They never recorded his reactions to the last effrontery and he never wrote again about Harding.

Harding and Daugherty evaluated the November 1922 election results and found the Republicans lost sixty-nine seats in the House and seven in the senate. The effect of stopping the railroad and coal strikes with a federal injunction and the use of forceful tactics cast a black mark on the Harding Administration. News about underhand dealings in the Veterans Bureau began to leak out to the press and to members of Congress. Calls for the impeachment of Daugherty started their rounds in congress.

President Harding told his friend Joe Chapple, "Some day, the people will understand what some of my former friends have done to me, in these critical times, when I depended so much upon them." A joke passed around at the time said, "The difference between George Washington and Harding was that Washington could not tell a lie. Warren Harding could not tell a liar." The significance of this joke was that Harding was innocent of all the thievery going on around him, but that is another story and maybe not true.

Attorney Wertz said Chancellor could be violating the postal code, if his writings brought on death threats to the President. This never happened. Late 1922, after Chancellor's book was confiscated and papers burned, a steady stream of threatening letters came to the White House announcing that they marked President Harding for death. The secret service increased their security but the letters came from people dissatisfied with the Daugherty and Harding's tactics of breaking strikes. None of these threats came because of Chancellor's writings.

Albert B. Fall resigned as Secretary of Interior and was soon put under investigation. Fall traveled to Russia with Sinclair of Sinclair Oil and the word got out that Fall had improved his ranch in New Mexico. Some of these improvements included a paved street to his remodeled ranch house and new automobiles. It did not take long to discover all of his back taxes he paid in full. Investigators began to look to find where the former Member of Congress got this money. Fall would serve time in jail.

In the spring of 1923, Charles F. Cramer under investigation committed suicide. He wrote a letter to President Harding who refused to read it. Then Jesse Smith the close friend and companion of Harry Daugherty become paranoid about being called to testify to the investigation committee. He told his ex-wife, men are trailing him and he feared for his life. One evening he shot himself in the head, and they found his body draped from the bed with his head over a wastebasket. No blood was found on the floor. Many believe they murdered him, just as some thought that they had murdered Jake Hamon.

Despite the deplorable press surrounding Harding, Harry Daugherty announced the president would seek a re election. Harding wanted a second term as President despite the bad press he was receiving. They planned to have President Harding to make a trip to Alaska and make speeches as his train went west. About thirty-five days into the trip Warren Harding died of a heart attack in California.

James Sloan the secret service man assigned to protect and do the bidding of President Harding had resigned and joined a brokerage firm in Cleveland, Ohio, before Harding died. The firm of Ungeleider and Company allowed Harding to trade freely and have an open account. The President owed this company about one hundred eighty-thousand dollars at the time of his death. His estate only partially paid the bill.

In 1924 Catherine Chancellor moved from the Neil Ave duplex and took an apartment on West Norwich in Columbus. Susan, Isabelle and David remained at the Neil Avenue address. Catherine started a new job as an assistant to Dean George F. Arps of the Ohio State University Education Department and would remain in that position for a year.

In 1925 Chancellor wrote another letter to the editor of the *New York Times* about Racism. He was stating his opinion about an earlier article that suggested poor people should not have children. Chancellor cited many examples that poor families in the past had given us fine men and woman. In this letter he also shows where he was in 1922 and something about the area.

Chancellor wrote, In 1922 I attended a Convention of 37,000 half-breeds on the shores of Lake Winnipeg, the whites, most visiting speculators, not included. All that the lake needs are railroads, steamship lines, industrial plants, settlers, workers, the sons and daughters of the poor. Also, the wealth of capitalists, and the direction of competent business minds.

What is true of Lake Winnipeg is true of many districts in the New World in one way or another. I have visited every state of the Union, every province of Canada and many other parts of the earth, sojourning in many different lands. It is plain to me that the defeatists simply have not the spirit of pioneers, the spirit of the poor whom they completely misunderstand.

I know a man, in Edmundston, Alberta, Canada, then in dire poverty, who 40 years ago went to central Alberta and settled with his wife, a point 300 miles from any railroad. He has today thirty-four descendants, more than 3,000 acres of land, and tens of thousands of cattle, swine, and horses. His is still 120 miles from any railroad, but he has a piano, a phonograph, radio, several motor cars, and every one of his sons went to a university.

That is a mere illustration. Room is plentiful for more people, several times as many as we yet have. Even Ohio has but one third the density of population of Connecticut. We are not yet done with building Cleveland and many of our Middle West cities.

At the mouth of the Saskatchewan River, where it empties its tremendous flood plain, into Lake Winnipeg, is a site for a vast city with a marvelous water power from the rapids through limestone. Lake Winnipeg is almost of the same area as Lake Erie. On its shores is room for another Buffalo, Cleveland, Toledo, or Detroit, for at least five million urban dwellers. The back country will grow wheat in a greater yield than any river valley in the United States or uplands. Great forests cover the lands and it holds mineral resources of immense value.

William Estabrook Chancellor wrote the above letter from Columbus, Ohio. He had finally returned to the United States and moved in with David and Isabelle on Neil Avenue.

The Peavevale School magazine commissioned Chancellor to write a series on education. Then he contracted to do a thirty-four-part serial on the private finances of the Presidents. As he said, he will write he will write, but he did not write about Warren Gamaliel Harding after his return to the United States.

Florence Harding took back to Marion, Ohio, papers she had not burned in Washington. As her health permitted, she culled through the papers and burned more of them. In the fall of 1924, just fifteen months after the death of Warren Harding, she died. Just about this time, President Calvin Coolidge tired of the contempt of Daugherty, asked him to step down as the attorney general of the United States. Coolidge learned that Daugherty was destroying various papers wanted by the impeachment committee. The Harding Era came to an abrupt and disgraceful close.

Isabelle displayed her artistic talent as she continued her studies to become an architect at Ohio State. She would comment often on how they condemned her for wanting to be part of an all male environment. Studying hard and under the careful guidance of her father she got excellent grades and her degree. She represented just one woman of that era, who graduated from Ohio State University with such a degree.

On September 29, 1925, the *New York Times* printed another Chancellor letter giving the professor's views on the fact that governor Alfred Smith was Catholic. He wrote this article from Columbus, Ohio. Chancellor took the side that the Democratic candidates' popularity would not offset religious prejudices in the United States. In this letter Chancellor mentioned he had recently spent eleven weeks in the State of Maine.

Harding biographers accuse the professor of being bigoted and a racist. In a *New York Times* letter to the editor the professor stated this position.

Chancellor wrote, for the *New York Times*. This propagandum of the race suicide goes still more than your correspondent suggests. I have seen it advocated that no widow or widower should remarry, as too, many children exist already. It that had been the legal controlling plan two centuries ago, we would have been no George Washington, the first child of Augustine Washington, by his second marriage. As an American, I prefer not to speculate on what this country would have been with no George Washington. With the race defeatists I have no sympathy whatever or with their birth control lists. They say that most mothers should not bear children more rapidly than every three years. Is there no room under right legal institutions, with the right social ideas in circulation, with free enterprise again encouraged?

Isabelle graduated from Ohio State University and by 1927 all of Chancellor's daughters were married except her and David was attending classes at the OSU. Isabelle received a commission from the Xavier University in Cincinnati, Ohio. Chancellor moved to Norwood, Ohio where he and Isabelle took up quarters in a large apartment building. David would live with the family in Norwood after graduation from OSU.

While helping Isabelle, Chancellor met Father Brockman, the Rector, of the Xavier University that is a Jesuit school. The two men got along well together and Father Brockman learned about Chancellor's experience in education. Men of his ability were uncommon and the College was in need of him. They ignored religion differences and returned the Professor to the class room. Chancellor reached his sixtieth birthday as he began his job as a professor of Economics at the Xavier University.

His pay as a Xavier professor was less then they paid him as a Hoge Professor at the College of Wooster. However, his love for teaching and being busy was reward enough for Chancellor. Letters sent by his formal students proved their love and admiration of their professor. Years after he left the institute, Chancellor received letters and cards from the University. He would teach at this school for fourteen years.

Hired to teach Economics he soon taught History of Commerce, American Economic History, Investment Advertising, Personal Management, Business Fundamentals, Economic Resource, Transportation, Marketing, Real Estate and he added "etc., etc., etc." This is a work load that would tire a younger man but he also found time to study law at Xavier and received his Doctorate from them in 1934. He wrote, "I did correspondence courses for five years, with the Blackstone College of law, taking thirty-five examinations." His thesis was "Conflict of Laws" and the degree he received from Blackstone was legally good in Illinois only.

Chancellor's affable manner endeared him to Norwood neighbors and he won a council seat in 1933. He would retain this seat until he lost by thirty-four votes, in an election to a former Xavier student. His popularity was such that another council member stepped down and gave the professor his seat.

When a youth he suffered from a gun blast close to his eyes and this would affect his sight for the rest of his life. Chancellor suffered from cataracts and this became more noticeable as he grew older. A family member related how he learned to fold a one dollar bill so he distinguished it from other dominations by the feel. He learned to type by touch only and had others check his letters for errors. Typing mistakes became more common in his letters as he grew older. Chancellor walked to Xavier from his Norwood home stopping at a traffic light before he crossed a busy street. He would listen to others who had to cross the street and when they moved he went with them.

Chancellor wrote that he traveled over five-hundred thousand miles in his life time which included visits to five continents. Where he went, what countries he visited I do not know. In the research of this book I had to travel more than four thousand miles to get letters and manuscripts stored in various archives. This I called the Chancellor Chase.

This chase started one evening while browsing the Internet and I learned about the rare book "Warren Gamaliel Harding, President of the United States," allegedly wrote by William Estabrook Chancellor. I found a copy at the Ohio Historical Society in Columbus, Ohio. They had told me only four books of this edition exist because the U.S. Government confiscated the rest. Given permission to *photocopy* the entire book I took it home and read it. I had a difficult time reading the book as it is not only poorly composed but the typesetters made many mistakes. Inconsistency was the hall mark of the book, but it did mention some interesting facts. Within days I was back to the archives of the Ohio Historical Society who houses what is left of the Harding papers. It was not long before I become skeptical of what other historians and authors wrote about Chancellor. I got permission from the College of Wooster to look at their archives.

March 1998, Tim, my youngest son, drove our car to Wooster, Ohio. As always, he took the back roads rather than a more direct route. Tim's claim is, since traffic is less on the back roads it is faster. We did seem to travel fast along the back roads of Ohio as the small farms and little towns whizzed past us. It was like going back in time. Most of the homes we passed, are early vintage, built at the turn of the century. This was much the way the rural America was at the time when Chancellor was alive.

About ten miles out of Wooster, I had my chance to tease my son. We came to a standstill waiting for a horse-drawn Amish carriage to clear the top of a hill before we could pass. His idea, that back roads are faster to travel, failed. This offered an excellent excuse to tease him about how fast the back roads were, which I did the rest of the way to Wooster.

It did not take us long to find the Andrews Library on the campus of the College of Wooster. Before long they seated us in the archive's library. Denise Monbarren and her assistant, Ms Synder, had materials out for us, more than I expected. I thought we would have to copy or make notes but soon discovered we could photocopy all the documents concerning William Estabrook Chancellor. Within less than an hour we found ourselves out of the Library and across the street at a campus-sponsored bookstore. Here I purchased a copy of the Reverend James Blackwood's book titled *HOWARD Lowry, A life in Education*. Of course, we bought College of Wooster T-shirts to keep as souvenirs.

Next we found the Wayne County courthouse and then the county recorder's office to see if Chancellor ever owned any property in the City of Wooster. The county records showed he had to rent while he lived in that town. At Wooster's town hall we tried to get information about William's tenure as a city council man. However, the room holding the records was in use to administer a civil test. Because I felt William's job as a city council member did not play an important role in the overall story we left the administration building. Our next effort was to find the local historical society building. Unfortunately, it was closed and would not open until sometime around two in the afternoon.

About noon we asked someone to recommend a good restaurant, and they mentioned the Parlor. In the Parlor we ordered our lunch. I took some papers out of my briefcase to get the address of the house Chancellor lived in while at the college. One paper said his home was on Beall Street. Three people were sitting at the oval-shaped counter, and I asked them how I would find Beall Street. Pronouncing the name as it read, Beall.

The three men at the counter, corrected me by saying it was Bell Street not Beall. They also said in Wooster they pronounced Bever Street as Beaver Street. You see, they explained, in Wooster we took the "A" from Beall (Bell) and put it in Bever (Beaver). They also said they pronounce Wooster "Worster."

Jokingly, I said, "Sure, just like your square, everyone tells us to go to the square and turn one way or the other. I cannot find the square."

One man said, "You must be from out of town."

"Yes, we are," I answered. "Could you tell us where the railroad station used to stand?"

A grey-haired fellow said, "That was down the street, but it is gone now. It was a really beautiful train station, but they had to tear it down. A train destroyed it. I was working near the old station when a train derailed and crashed into the old depot. The crash created the biggest noise and racket you would ever want to hear. They tore the old station down because the damage was so extensive." They have told me it was a classical train station and a source of pride in Wooster.

The man who told us how to pronounce Bever as Beaver, I was soon to find out, was Anthony J. Biggio, a dentist from Wooster. Biggio asked me what I was looking for. I told him I was looking for information about William Chancellor, a former professor of the College of Wooster. Biggio immediately replied, "William Estabrook Chancellor?"

In my experience researching history, I have always found a local resident who has done research on whatever I was looking for. These self-taught historians usually gave me reliable information about the vicinity. Information, I doubt I would have found any other way. This person was about to really surprise me.

Anthony Biggio, came over to our part of the counter and introduced himself. Then he asked how long we were going to stay in town. I told him that at the most, a few more hours.

"Look, if you could come to my office at five, I want to take you to my home. I purchased the house and farm from one of Chancellor's daughters and

The Indictment

I have in the attic some boxes of stuff you may want to have."

My heart jumped. I said to Biggio, "We will be leaving town when we leave your house!"

My son and I went back to the historical society's building after spending an hour at the local Library. The Wooster's Historical Society's building was the original home of Colonel Beall who had settled the area in 1803. His heirs had donated the Beall home to the College of Wooster, who then gave the rights for the local society to use if they wanted. The year before we got there, the basement of the historical society had flooded, damaging valuable records. So, the Historical Society could not help in my research.

At 4:50 Tim and I sat in Biggio's waiting room. The good doctor came out and told us he would not be long. Doctor Biggio had me ride with him out to his home in his pickup truck and my son followed with our car. Anthony asked me about Chancellor and, of course, what other books I had written. We talked about Chancellor briefly and then Ohio history, which was a real interest to him.

They originally built Chancellor's daughter house, now owned by Biggio, about the year 1850, bricked on the outside and brick on the inside. The Biggios tastefully retained the flavor of the old house, not only in decorating but in construction. It is a beautiful home nestled in a super setting. I walked around the home's first floor as Anthony excused himself to change into some old clothes. He said the attic was really dirty.

As I waited, Mrs. Biggio (Maryanna) came home. Evidently, Anthony told her I was inside. I talked with Maryanna as Doctor Biggio went into the attic.

Soon four boxes and then another sat on the Biggio's kitchen table. Accumulated dust from over the years covered the boxes. They may have been sitting in the attic some forty to fifty years. We tried our best to clean them off, and dirt and bits of old paper soon covered the kitchen floor and table chairs. Carefully, we opened each box.

We counted nine unpublished manuscripts nicely typewritten and carefully stored in the original typing paper boxes by Chancellor. On these boxes were black block letters telling of its contents. WAGES, HUMAN ECOLOGY, ECONOMY, IN THE WORLD'S WILDERNESS, INDUSTRY, COMMERCIAL AND GEOGRAPHICAL OF THE UNITED STATES AND AN ACCOUNT OF EACH STATE, FIVE CORNERS, PASTIMES AND PLAYS WITH WORDS AND COMIC WORDS BOOK. All added to the phenomenal works already credited to Professor Chancellor. Included with the collection was his thesis given at the University of Amherst, "An Inquiry into Poverty" written in 1896, more than 100 years ago. Later I found seven more manuscripts hidden in unmarked boxes.

Professor Chancellor's wife Louise had died in 1908, four weeks after she gave birth to his only son David. Included in this collection were some of her diaries and poems she had written. I told Dr. Biggio and his wife, these were significant in the fact that Louise was a niece of Harriet Beecher Stowe the author of *Uncle Tom's Cabin*.

I was to discover later, that Louise had published at least three books, including a 1903 book about education titled, *An Easy Road to Reading* and another titled *Players of London*. They published the *Players of London* in 1909, a year after she died. The hardcovered book is lilac in color and embossed. The title and author's name were done in gold. Each page is bordered printed in lilac enclosing the script, an expensive book to print in 1909 a work of love. They adapted this book, Players of London, to a play titled "No Bed for Bacon." The book and play were about Shakespeare falling in love.

That same year, Chancellor published a book titled, *Transitus in Lucem and Other Verses in Memory of Louise Isabelle Beecher Chancellor*. This book was no more than twelve pages in size and can be found in the Library of Congress. Chancellor, a private man, left few private letters, and he never remarried. He raised his family without complaint.

I glanced through the professor's scrapbooks containing newspaper clippings of political events up to and including the Korean War. One scrapbook had a news clipping of how an organization in Zanesville, Ohio, had named him the father of the year. Only a few of these letters had any reference to the Harding era. A letter from a friend, noted Mally Daugherty, the brother of Harry Daugherty, had died in a run-down home owned by a colored man. The ex banker died broke.

Letters written on Xavier University stationery included a picture of William when he was in his sixties. Dated family letters, old checkbook stubs and a few other items were in the boxes. We found a letter addressed to the professor that turned out to be a rejection slip from a publishing company. It stated "we have no interest at this time for your manuscript," the dread of every author. We dated the letter in mid 1940. Many rejection slips are in this collection that I call the Biggio papers. Chancellor would never publish after the banning of the book that he never wrote.

We discovered three hard bound books in Biggio's papers. One book is, Gaston Mean's, *The Strange Death of Warren G Harding*, a self-published book that became a bestseller. Most used bookstores sell this edition for about twenty to forty dollars depending upon its condition. Because Chancellor had written his name in this book, it might be worth one hundred fifty dollars or more, to a knowledgeable collector.

A book by Joe Mitchell Chapple titled *Warren G Harding the Man*, published in the year 1920, was also in the collection. Current price on this book is about two dollars. Handwritten notes in the margins by Chancellor gave me the insight that Chancellor had used this book in his research of Harding. That book I kept for my research.

The professor wrote on the inside leaf of Chapple's book, "All wind, signifying nothing." Opposite page thirty-two of this book is a picture of Warren's father, George Tyron Harding. This photo, not retouched, shows the swarthy skin coloring of the man. Chancellor wrote in the margin, "Throughly Mulatto."

On page fifty-one, on the bottom, Chancellor wrote about Mrs. Votaw, "I appointed a Mrs. Votaw as a Black woman to the colored schools." Page sixty-five in Chapple's book shows two pictures of Charles and Mary Ann Crawford Harding, supposed to be pictures of Warren Hardings grandparents. Chancellor writes, "Are these fakes? Text says Amo's picture caption says Charles. Text says nothing, pictures captions says Mary Ann Crawford, people say Mary Ann Dixon. She may be Charles (Amos) second mate." Twice in this book Chancellor notes that Warren G. Harding's eyes are not blue but light brown and yellow.

Chancellor's book on American History published at the turn of the century and so was a book on spelling in this collection. The spelling book, he wrote while Superintendent at the District of Columbia schools.

We looked through this amazing collection. Dr. Biggio asked if we wanted to go to town for supper. At this time I realized how late in the day it was. I thanked the good doctor for his offer but declined. Then I answered Dr. Biggio's earlier question about whether I wanted the collection. I told him no and explained, "First because these are unpublished books by Chancellor, I could not use any part of them without the written permission of the heirs. In 1963, the year the professor passed away, he left more than seventeen great-grandchildren. It would not be an unsurmountable task to get individual permission from each heir for intellectual rights, but a tedious one."

I suggested to Biggio that they should make the Chancellor family aware of the collection and then have them donate it to a historical society. My first choice would be the College of Wooster and the second would be the Ohio Historical Society in Columbus, Ohio. The College of Wooster declined and the collection is now at the Ohio Historical Society.

"You see, Doc," I said to Biggio, "Chancellor's story center's around Harding's ancestry and I care less if Harding had black blood. That is not the entire story, and is not the point. In the banned book, Chancellor reveals the morals of Harding who had an affair with the Phillips woman. He tells how hard cash purchased delegate votes at the Republican Convention in 1920. Chancellor's insight into a possible war with Japan and Germany is amazing. A man like Chancellor or anybody for that matter, are supposed to have the right to say what he wants in this country, the first amendment states this. The professor's stand on Harding's ancestry was the justification by Harding and the government to stifle this man."

"We are looking at hundreds of hours of writing done by a really amazing and brilliant man. All of this work was a waste of time. The action of Daugherty, Harding, and the power of the government crushed this man in the year 1922 and the stigma stuck that he was a racist. They blackballed him as an author for the rest of his life. Living proof sits on your kitchen table. Doc, it would be no different from the FBI raiding your office, destroying all your tools and humiliating you in front of the world on some trumped up charge. All did in the name of so-called justice." Doctor Biggio looked at me, then at the boxes on his kitchen table, and said, "It is a shame, it is a shame."

The Chancellor chase took me to Bucyrus, Blooming Grove, Galion, Norwood and Cincinnati to mention some places I visited. Two separate trips to Washington, D.C. highlighted my quest for information about Chancellor. The miles I traveled to the archives and libraries in Columbus are just too many to list. Now my search is over and the true story of the Chancellors' affair is now public.

They listed Dr. Chancellor in Who's Who as early as 1904 and then after his death they listed him in "Who Was Who." He listed the number of speeches and lectures to the number of four thousand and that he separately tells about the lecture Rivers of Life. In the papers found at Dr. Biggio's was a four-page brochure telling about this lecture.

The brochure states, "A Lecture, for general entertainment or lecture courses and for evening meetings of churches, societies, institutes and other organizations." Press notices, claim this lecture as the most fascinating, full of wit and good cheer. In Chicago they said, "After the lecturer finished, an audience that packed the theater called him back three times to acknowledge applause."

Chancellor stood about six feet and maybe a little taller when he gave this speech, which he mentioned often in his writings. A grand daughter remembers him as a big man with a booming voice that was also pleasant.

Fittingly the final act to write about Dr. William Estabrook Chancellor should be his Rivers of Life lecture. Actual copies of his speech have not been found, but his brochure aptly outlines enough to give us an idea of what he had to say.

Is life more abundant now than it was two thousand years ago? From personal experiences in public office for many years, and lifelong business affairs, and out of a fund of stories, I will try to answer this question.

We all want overflowing vitality. The average American enjoyed better health, is stronger, can do more, enjoys life more than did any civilized persons in ancient times. Diet, sanitation, housing, modes of exercise and recreation have improved wonderfully. Then, seventy thousand people were on earth, and now we have 170 million. When Ohio reaches the density of population in Connecticut, she will have twenty-two million people! Terrible as has been war of all nations, in only six countries has population decline by excess deaths over births.

The average age at death used to be twenty-eight years, now it is forty-five years. The known world extended over but one-tenth of the real surface of the globe. Now men know every part of the earth and are at home everywhere and anywhere. In these two thousand years we have learned to measure and to count the stars. We have discovered cells, microbes, and the elements of which they make the universe. We travel under land and sea, upon their surfaces and through the ocean of air. Over the time span we have made ten thousand scientific discoveries and technical inventions.

With the compass and the wheel, with fire and an almost incredible variety of tools and machinery, the microscope, the terrific steam locomotive, test tubes of the chemist and the forge of the metallurgist, with electricity and dynamite, we profit by and enjoy all of

The Indictment

the nature. They have turned night into light, and warmed indoor winter into summer and we will yet to cool the tropics to make homes for men. We have tapped the earth for hot water, and we will have cool breezes in home and factory.

Then, the average cow weighed three hundred fifty pounds and the average horse six hundred pounds. Now the average cow weighs nearly three times as much and gives twelve times as much milk. The average horse has doubled that weight and trebled its strength and its speed. Ancient Palestine, regarded four bushels of wheat per acre, a good crop. Today one hundred bushels are common.

The equipment of the ordinary home of today would astonish even a Roman Emperor in his mile long marble place. The Emperor imagined himself a god, but he could not draw water from a tap in the second story of his palace. He could not talk with his servants at opposite ends of his palace and he could not read the news of the little Roman world in a paper at breakfast. He thought he went fast in a "chariot and four," at twelve miles an hour on a cobblestone roadway. Our motor cars go forty miles an hour, our trains sixty, and our aero planes one hundred and fifty.

Then, nine-tenths of all men were either slaves to the lords of wealth and power or ignorant barbarians. Now slaves and barbarians are but a very small fraction of earth's people. Parents and elders arranged marriages and husbands owned heir wives and could divorce them at will. Fathers were the absolute rulers of their children. Now those who marry choose their mates in freedom, and in American homes parents and children are all sharers in freedom according to their abilities. We have created many voluntary societies in which all may fearlessly and freely meet kindred minds and cooperate in many ways.

Two thousand years ago almost every disease and major accident was fatal. Now the positive diseases are but few, and even of the wounded in battle, 90 per cent recover. Then, not one person in a hundred could read and write. In some states, ninety-seven out of a hundred can read and write. We are opening wide the gates of knowledge to all men.

Superstition ruled all lives. Now we are freed from superstitions including fear of the ghostly dead. Priests do not own God, nor do they have keys to the gates of Heaven. We are winning freedom for all men in America and fighting for freedom for all men everywhere. They will outlaw war, as we have conquered polygamy, slavery, brigandage and piracy. We are now conquering and outlawing the saloon. We no longer confuse the insane with the criminal, and we are merciful to the poor and ignorant. Never was there a century when humanity was better-off than it is right now. In a world of truth, big as this earth is, there is no room for a pessimist.

The Indictment

Already we have worked out vast federations of peoples living in friendship. We have ended the quarrels and feuds of families, clans and tribes and peoples. Certificating passports were once required even from village to village. Steadily, surely, humanity grows into harmony and social unity. Poison is more dangerous than a false idea. Political democracy is growing into a social democracy and universal self-government. We live where run the rivers of life, rivers of truth, of art, of wealth for all, rivers of justice, of freedom and good will.

Reverend James R. Blackwood wrote about the professor and discovered that William Chancellor was in an old age home in Wooster, Ohio and visited him there. He is the only author I know of that took the time to visit this controversial and interesting figure.

Russell Francis in 1964 had planned to talk to Chancellor but when he came to Ohio, Chancellor had passed away the year before. Samuel Hopkins Adams when he wrote his book, the *Incredible Era* traveled to Wooster, Columbus and Dayton, Ohio, to finish his research but never met the professor. Adams listed the Xavier University erroneously as the University of Cincinnati, but he was close enough to Norwood, Ohio, where Chancellor was living at the time, to find the truth. Maybe, Adams was one of three people who had asked Chancellor for his notes, this is unrecorded and Chancellor nor Adams, ever released this information.

Mr. Blackwood told me that Chancellors was very respectful to everyone around him, even the colored nurse that helped to care for him. He remembered the Professor as a congenial person and to my knowledge the two men, never discussed the run-in he had with President Harding. Mr. Blackwood was very happy to hear that Chancellor did not write the banned book, as he always suspected it was below the man's dignity. At the old age home in Wooster, Ohio, the professor passed away in the year 1963, near the College of Wooster that he loved so much. Ironically the old age home was near the same building that housed the Wooster post office, where Chancellor faced the postal inspector Zimmerman for the first time.

At the Ohio Historical Society, is the collection of Cyril Clemens a descendant of Mark Twain. For years Cyril collected data about Harding with the intent of writing a book. This never happened. Clemens wrote to those who were alive at the time and that included William Chancellor. In a letter to Clemens, Chancellor talked about the Korean War and his view point on the Democrat Smith, but nothing about Harding. One letter Chancellor signed with a shaky scroll. On this letter he noted at the bottom, "Excuse the errors as I am totally blind." This was in 1948.

So ends the story of Professor William Estabrook Chancellor... Person extra ordinary.

APPENDIX

William Estabrook Chancellor
b. Dayton, Ohio. September 25, 1867 d. December 4, 1963
Parents: David W. and Harriet (Estabrook) Chancellor
Education:
    Amherst College, A.B. 1889 magna cum laude, valedictorian.
    Long Island Medical College
    Harvard Law School 1892-94
    Xavier College Law LL.B. 1934
Wife:
    Louise Beecher December 14, 1892 d. August 18, 1908
Children:
    Marie Louise [Mrs. Roy C. Miller] A.B. Barnard College, Columbia
       University 1916
    Susan Beecher [Mrs. Harold L. Borst] College of Wooster 1919
    Catherine Beecher [Mrs. James A. Howenstine] Wooster Academy
       1918
    Isabel Beecher [Mrs. Albert E. Hill] OSU 1926
    David Beecher OSU 1931
Employment:
    President of Western College and Polytechnic Institute, Lincoln
       Nebraska.
    Instructor Delancy School, Philadelphia 1895-96
    Head of History Department, Enamus Hall High School NYC 1895-96
    Lectured Sociology Brooklyn Industrial Arts and Sciences 1895-98
    Superintendent of Schools, Bloomfield, N.J. 1897-1904
    Superintendent of Schools, Paterson, N.J. 1904-1906
    Superintendent of Schools District of Columbia, 1906-1908
    Superintendent of Schools Norwalk Conn. 1908-1912
    Assoc. Professor of History and Mathematics, Summer Quarter,
       University of Chicago, 1907-08
    Instructor Summer School in Education and Sociology, 1909-15
    Associate Director, School of Administration, Summer School,
       Dennison University, 1909
    Professor of Psychology, Conn. Normal School, Bridgeport, Conn
       1908-1912
    Acting Professor in Political Science, College of Wooster 1914-15
    Department of Political and Social Sciences College of Wooster 1914-
       1919
    Hoge Instructor of Morals and Sociology, College of Wooster 1917-19
    Hoge Professor of Political and Social Sciences College of Wooster
       1915-1920
    Professor of Economics and Law, Xavier University, Cincinnati, Ohio

1927-1940

Lectured at:

Economic and Natural Sciences, Pratt Institute

History and Mathematics, Summer School New York University 1906

Education, Teachers College, George Washington Univ. 1906-1907

Philosophy, John Hopkins University

Lectures. History Brooklyn Polytechnic Institute

More than 5,000 lectures, Rivers of Life, 281 times.

Editorial

Educational Foundation and School Journal, New York City 1912-14

School Journal 1912-15

Ohio Teacher 1915-1920

Associate Editor, Neale's Monthly   1912-1914

In Canada:

Bond Business, Edmonston, Alberta, Canada 1921-1922

Political:

Ohio Presidential Elector 1916

City Councilman, City of Wooster 1919-1921

City Councilman, City of Norwood, Ohio 1933-1940

Fellow Ships:

Royal Economic Society

A. A. A. S.

James Buell, New York University 1904-06

Member of:

America Economics Association

American Political Science Association

National Education Association

National Economic Council

New York Press Club

Cosmos Club

Authors Club

Authors League of America

Royal Arch Masons

Century Club

Intercollegiate Athletics Association, Xavier University

Alpha Delta Phi Beta Kappa

Masonic Lodge

Thesis: A. M. Amherst College, 1895, LEGAL CAUSES OF POVERTY, WITH SPECIAL REFERENCE TO LAND TENURE CHANGES OF THE ENGLISH REVOLUTION

Published Books:

Essential elements' 1901

Fundamental elements' 1901

Numbers   1901

The Indictment

Standard measurements' 1901
Children's Arithmetic by Grades 1901
Arithmetic Intermediate, Essential Principles 1902
Arithmetic Primary (second and Third grade Ratio and Numbers 1902
Commercial Affairs   1902
A Text book of AMERICAN HISTORY 1903
The United States: A History of Three Centuries 1903
Primary ratio and number   1903
The United States, A History of Three Centuries 1904
Reading and Language, lessons for evening schools 1904
Studies in English for evening schools 1904
Our Schools, their administration and supervision 1904
Grammar school arithmetic, Geometry, and Algebra 1904
Graded City Speller 1904
Our Schools their direction and management 1904
Graded City Speller 1905
History and Government of the United States 1905
OUR SCHOOLS, Their administration and supervision (1905)
OUR SCHOOLS, Their administration and supervision (1906)
Intermediate principles 1906
THE Washington Word List 1906
A Theory of Motives, Ideals and Values in Education 1907
Elementary school mathematics by grades   1907
Graded school speller 1907
Graded city arithmetic 1907
Our City Schools: their direction and management 1908
The Washington Word List 1908
Our City Schools, Their Administration and Supervision 1908
Our City Schools, Their Direction and Management 1908
Elementary school mathematics by grades   1908
Transitus in Lucem, and verses in memory of Louise Beecher 1910
Class Teaching and management 1910
An argument for disability pensions 1911
Standard Short Course for evening schools 1911
Our Presidents and Their Office 1912
Reading and Language, for Evening Schools 1912
A Life of Silas Wright, 1795-1847 1913
 Studies in English for Evening Schools 1913
History and Government of The United States   1914
Our Schools: Their administration and supervision 1915
Graded City Speller, seventh grade level 1915
Educational Sociology 1919
The Health of the Teacher 1919
History and government of the United States   1921
Magazine Articles-Too many to list.

Bibliography

Adams, Samuel Incredible Era, Boston: Houghton Mifflin Company 1939

Alderfer, Harold F. The Personality and Politics of Warren G. Harding Ph. D dissertation, Syracuse University, 1928

Allen, Frederick Lewis, Only Yesterday, New York: Bantam Books, 1946

BaKhufu, Auset The Six Black Presidents, Black Blood: White Mask U.S.A. Maryland: A & A Distributors, 1974

Baughman, A. J. History of Morrow County Ohio New York: The Lewis Publishing Company, 1911

Blackwood, James R. Howard Lowry, A Life of Education Ohio: The College of Wooster, 1975

Boroson, Warren, Fact: Volume One, Issue One, January-February 1964

Britton, Nan. The Presidents Daughter, New York: Elizabeth Ann Guild, 1927

Caesar, Gene. Incredible Detective, The Biography of William J. Burns. New Jersey: Prentice Hall, 1968

Chancellor, William Estabrook, etal, Warren G. Harding, President of the United States, Sentinal Press, 1922

Chapple, Joseph Mitchell. Life and Times of Warren G. Harding. Boston: Chapple Publishing Co. 1924

Chapple, Joseph Mitchell. Warren G. Harding, The Man Boston: Chapple Publishing Company, Limited, 1920

Cox, James M. Journey Through My Years. New York: Simon and Schuster, 1946

Daugherty, Harry M. The Inside Story of the Harding Tragedy. New York: Churchill Co. 1932

Davis, James Kirkpatrick. Spying on America. Conn. Praeger Publishing, 1992

Downes, Randolph C. The Rise of Warren Gamaliel Harding Columbus: Ohio State University Press, 1970

The Indictment

Ferrell, Robert H. The Strange Deaths of President Harding Missouri: University of Missouri Press, 1996

Fields, A.N. Lily Whiteism and how it Started Chicago: Abbot's Monthly, 1932

Giglio, James N. H.M. Daugherty and the Politics of Expediency Ohio: Kent State University Press

Greer, David C. Sluff of History's Boot Soles, Wilmington, Ohio, Orange Frazer Press, 1996

Gross, Edwin, Vindication of Mr. Normalcy. New York, American Society for the Faithful Recording of History 1965

Halderman-Julius, E. The Serious lesson in President Harding's case of Gonorrhea, Halderman-Julius Company, 1931

Howe, Henry, LL.D. Historical Collections of Ohio, vol. I & vol. II, Cincinnati : G. J. Krembel & Co., 1903

Hunt, William R. Front page detective: William J. Burns and the detective profession 1880-1930 Ohio: Bowling Green State University Popular Press, 1930

Johnson, Willis Fletcher, A.M., L.H.D. The Life of Warren G. Harding, USA: W. F. Johnson, 1923

Labor Defense Council The Burn's and Daugherty's attack upon labor and liberty Chicago: Labor Defense Council, 1923

McLean, Evalyn Walsh, Father Struck it Rich, Boston: Little, Brown & Company 1936

Means, Gaston B. The Strange Death of President Harding. New York: Guild Publishing Co. 1930

Mee Jr., Charles L. The Ohio Gang. Evans and Company New York, 1981

Moore, Opha History of Franklin County Ohio, vol. I, vol. II, vol. II, Indianapolis: Historical Publishing Company 1930

Notestein, Lucy Lilian Wooster of the Middle West, Vol. II Ohio: Kent State University Press, 1971

Rogers, J. A. The Five Negro Presidents Florida: Helga Rogers, 1963

Russell, Francis, The Shadow of Blooming Grove, New York: McGraw-Hill Book Co., 1968

Sinclair, Andrew The Available Man, the Life behind the masks of Warren G. Harding New York: MacMillan Company, 1965

Tumulty, Joseph P. Woodrow Wilson As I Know Him New York: Doubleday, Page & Company, 1921

Archives and Libraries

Special Collections: College of Wooster, Wooster, Ohio

Special Collections: Ohio State University, Columbus, Ohio

Special Collections: Xavier University, Victory Parkway, Cincinnati, Ohio

Harvard University Archives, Pusey Library, Cambridge, MA.

Archives Association of British Columbia, Vancouver, B.C., Canada

Montgomery Historical Society, Dayton, Ohio

Montgomery County Records Center and Archives, Dayton, Ohio.

Ohio Historical Society, Columbus, Ohio

National Archives and Records Administration, College Park, Maryland

Library of Congress, Washington, D.C.

Dayton & Montgomery County Public Library, Dayton, Ohio

Main Branch Columbus Library, Columbus, Ohio

Norwood Library, Archive and Historical Data, Norwood, Ohio

Public Library of Cincinnati and Hamilton County, Vine Street, Cincinnati, Ohio

Public Library of Wayne County, City of Wooster, Wooster, Ohio

Public Library of Bucyrus, Bucyrus, Ohio

Public Library of Mt. Gilead, Mt. Gilead, Ohio

The Indictment

United States of Department of Justice, Pennsylvania Ave, Washington, D.C.

United States Postal Inspection Service, Cleveland, Ohio and Washington, D.C.

United States Department of the Treasury, Secret Service, Washington, D.C.

Index

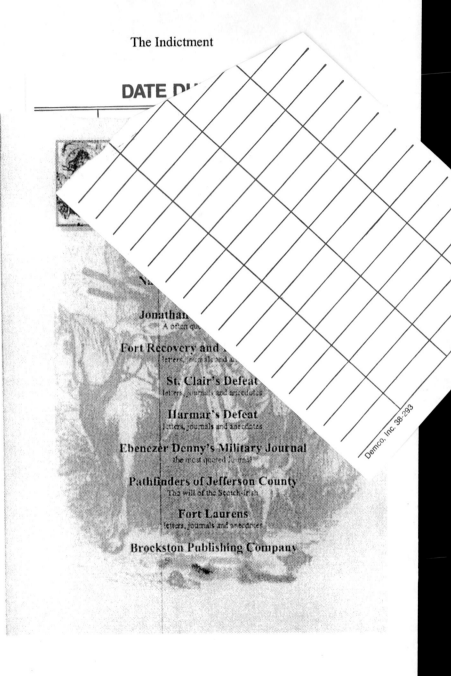

DATE D...

Jonathan
A often qu...

Fort Recovery and
letters, journals and a...

St. Clair's Defeat
letters, journals and anecdotes

Harmar's Defeat
letters, journals and anecdotes

Ebenezer Denny's Military Journal
the most quoted journal

Pathfinders of Jefferson County
The will of the Scotch-Irish

Fort Laurens
letters, journals and anecdotes

Brockston Publishing Company

Demco, Inc. 38-293

The Indictment

ISBN 0-918052-03-3

9 780918 052032

51995 >

BROCKSTON: INDICTMENT